LINES OF DEFENCE OF THE BIBLICAL
REVELATION

LINES OF DEFENCE

OF THE

BIBLICAL REVELATION

BY

D. S. MARGOLIOUTH, M.A.

LAUDIAN PROFESSOR OF ARABIC IN THE UNIVERSITY OF OXFORD

London

HODDER AND STOUGHTON

27, PATERNOSTER ROW

—

1900

PREFACE

FOR much of the matter contained in the
following pages I am indebted to Arabic and
Hebrew texts. Of the former the largest
number and the most important have been
published at Cairo or Boulak ; but many of
great value have also been issued by scholars
in Holland, Germany, Turkey in Europe, Syria,
and India ; and several other countries have
contributed a few. With these works on our
shelves it is now possible to treat the Old Testament as a part of Arabic literature, just as it
has long been possible to treat Hebrew as a
dialect of Arabic. That in the language and
literature of the Arabs we get the points of view
whence those of the Israelites can be best understood is eloquently attested by the fact that

after centuries of neglect Hebrew developed a
new life when once the Jews had learned to
think, to write, and to speak in Arabic.

The value of Hebrew texts is different, but
should not be underrated. The Jewish traditions were committed to writing very late—
Rashi, in the eleventh century, speaks of this
event as having happened almost in his own
time,[1] but they preserve the memory of many
ancient controversies, and also introduce us to
modes of thought which varied little from the
time when, owing to the Exile, the Rabbi and
the Synagogue took the place of the Priest and
the Temple. Somewhat as the books of the
Arabs provide guidance for the period before
the Exile, so those of the Rabbis provide it for
the period after the Return.

The references to Ecclesiasticus will be found
rather numerous, but the keys to that book
have so often been flung away with contumely
that it is like the private property of any one
who will use them. It is not for nothing that
the Greek translator tells us his relation to the

---

[1] On *Baba Mezia*, 33*a*, in the correct editions.

author of the book ; we learn thereby that his
translation has almost the value of an autograph
of the original. The observation given in Chapter VII. below, that in repeating what Genesis
says about Abraham, the author adds a syllable
in one case, and omits some syllables in another,
conducts us to the valuable result, that with
Ben-Sira a syllable is a matter of importance,
i.e., that he writes *in syllabic metre ;* and since
those two clauses can be restored with certainty,
we learn from them what his rhythm was ; and
that rhythm is, as we should expect, analogous
to the rhythm employed in the contemporary
Canaanitish document, the Punic of Plautus :
both are imitations of Greek metres. The
metre employed many centuries afterwards in
the Persian *Pand-nameh* and the Ouigour
Kudatku Bilik, of which the contents are analogous to those of Ecclesiasticus, differs very
slightly from Ben-Sira's.

That Ben-Sira's metre will one day be regarded as a stone of great importance in the
edifices of Hebrew Grammar and Biblical Criticism, is not, to my mind, doubtful ; but of the

length of time that will intervene before its
importance is appreciated it is difficult to form
an idea. If, however, in the case of any result
based on sound premises we waited till it had
obtained general assent before utilizing it, most
of the time that should be given to the further-
ance of knowledge would be wasted.

It is worth observing that Ben-Sira lets it be
known that Scripture was beginning to be discredited even in his day. " Give testimony,"
he prays his God, " to Thy *In the beginning
created*, and fulfil the prophecies in Thy name."[1]
By the *In the beginning created* he means the
Bible, which commences with those words, and
can be called by them, as the Romans speak of
Arms and the man for the Aeneid, and Arabic
writers of *Stand weep we* for the Muallakah of
Imru'ul-Kais. Clearly, then, the *In the beginning created* had already been attacked, else the
Divine testimony to it would not have been
solicited. During the 2,100 years that have
elapsed since then it has been constantly be-

[1] Ecclus. xxxvi. 20.   תֵּן עֵדָה לִבְרֵאשִׁית בָּרָאֶךָ
וְהָקֵם נְבוּאוֹת בִּשְׁמֶךָ

sieged, yet has succeeded in holding out. A
position so difficult to capture seems to merit
the name Impregnable bestowed on it by the
great political leader.

My best thanks are due to Dr. Robertson
Nicoll, at whose invitation these papers (with
the exception of Chapter VII.) were contributed
to the *Expositor* for 1900.

CONTENTS

CHAPTER I

xii CONTENTS

CHAPTER VI

CHAPTER VII

I

THE BIBLE OF THE GENTILES

THE Old Testament is the treasure of the Israelites, but other races have utilized it more than they. The same talent which committed to the Jews produced little, having been committed to the nations of Europe and Asia has produced much. Gentiles have taught the Jews to translate their Bible, to perpetuate its pronunciation, to comment on its matter and language, and to codify its precepts; if the Gentiles would have had no Bible save for the Jews, the Jews but for the Gentiles would have had no literature besides. By communicating their treasure to the world, the Israelites have thus gained more than if they had succeeded in keeping it to themselves.

The first translation of the Bible into another language is associated with the name of Ptolemy Philadelphus, whose reign lasted from 285 to 247 B.C. The LXX. translation is stated by both Greek and Hebrew writers to have been

executed by his order ; the ancient Calendar of
the Synagogue [1] commemorated the undertaking
by a fast-day ; whereas, if we may believe
Josephus, King Ptolemy himself celebrated it
by a feast-day.   Let us endeavour to get some
idea of the occasion which led to the introduction of Jewish literature into the Hellene world.

Of the poets who flattered Ptolemy Philadelphus the idyllist Theocritus has always enjoyed
a large share of popularity.   This writer's Greek
is frequently of a sort which makes it difficult
to believe that Greek was his native language ; [2]
and the information which we possess concerning his birth and domestic history seems
mainly to be based on statements of his own,

[1] Kardizi, *Feasts of the Jews*, No. 13.

[2] He is included by the most eminent Greek scholar
of the nineteenth century (G. C. Cobet, *Variæ Lectiones*,
p. 396) among those who "constantly make disgraceful
mistakes."   His native language was probably Hebrew
or Syriac, for he cannot distinguish between *daughter-in-
law* and *bride*, just as the LXX. (Gen. xi. 31, &c.) cannot ; xviii. 15, τεὰ νυὸς ἀδε could only mean "This is
thy daughter-in-law" ; and it is even doubtful whether
xv. 77 would be tolerable, though doubtless "*the*
daughter-in-law" could be said in lieu of "the bride."
xviii. 49 contains a curious mistake : "Letters shall be
written in bark, that the passer-by may read in Doric,
' Reverence me,' &c.," where clearly the words in Doric
should be those of the inscription ; they are not in
Doric, but the Doric verb for *to read* is used !   The
mistakes in xxii. 2 (ἐρεθίζειν for ἐρίζειν), xv. 129, and
xxvi. 29, also betray the foreigner.

not all of which are intended to be serious. Several of his Idylls, however, can be accurately dated, whence he is a valuable witness. In Idyll xvi., which is of the year 270 B.C., or thereabout, he observes (line 40) that certain princes had got no good out of their wealth "when once they had *emptied out* their sweet soul into the broad raft of the grim old man (Charon)." To "empty out"[1] one's soul is, of course, incorrect and absurd Greek,[2] but a very tolerable Hebraism for "to spill" or "to pour out"; since the old Semitic verb[3] which means "to shed" or "to pour," is in Hebrew confused with a word meaning "empty," whence the verb gets the double sense. We can, moreover, trace this Hebraism to its source. That is the third verse of the Song of Solomon, where the LXX. has "Thy name is like ointment emptied out" (with the same compound verb as is here employed by Theocritus) for "poured out."[4] Now identity of mistake is regarded as important evidence in law when questions of infringement of copyright are discussed. We see that Theocritus has mistaken the sense of this Greek verb in the same way in which the LXX. translator of the Song of Solomon has

---

[1] ἐκκενοῦν. The mythology seems erroneous.

[2] An editor says *nove dictum*.

[3] Arabic *harāka :* used of tears in the earliest Arabic we have. [4] הורק.

mistaken it ; but the LXX. translator's mistake
is due to the fact that he is translating from
Hebrew, which is not the case with Theocritus.
Unless, therefore, Theocritus be himself the
translator of the Song of Solomon, there is a
strong presumption that in Idyll xvi. 40 he
was misled by the usage of the LXX. Song
of Solomon ; whence we infer that the LXX.
Song of Solomon is earlier than 270 B.C.   If
we find in Theocritus further traces of the
influence of the Song of Solomon, this presumption will rise into a certainty.

The most striking of these are to be found
in Idyll xviii., the Epithalamium to Helen, a
performance which, both from the point of
view of language and of taste, contains much
that is objectionable.   In line 30 Helen is
compared (among other things) to a *Thessalian
mare in a chariot.*   That such a comparison is
extraordinary in a Greek poet must strike
every one.[1]   It struck Vergil, who, though he
imitates some of this passage (Ecl. v. 32–4),
omits the mare in the chariot.   Hence Theocritus must have got it from some non-Greek
source ; and this is clearly the Song of Solomon,
almost at the commencement of which we read
(i. 9), " To my *mare* in the *chariots* of Pharaoh
do I compare thee, my kinswoman."   The word

[1] Alcman, in Bergk's *Lyrici Græci*, iii. 39, compares a
beauty to a horse among *cattle*.   The text of Theocritus
is that of Ahrens in the Teubner series.

Thessalian is got from an oracle in which it is stated that the best horses are from Thessaly, just as the best women are from Lacedæmon ; but the idea of the mare being the pride of the chariot, just as Helen is the pride of the Lacedæmonian women, is from Solomon.

Two comparisons that are more in accordance with Greek taste occur at the commencement of the paragraph : " The rising dawn gives a glimpse of its fair face : the lady moon at night." The word *moon* is introduced by conjecture, but the scholar who introduced it does not seem to have been thinking of the Song of Solomon. These two comparisons are found in the Song in the same order (vi. 9) ; " Who is this that peereth forth like the dawn, fair as the moon ? "

The theory that *swarthiness produced by sunburning* need not be regarded as disfiguring a woman is the subject of some pretty verses in Idyll x. 26–29. A distinguished German commentator compared the Greek " popular song " (as he termed it) " I am swarthy, yet fair." This " popular song " is from the Song of Solomon (i. 5), where it is further explained that the swarthiness is, as in the case of the girl in Theocritus, produced by sunburning.

The picture of foxes munching grapes is one that took Theocritus' fancy, and is found twice in his Idylls (i. 47, v. 112). It seems to be drawn from the Song of Solomon (ii. 15),

" Seize for us the little foxes that spoil the vines."

The greater number of the Idylls show much prettiness and wit, but little originality ; yet their author is the *founder of a style*—Bucolic Poetry. That Theocritus was the first Bucolic or Pastoral poet is attested by Vergil (Ecl. vi. 1), an excellent authority ; and the silence of the Poetics of Aristotle, which was composed but little before the time of Theocritus, bears out Vergil's statement. That this style, in which highly artificial performances are put in the mouths of shepherds and cowherds, should have originated in Greece would be surprising ; for the persons who followed those callings were ordinarily slaves, or humble hirelings, whom the classical writers treat with little respect. But from the time of Theocritus their profession becomes associated with the poetic art. The shepherd's clothes are donned by Vergil, Spenser and Milton. The existence of the LXX. translation of the Song of Solomon gives us the explanation of this fact. The Song of Solomon is a Pastoral Poem, but *its pictures are true to nature*. The father of the writer, himself both a king and a poet, had kept sheep. The combination of the court life with country life, which in Theocritus seems so unnatural, was perfectly natural in pre-exilic Palestine. Hence the rich descriptions of the country (ii. 12) beside the glowing descriptions

of the king's wealth (iii. 10). Theocritus can
match both (Idylls vii. and xv.), but it may be
doubted whether he could have found any
Greek model for either.

There is, if I mistake not, a certain trace of
another Biblical book in the Idylls of Theocritus. In Idyll xxiv. ("the little Heracles")
two verses (86–7) are introduced into an oracle,
which are apparently unconnected with their
context : " There shall be a day when the
ravening wolf shall refrain from harming the
fawn, though he see her in her lair." These
lines remind us of Isaiah xi. 6, " And the wolf
shall feed with the lamb." But what makes it
practically certain that the verses are modelled
on Isaiah is that the preceding line in Theocritus runs, " Who sent these burrowing mon-
sters (*i.e.* serpents) to harm the babe." Now
since, in Isaiah xi., the verse quoted is almost
immediately followed by " and the little child
shall put its hand on the holes of asps," the
connexion in thought becomes intelligible, if
we suppose Theocritus to have had the passage
of Isaiah either before him or in his mind.
For the subject of Idyll xxiv. is "serpents
attacking the infant Heracles." The epithet
" burrowing" or "living in holes," which he
applies to the serpents, is surely suggested by
the verse in Isaiah also. Several editors,
indeed, regard verses 86 and 87 as interpolated ;
but this cannot be, since Vergil knew them

and imitated them in his Messianic fourth Eclogue.

Since, then, Idyll xxiv. implies that the LXX. translation of Isaiah already existed, it is worth while trying to fix the date of Idyll xxiv. Idyll xvii. was composed before 260 B.C., because the author there glorifies Cos in a way which would have been impossible *after* the defeat sustained by Ptolemy off Cos about the year 260.   But in Idyll xvii. Theocritus speaks of his Praises of the Demigods as well known. One of these may well be Idyll xxii., which deals with Castor and Pollux.   The others must be some of the Heraclean collection, *i.e.* xiii., xxiv. and xxv.   But xiii. is later than xxiv., for at the commencement of xiii. there is a reference to the list of Heracles's accomplishments which is given at length in xxiv.   The Theocritean authorship of Idyll xxv. is abandoned by most scholars.   I am unable to agree with their opinion ; but every one must grant that the style is sufficiently different from that of xxii. to mark a different period in the poet's life.   On the other hand, Idyll xxiv. belongs to the same period as xxii., for Pindar's Nemean Odes are imitated in both. Therefore Idyll xxiv. is earlier than Idyll xvii., and so is earlier than 260 B.C.   Therefore the LXX. translation of Isaiah is earlier than 260 B.C.

A little internal evidence in support of this

result is worth extracting. An unusual word for " cup " which occurs in Isaiah li. 17 and 22 is rendered by the foreign word κόνδυ. Now on this word there is an interesting article by the archæologer Athenaeus, who quotes for it two authors of the New Comedy, who flourished about the year 320 B.C., *i.e.* within the century in which we suppose the translation of Isaiah to have been made. Since the word appears only to occur in this period, it is probable that these comedians introduced it, that it was in vogue for a short time, and then fell into disuse. Athenaeus's authorities point out that it was an Asiatic (not Egyptian) cup, whence the LXX. translator appears anxious to reproduce the foreign appearance of the word in his text.

The translation of the Pentateuch is certified as Ptolemaic by the intentional avoidance of the Greek word for " hare " (λαγώς) in the list of unclean beasts : for the tradition that the king was sensitive about the name of his ancestor Lagos is shown to be true by the fact that Theocritus intentionally alters its quantity : " *Lāgīdas* " (Idyll xvii. 14) is meant to suggest not " hare," but " leader of the people," a far more princely name.

It was desirable to get some external evidence to show that Ptolemy's translation included all three divisions of the Old Testament ; and that evidence has now been produced.

But how came Ptolemy Philadelphus to know

of Jewish literature? and what interest had he in procuring a translation of it? These questions can at present be answered hypothetically, but the following hypotheses seem to have some probability.

It is clear that some specimens of a literature have to be translated before it becomes worth while to organize a translation on a large scale. Neither the Song of Solomon nor Isaiah is likely to have been the first Hebrew book rendered into Greek; for neither of these exhibit signs of being specially intended for the Greek market. The whole tendency of translation in antiquity is from the less to the more literal. The work in the whole LXX. which shows the clearest signs of being intended for Greeks is the *Wisdom of Solomon.* That this book is a translation from the Hebrew is practically certain. For there is a paragraph in the disquisition on idolatry which this book contains (*c.* xiv.) in the middle of which occur the following sentences : " For that which was *done*[1] shall be punished together with the *doer ;*[2] for this reason also there shall be visitation on the idols of the Gentiles " (*vv.* 10–11). Those who are accustomed to think while they read will at once detect a mistranslation here ; for how can the thing done be punished apart from the doer ? And the source of the mistranslation is easy to find ; for the word which in Aramaic

---

[1] πραχθέν.   [2] δράσαντι.

means " to do " means in Hebrew " to worship."
Hence the original sentence must have meant
" for that which is *worshipped* shall be punished
together with the *worshipper* " ; and from this
the next sentence follows logically. And we
learn from Josephus that at the time of the
LXX. translation Aramaic was better known
than Hebrew, though the two languages were
known to be alike ; nor need we quote examples
of mistakes due to homonymy in the languages,
since these are common in the LXX. What,
however, takes the reconstruction of the above
verses out of the region of probability into that
of certainty, is that the original (or a paraphrase
of it) is preserved in the Midrash[1] on Genesis
xlvii. 49. We are there told that Jacob disliked
being buried in Egypt for fear of becoming an
object of worship to the Egyptians ; " for just
as the *worshipper*[2] is to be punished, so also is
the *object of his worship* ;[3] wherefore it is written,
' And on all the gods of Egypt I will execute
vengeance ' " (Exod. xii. 12). But these verses
are found in the middle of a paragraph, which
is closely reasoned. Therefore the quotation in
the Midrash is sufficient to certify a Hebrew
original for the whole of the Wisdom of
Solomon.

Confirmation of this result meets us everywhere as soon as it has been ascertained. In

---

[1] See the collections called Rabbah and Tanchuma.
[2] העובד.   [3] הנעבד.

i. 12, "do not emulate [1] death" is parallel to
"do not attract destruction"; clearly "emulate"
is a mistranslation for "acquire," as it is in the
LXX. of Isaiah xi. 11;[2] this mistranslation is
also due to the disappearance in Aramaic of a
sense which the Hebrew root retains. In xii.
24, "thinking gods the dishonourable among
the beasts of the enemies" is assuredly a mistranslation: for what are beasts of the enemies?
The phrase should have been rendered "beasts
of prey."[3]　In i. 3 "the power reproveth" is a
fairly obvious misrendering for "reproving reproveth."[4]　Other cases will be quoted in the
sequel.

The fact that the Wisdom of Solomon is
translated from Hebrew is therefore sufficiently
certain to be made the basis of inferences; if
it is not certain, then little in the history of
literature is certain;[5] and we must date the
thought by the language, not the language by
the thought.

Three facts strike us about the Greek of this

---

[1] ζηλοῦτε.

[2] Hebrew תקני and תקנאו.

[3] Probably Hebrew השנים (intended for "of the
teeth," as in Syriac).

[4] הֹכֵחַ תּוֹכִיחַ (cf. Levit. xix. 17; Job vi. 25, xiii. 10).

[5] The words of Epiphanius de Mens. et Pond. § 4 and
Adv. Haer. i. § 6 imply that the book was in Hebrew, so
that we have a combination of internal and external
evidence.

work. First, it is the Greek of an educated foreigner, who is anxious to display his acquaintance with the resources of the classical language. There are not a few happy reminiscences of Greek poets, and adaptations of the technical language of the schools. The translator has done his utmost from this point of view to render the work of the Hebrew writer attractive to Greek readers. Secondly, he resolutely avoids mentioning the names of persons. Instead of speaking of Adam, Noah, Lot, Joseph, Moses, Joshua, he uses allusive expressions, such as "the father of creation," "the just," "the holy prophet." The reason for this is evidently that he does not wish to spoil the appearance of his Greek. The introduction of barbarous words would seriously mar the effect of his eloquence. Thirdly, he scrupulously avoids mentioning *Egypt.* The deliverance from Egyptian bondage is perhaps his chief theme ; and the name of Egypt nowhere appears !

From this third fact we may draw two inferences. It is evident, in the first place, that the omission of the name of Egypt is due to the *translator ;* for in the verses preserved in the Midrash it is on the gods of *Egypt* that vengeance is threatened, not on the gods of the Gentiles generally. And indeed we learn that Wisdom xiv. 11*a* is a quotation from Exodus xii. 12, brought in to illustrate the paragraph. Now the substitution of the generalizing

"nations" for "Egypt" must have a purpose;
viz., to avoid offending the Egyptians, for whom
the translator was working. He thought (probably with justice) that whereas a threat of
vengeance on the idols of the *nations* would
escape notice, an attack on the idols of Egypt
would ruin Solomon's chance of obtaining
popularity in that country. But if he deliberately omitted the proper name in this place, he
probably omitted the proper names deliberately
everywhere; and hence an Egyptian might read
the book from beginning to end and need never
even fancy that his own country was being
attacked.

But this fear of offending the Egyptians
could only have been felt before any considerable portion of the Old Testament was translated into Greek. For with the deliverance
from Egyptian bondage the whole Old Testament rings. Any one who had the most
elementary acquaintance with the history of
Israel must have heard of the relation of Israel
to Egypt. The miraculous deliverance of the
Chosen People from that country is the fact in
their history which overshadows all others.
Now it is worth while concealing a matter only
if it is not known. When it is a matter of
common knowledge, it is taken for granted.
People become callous about it. Hence the
Wisdom of Solomon must have been translated
into Greek before any considerable portion of

the Old Testament was known to the Egyptians. And since the translator has done his utmost to give the Greeks a favourable impression of the literature of the Hebrews, we are justified in concluding that this was the first Hebrew work translated into Greek.

A little external evidence would be desirable to support this result, and this we have in the LXX. of Isaiah iii. 10. The Hebrew has there, " Say of the righteous, It is well : for they shall eat the fruit of their works ; Woe to the wicked, it is ill." For the first of these sentences the LXX. has " Saying : Let us bind the righteous, for he is grievous unto us." It is very clear that the LXX. can here make no claim to represent the original ; the correctness of the Hebrew is certified by the antithesis. The word " bind," moreover, seems a mistranslation of the Hebrew " say," resulting from the similarity in some scripts of the letters M and S.[1] But the wilful substitution of "grievous " for " well " or "good" requires further explanation : and this is to be found in Wisdom ii. 12, where, in the middle of a discourse which is put into the mouth of the wicked, occur the words, " *Let us waylay the righteous, for he is grievous unto us*, and opposes our works, and taunts us with transgression of

[1] אסר for אמר. For the insertion of the word " saying " compare viii. 17. The LXX. rendering of this verse attracted attention very early ; see Justin, *Dialogue* § 137.

the Law." The discourse in Wisdom bears considerable resemblance to that in Proverbs i. 11, where the word for "let us waylay" occurs ; it bears none to the passage of Isaiah. Hence it seems clear that the LXX. translator of Isaiah, having by a misreading substituted " bind the righteous " for " say of the righteous," *interpolated* the rest of the passage from the discourse in Wisdom, which he remembered. But in that case the LXX. translation of Wisdom must have existed before the translation of Isaiah.

We are justified in assuming that the translator of Isaiah would alter his text on account of a reminiscence, because he does so elsewhere. In xlv. 9, where he finds curious difficulty in translating, he inserts a clause "shall the plougher plough the ground the whole day ? " from xxviii. 24, because the consonants of xlv. 9 bear some resemblance to those of the other verse. Likewise in lxv. 4, where the text has "they pass the night in caves " he adds *for the sake of dreams*, undoubtedly with a reference to the Greek cave-oracles, of one of which Plutarch gives us a vivid description. Hence in the preceding verse, where the original has "they offer incense on the bricks " and the translator adds *to the demons who are not*, it seems reasonable to see a reminiscence of Wisdom xiv. 13, where we are told distinctly of the idols that "they were not from the beginning, nor ever shall be."

A much clearer reminiscence of Wisdom occurs in xxxv. 6 : " Then shall the lame man leap as a hart, and the tongue of the dumb shout." The word here rendered " shout "[1] is a favourite word with Isaiah, and is ordinarily represented correctly by the LXX. translator : why then does he here render " the tongue of the dumb shall be *clear* "—using for " clear " a word that is found nowhere else in the canonical LXX. ? It is evidently a reminiscence of Wisdom x. 21, "Wisdom has made *clear* the tongues of the speechless." It would seem that the jingle of the Hebrew word in Isaiah with the Greek word used in Wisdom was what suggested this inaccurate but elegant rendering.

Wisdom can scarcely have failed to win a favourable reception at Alexandria. The language employed by writers at Ptolemy's court was very similar in character to that which this translation exhibits. It is very far removed from Attic simplicity ; but it is rich, learned, and melodious. Moreover the brilliancy of the thought is but little tarnished by the faults of the style. Many of the themes handled are such as may be relied on to evoke warm approval from any fairly educated audience.

I am inclined to find a trace of the Wisdom of Solomon in certain lines of Lucretius, who lived at a time when Alexandrian literature

---

[1] תרן, τρανάς.

was greatly admired in Italy, and who may possibly have used the Wisdom of Solomon at second hand. "Men often," he says (iii. 912), "when seated at banquets holding cups in their hands, and with their brows shaded with crowns, say bitterly : 'This enjoyment is of brief duration for us poor mortals ; soon it will be past and beyond recall.'" The four ideas of the banqueters, with cups in their hands, and crowns on their brows, saying that life is short, all occur in the fine passage of Wisdom ii. 2, and 7, 8 : "They say in themselves, reasoning falsely, 'Our life is short and grievous ; presently we shall be as though we had not been. Come, then, let us enjoy our present goods ; let us be filled with rare wine and ointment; let us crown ourselves with rose-blossoms before they fade.'"

We may suppose, then, that the success which attended this translation led to the rendering into Greek of another work by Solomon. This would naturally be the Song of Songs, the matter of which, being erotic, would be suitable to Alexandrian taste ; for with the Alexandrines love was a favourite theme. Assuredly the translator made a fortunate choice ; for the form of love which this book *appears* to glorify is of a sort which would give it a peculiar interest to Ptolemy *Philadelphus*. His marriage with his sister Arsinoë deeply offended Greek sentiment ; Sotades earned a martyr's crown by publicly rebuking the king for it. Now in the Song of Solomon the bridegroom seems to be a king, and the very king to whom the noble philosophy of the Wisdom of Solomon is ascribed ; and he and the bride repeatedly call each other *brother* [1] and *sister*. Apparently, in order that there may be no mistake, " my kinswoman " is substituted sometimes for "sister." Of course in the Hebrew these words are used with the most harmless intent ; for among Oriental peoples a husband calls his wife " my sister " or " my cousin." But this was not a Greek custom ; the matrimonial relation was so very distinct from the erotic relation that the forms of address between husband and wife were far more cold and respectful ; and in the ode of Callimachus (preserved to us in a translation) called Berenice's Lock, the poet is careful to imply that Berenice's love for her husband was due to the fact that he was her brother ! Since we have seen that Theocritus's acquaintance with the Song of Solomon can scarcely be questioned, and Theocritus was a flatterer of Ptolemy Philadelphus before he became a Pastoral poet, and endeavoured to please the king by justifying his marriage with his sister : we have in this fact about the Song of Solomon what at any rate is an adequate reason for Ptolemy's in-

[1] ἀδελφιδός could probably be regarded as a diminutive of ἀδελφός.

terest in the literature of the Jews ; for when
men violate the well-grounded sentiments of
their contemporaries, they are grateful to any
advocate who will speak in their favour.

We have, therefore, acquired the date 270 B.C.
as the *terminus ad quem* for the LXX. translation of the Song of Solomon. Now if that
translation were accurate, it would be a help
to the understanding of the Song of Solomon,
but would tell us nothing of the state of the
Hebrew language at the time when it was
made. As, however, it is a literal but incorrect translation, something may be learned
from it in regard to this point also. For if a
translator of the year 270 B.C. interprets a
Hebrew word X as Z, it may reasonably be
inferred that the meaning X was obsolete by his
time.

Naturally we should like to know who the
translator was, since the assertion of Josephus
that the LXX. were the best scholars of the
time does not necessarily settle the point. It
seems, however, clear that the translator must
have been an Israelite, with whom Greek was
an acquired language. The geographical and
historical references could have been understood by no one other than an Israelite.
Moreover one who had had a Greek education
would have avoided many errors that are clearly
due to imperfect acquaintance with Greek.

The translator's geography is remarkable

both for what he knows and what he does
not know. He knows that in iv. 4 *Thalpioth*
is the name of a place. This must be regarded
as an out-of-the-way piece of knowledge, for
it seems to have escaped most commentators.
Yet a place bearing this name is mentioned by
the Arabic geographer Yakut in such a way
as to leave little doubt of the correctness of the
LXX. interpretation. " Talfiatha," he says, " is
one of the villages of the Ghutah of *Damascus ;*
it is mentioned in the tradition of Abu 'l-'Amaitir
Al-Sufyani, who revolted in the days of the
Caliph Al-Amin " (ninth century A.D.). It also
figures in history in the reign of his immediate
predecessor, the Caliph Harun Al-Rashid.[1] Evidently the translator identified " the tower of
David built towards Talpioth," with " the tower
of Lebanon which looks towards Damascus " of
vii. 4. As a proper name the word admits of an
easy derivation ; it is the Hebrew for " Edge-
hill," or " the Mound of Edges," so called after
its shape. Since in other places geographical
names are translated, and the meaning of words
guessed at, it seems clear that had not the translator known the local name Talpioth, he would
have rendered the passage by some ingenious
guess, as others have done.

This being so, we have reason to infer that
in his time those geographical names which he
does not know were obsolete. The most striking

[1] Ibn Al-Athir's *Chronicle*, vi. 88.

of these is *Thirzah*, at one time famous as the capital of the northern kingdom; but apparently the river *Amanah* also had already changed its name, since he misrenders this word by "Faith."

But what is more important is that we may infer from a study of this translation that the Biblical Hebrew was a dead language in the translator's time. He stumbles where we stumble ; in some cases he is misled by modern usage so as to mistake what to us is the obvious meaning of a passage—obvious, because most of us are more familiar with Biblical than with late Hebrew. Throughout the book he mistakes the old word for "love" (*dodim*) for "breasts" (*dadaim*), a favourite word in New Hebrew.[1] Hence *dodim* must have been obsolete in his time.

A most interesting mistake is his mistranslation of the word for "veil"[2] by "silence." This word properly signifies a "juncture,"[3] and refers to the juncture of the hood which comes over the head with the veil that comes up over the face. In the costume of Egyptian women of the present day the juncture itself is effected by a short chain or ribbon ; but the advantage of the method is that it allows the eyes and temples to appear, as was the case with the veil spoken of by Solomon (iv. 1, 3). Evidently to

[1] B. *Baba Mezia*, 87*a* ; Kohut, *Aruch Completum*, iii. 24.

[2] צמרתך.   [3] Arabic d*ammah*.

the translator this sort of veil was obsolete, as
he was not acquainted with its name ; for from
this it may be inferred that the custom itself
was obsolete. But since the name must have
been preserved in Canaanitish from pre-historic
times, it seems to follow that it must have been
lost during some great break in the national
continuity—*viz.*, during the exile.

The absurd rendering "silence" is also of
value. The word s*amt* is ordinary Arabic for
"silence"; and it is old Arabic, for among
examples of early words is the name of a
desert called *Ismit, i.e.* Hush! The rendering
of the word by Silence can therefore be no
accident ; yet we should not be justified in
supposing that the LXX. translator could
do as we do on any emergency in our
Hebrew studies—look out the word in an
Arabic dictionary. The word must have been
known to the translator either as an old
Canaanitish word, or as a recent importation
from Arabia ; and the latter is the only possible account to be given of it. We have then
in this translation a confirmation of the statement in Nehemiah about the loss of the "purity"
of the Hebrew language which suggested to him
the necessity of preventive measures.

In viii. 5 we have a remarkable case of two
guesses side by side from the Arabic : "Who is
this that cometh up *clad in white, leaning* on
her cousin?" For the two words italicized the

original has only one word.[1] The analogous
Arabic word is employed in an Arabic tradition:[2] "Who is so-and-so?" *Answer:* " The
white, the leaning." So the tradition is rendered ; but, since another derivative of this
stem is used with the sense of "white," it
seems likely that the answer in that tradition
should be rendered "the white, the clad in
white,"—thus making the second word explain
the first. Whether this comparison be just
or not, it is certain that the word rendered
"leaning" occurs nowhere else in the Old
Testament ; and it is also certain that it belongs to a numerous family of Arabic words—
a family which contains the word for "elbow,"
which also appears in late Hebrew. The
word, therefore, employed by Solomon is old
Canaanitish ; the double rendering in the LXX.
implies that the translator had a doubt about
it, and apparently interpreted it with hesitation
from the Nabatæan usage, which in this case
had reintroduced into Palestine a stem that had
disappeared.

Nabatæan is not the only foreign language
which the translator consults. He translates
one word from the Aramaic : the modern
authorities follow him, but probably he is
wrong. He has also found many followers

[1] מתרפקת.

[2] See *Nihāyah* of Ibn Al-Athir (brother of the
historian).

in interpreting a word from the *Greek*—by
evidently a mere guess ; for the text is thus
made to say that Solomon made for himself
a *bier*, whereas a very different kind of couch
is intended.

What I desire to prove in this paper is that
a book of the Old Testament presented to a
Jew of the year 300 B.C. or thereabouts much
the same appearance as it presents to one of us.
It is in a dead language. Many verses we are
inclined to give up altogether ; too little is
known of their meaning to allow of any chance
of a satisfactory conjecture. Elsewhere from
what we know of cognate or contemporary
tongues we can perhaps satisfy ourselves ; but
our ignorance of many ancient customs, and of
matters historical and geographical, is likely
to mislead us constantly. That we can interpret the Song of Solomon better than the LXX.
translator is due to the fact that many sources
of knowledge are open to us now which were
not then accessible to him. The Song itself is
evidently pre-exilian, and the tradition which
ascribes it to Solomon is most likely to be
correct ; but the traditional interpretation
which very likely accompanied it seems to
have perished during the Exile. Had it been
current in the LXX. translator's time, he would
assuredly have employed it.

The evidence of the translation of Isaiah is
too bulky to be collected here, but it fully bears

out that of the Song of Solomon. In one place
the translator gives a word in his native language—*Geioras* for "stranger" (xiv. 1) ; and it
is Syriac. In another [1] he interprets a Hebrew
word—which ought to have occasioned him no
difficulty, from the Arabic, or, more probably,
Nabatæan—"curse," for "confusion." That the
language of the prophet is as much a dead language to him as it is to us does not admit of
question.

It follows that we must deny the post-
exilian origin of any performances in classical
Hebrew, and thus restore the bulk of Scripture
to pre-exilian times. For it is certain that the
philological sense failed the ancient Hebrews
altogether. The way to save the old language
would assuredly have been to register it in
grammars and dictionaries ; but such an idea
did not occur to Nehemiah : he tried far more
drastic, yet far less effectual methods. Now
even when a language has been thus registered
it is difficult to write in a style that does not
betray the century in which the work is written ;
even in such artificial performances as Latin
Hexameters or Greek Iambics a competent
judge ought to be able to tell the work of the
nineteenth century from that of the eighteenth,
and indeed the work of the first half of this
century from that of the second half. The pro-

[1] lxv. 23. The word *ibtihāl*, "mutual execration,"
occurs in the Tradition of the people of Najran.

cess of judging is not *divining*, but perfectly scientific : the judge ought to know exactly what rules were known to composers at each of those periods, and the records of the progress of knowledge give him exact dates. But if we possessed complete knowledge of the ways of the ancients, this criterion would in the case of the best work be inapplicable. Hence, in dealing with the work of a nation that possessed no sense of grammatical science at all fabrication ought to be very easy of detection A man who had possessed the skill to analyse the old Hebrew idioms would probably, by starting the science of philology among his countrymen, have won more permanent fame and gratitude than he could ever have won by fabrication. But it is certain that the study of Hebrew grammar is not older than 850 A.D. The Mohammedans were compelled by circumstances to compile grammars, vocabularies, and commentaries ; and since the Jews flourished in Mohammedan states, they imitated their example.

There is, moreover, another reason for paying great attention to the traditional dates and authors of the Biblical books. Science detests the uneven balance ; to use a line of argument when it leads to a desirable conclusion, but reject it when it leads to an undesirable one is an abomination in her eyes. Now let us think how it comes that we can read Hebrew texts at all. The vowels remained unwritten from the time at which those texts were composed until about 750 A.D.—about 1,250 years after the death of old Hebrew, and about 700 years after the death of new Hebrew. The correct pronunciation of the words was handed down from father to son, from teacher to pupil. In sporadic cases it could be tested by transliterations ; but owing to the fact that till the most recent times no scientific method of transliteration had been invented, this test was absolutely insufficient. A test has at last been discovered, and this will confirm many remarkable peculiarities of the traditional vocalization. We trust the tradition, then, for such minutiæ as vowel points through a period of more than a thousand years and find that trust justified ; but when it comes to important questions, such as the authorship and dates of Isaiah and the Psalms, we discard the tradition with scarcely a hearing !

In judging questions of authorship, we had best be guided by experience ; the closer we follow what it tells us the more likely we shall be to hit the mark. Anonymous works, except when they are humorous, are rarely, if ever, good. A good writer is not anxious to shirk either the responsibility or the honour of what he writes. And posterity is not ordinarily unmindful of those who have served the race by their pens, but preserves and reverences their

names. The Song of Solomon was, as we have
seen, a work of such striking beauty that Greece,
so rich in literary forms, borrowed from it a new
style. If any other than Solomon had written
it, his name would doubtless have been handed
down, as has happened with such authors as
Archilochus, Sophron, and Menippus. Moreover, if the tradition that it was by Solomon
was pre-exilic, we assuredly have now no power
of checking it. The historical facts that shine
through show us Palestine united and peaceful,
such as it was only in the great king's days.

Hence the fact that it was by Solomon gave
it a place in the Bible ; and that place was
utilized by Providence to introduce the pre-
paration for the Gospel. The Law and the
Prophets can be appreciated by a trained taste
only ; but every one is attracted by the rich
fragrance of the country. " Beauty and grace
doth thine eye desire, but most of all the green
of the fields." The Rabbis, who do not ordinarily show themselves impressionable, speak of
the Song of Solomon as the gem of the Bible.[1]
It has about it a bloom and a freshness which
reflect the halcyon days wherein it was composed.

But were those who gave it a place in the
Canon because it was by Solomon in the right ?
Did the Bible condescend to entertain an erotic
poem in order that the Gentiles might one day

[1] *Yadayim,* § 3.

be won, or is the theory more true that its love and wine stand for something very different from what they ordinarily signify? Here again we had best be guided by experience. There is no poet more highly prized in Persia and India than Hafiz; scarcely one more popular where Arabic is spoken than Ibn Al-Farid; these authors apparently are occupied only with love and wine; but no one believes that they in reality are dealing with either. In many cases there is a traditional interpretation of their verses; this is not always easy to understand, because to those who spent their lives in certain forms of meditation, certain concepts would be familiar which to others convey little or no meaning. But occasionally the inner sense is plain. Sometimes the verses are so clearly mystical that no one could suppose the literal meaning to be the sense intended; whereas at other times, without the tradition to guide us, we might fancy we had before us commonplace wine-songs or love-songs. Thus the first ode of Ibn Al-Farid, where the wayfarer is asked to tell certain of the tribe of Tay that he is sick of love, that the physician had told him there was no cure for his complaint, that the tie which bound him and *her* in the code of love was nearer than that of brother and sister, seems at first sight so clearly erotic that we have difficulty in assimilating the mystical rendering. But the same writer's *Tā'iyyah*, probably the most celebrated of the mystic poems of the East, scarcely veils its meaning from the first, but lands us almost at once in Pantheism. Somewhat similarly in the Song of Solomon the last chapter is mystical, one might say, without question ; its allegorical character is on the surface ; thence we are justified in arguing that the same is the case with the other chapters ; they are mystical too, but the fact is less conspicuous.

II

THE WISDOM OF BEN-SIRA AND THE WISDOM OF SOLOMON

SINCE we shall be occupied in this chapter with the Wisdom literature as it is called, let us endeavour first to obtain a clear idea of what the Old Testament means by "Wisdom." The author who tells us most clearly what is denoted by it is Ben-Sira.[1] Wisdom, he tells us, is higher than heaven, broader than earth, more unfathomable than the abyss; it has been steadily built up from the beginning;[2] God only knows it, has measured it, and spread

---

[1] Ben-Sira's verses can ordinarily be restored by simple retranslation from the Greek, remembering that the verse must have the rhythm ‿ ˊ ‿ ‿ ˊ ‿ ‿ ˊ ‿.

[2] Ecclus. i. 3, 4 :— גְּבֹהַּ שָׁמַיִם רֹחַב אָרֶץ
וּתְהֹומֹות כַּמָּה מִי יַעֲקֹב
מִכָּל־אֵלֶּה רָבְתָה הָכְמָה
וַתִּבָּנֶה בָנֹה מִקֶּדֶם.

it over His works.[1]   At the commencement of
the world it took up its residence with Adam
and abides with his posterity.[2]   Fear of the
Lord is the commencement of it ; yet all mankind have some share of it, only those who
fear God have the largest share.   Similarly
he states that the whole process of creation
was done in the presence of Wisdom ; and that,
being given the choice of all the world, Wisdom,
while reserving to herself a *pied-à-terre* in every
race, chose Jerusalem, David's city, for her
headquarters.[3] And finally he identifies Wisdom
with the Bible as it was then known to him.
" All this is the Book of the Covenant of the
Most High God, with the Law that Moses
commanded us, the heritage of the Synagogue
of Jacob."[4]

Ben-Sira is not an original writer, but a
poetical paraphraser of the ideas of the Old
Testament ; and the ideas of these paragraphs

Ecclus. i. 6, 7 :—   אֶחָד הוּא חָכָם נוֹרָא לָחַד

יוֹשֵׁב עַל כִּסְאוֹ יְהֹוָה הוּא

בְּרָאָהּ וְרָאָהּ וַיִּסְפְּרָהּ

וַיַּשְׁדֶּנָּה עַל כָּל־מַעֲשָׂיו (*sic*).

[2] Ecclus. i. 13 :—   עִם אָדָם מִיסּוֹד עוֹלָם הָתְקַנּ־

נְכָה וְעִם זַרְעוֹ תִּתְאַמֵּן

[3] Ecclus. xxiv. 11 :—   בְּעִיר דָּוִד בֵּן הֱנִיחַנִי

וּבִירוּשָׁלַיִם שָׁרִיתִי

[4] Ecclus. xxiv. 22.

4

are also to be found separately or together in the Proverbs, Job, and the Wisdom of Solomon. His identification of Wisdom with the Bible seems however to be his own. And the noble truth that Israel only had a larger share of the treasure in which all races participated to some degree is assuredly nowhere stated so distinctly as in the verses that have been quoted.

What then is this Wisdom? What is there known to us which will suit these descriptions? The answer is of course *science*. It is the privilege of man that he has insight into the works of God ; here and there he can grasp their meaning, and the processes by which they are accomplished ; not unfrequently he can imitate them. Between instinct and reasoned action there is a gulf that can never be spanned. In the one case the actor and the designer are one; in the other they are wholly different beings. Man is in the image of God, because God as revealed in nature uses the same instrument as man can use ; the syllogism with its major premise of a universal law. So far as the world is carried on by the working of laws, the difference between the work done by nature and that which is performed by man is quantitative rather than qualitative; the building of a human frame and the building of a steam-engine are processes which differ in complication rather than in any other

respect. Hence what Ben-Sira says of Wisdom
in the passages quoted is literally true and
exact, if we interpret Wisdom as *science*. It
was present at the Creation ; for the whole
universe is the solution of a scientific problem.
It took up its abode with Adam at the commencement of human society, because man is
the only rational agent who mixes with that
society. He only acts because he is acquainted
with the laws that make effect follow cause ;
and the longer the chain of reasoning whereon
his conduct is based, the more far-reaching
the effects which it contemplates, the more
Godlike is his conduct. But on the other
hand science has been constantly *built up* from
the beginning ; not science as known to God,
but as known to man. It is an accumulation
of observations and deductions from the time
when man first became a reasoning being.
With constant accumulation facility of con-
servation and assimilation has also increased.
What to one generation has seemed a mighty
fabric of science to a later one seems a humble
erection : it has *gone on building from the
beginning ;* no one can prophesy how high
the fabric is destined to rise. We are like
those insects who contribute (if we are fortunate
enough) our grain to the hill, but the ultimate
height and shape of the cliff is beyond our
ken.

But further, the fear of the Lord is the

commencement of the whole.[1] Without morality
the continuance of the race would be possible,
but its progress would not be possible. Fear,
or self-restraint, for however short a period is
the necessary condition of all science. The
savage who, instead of devouring his captive,
makes a slave of him, has started science and
civilization ; for in view of a future gratification
he has restrained a present appetite. And
when the pursuit of science itself becomes the
absorbing interest, apart from all other gratifi-
cations, all of which are sunk in that of the
contemplation of the works of God, and inter-
course through them with Him, then the fear
of the Lord may be said to be a satiation with
Wisdom.[2] For the whole being has then
become filled with it.

This is not forced into the Hebrew writers,
but is the only explanation of their words
which will suit every portion of the description.
Viewed as God's, science is before the worlds ;
viewed as man's, it is coeval with him, and
has been steadily growing with the growth of
human society. Viewed as an instrument for
ameliorating man, it is the most effective that
Christianity can employ ; for by inventing anything you possibly divert an unlimited number
of human beings from preying on the others
and turn them into co-operators for the general
welfare. The more each one of us becomes

[1] Ecclus. i. 12.   [2] Ecclus. i. 14.

dependent on all, the more are the interests of all made identical.

Ben-Sira, as we have seen, identifies "Wisdom" with the Bible; thinking, evidently, that the Bible was the complete store of science. And in thinking Scripture science he was right; for clearly morality is no less science than chemistry; and science cannot dispense with history, which furnishes matter for her syllogisms. But in regarding Scripture as the sum total of the knowable he was mistaken, and indeed it may be doubted whether he could have coolly maintained such a view.

The Hymn to Wisdom which forms chapter xxiv. of his Proverbs was composed about 200 B.C. Speaking of Scripture as a whole, then, he says that it is identical with that Wisdom of which so glowing an account is given in chapter i., that the first man did not fully know it, and that the last shall not sound it to the bottom, for it is deep as the ocean, and perennial as the Euphrates. Surely no man could use such language of a book that did not occupy a unique position, such as can only be acquired by long familiarity and reverence. And by Wisdom he means not the Law in the narrower sense, but the Old Testament in the wider sense. For he states that his own work consists of gleanings from it; his book is a rill taken from the great river. Therefore if we can

trace the source of his imitations, we know
what his Bible was, and what he identified with
the Wisdom that helped at the creation of the
world. It is not necessary to prove here that
Ben-Sira draws matter from all three collections
of Biblical books ; that may be taken as generally known. But the question that is clearly
apposite is—If a collection of books had in 200
B.C. acquired such tremendous authority that a
writer of unusual common sense could identify
it with the Divine Wisdom—in other words
speak of it as Mohammedan writers speak of
their Koran—how could any fresh matter be
smuggled in to that collection later than 200
B.C.? We might conceive an occasional word
or an occasional verse being interpolated, though
even this would be difficult: for in Oriental
countries a man is not supposed to know anything that he does not know by heart. The
Semitic writing is somewhat of a *memoria
technica* rather than an accurate representation
of sounds. There would be no difficulty in
finding Israelites now who could repeat the
whole Old Testament verbatim. Such persons
would testify to the spuriousness of a new
chapter at once ; they could also testify to
the spuriousness of a new verse or even a new
word. If we consider the conservatism which
characterizes such persons, it may be doubted
whether the introduction of a work of any
considerable dimensions into their canon could

be executed : if such an operation were performed, the probability is that posterity would hear something of it.

The facts of the Greek translation of Ben-Sira's book being dated and the work of a known man, render it suitable for building inferences. Therefore attention should be called here to some points about the book which show us that since the completion of the canon Hebrew literature and Hebrew society have greatly altered.

The poetry of the Bible is unmetrical. Attempts to reduce it to metre are utter failures. If there were any metrical laws, they would not shun the light, but be plain and obvious as is the metre of the Vedas or the rhyme of the Koran. But it has no such artifices because it does not require them. " The word of the Lord is tried." It will win approval on its merits only. It thrills more than any other poetry, albeit it is not rendered attractive by such gay costume as other poetry puts on. Such performances as the second or the forty-fifth Psalm are like mountain torrents ; the thought of hemming *them* in with locks and regulating their pace with sluices is too absurd for consideration. But by Ben-Sira's time things have changed. Some of the ideas of Greece have found their way into Palestine,[1]

---

[1] To Æsopic fables there are allusions in Ecclus. iv. 30 and xiii. 2c ; to the Seven Sages in xi. 26 ; and to Homer in xiv. 18.

and the measuring of syllables is probably one
of them. Since inspiration flows now in no
such torrents, art has to do something to com-
pensate for the loss. The fact, then, that Ben-
Sira's work is metrical shows the gulf that
separates the Psalms from 200 B.C.

Secondly, let us compare the society addressed by the author of the second or the
forty-fifth Psalm with that to which Ben-Sira
speaks. "Be wise now, therefore, O ye kings :
be prudent, ye that judge the earth." "Hearken,
O daughter, and give ear"—this is how the
author of Psalm xlv. addresses a queen! But
Ben-Sira's audience is very much humbler.
"Make thyself agreeable to the synagogue, and
bow thy head before the Rabbi."[1] "Among
Rabbis do not exalt thyself, and where there
are presbyters do not talk much."[2] What a
descent ! From a congregation of kings and
queens to one in which the Rabbi of the
synagogue is the towering figure ! After
enumerating the great men of his race the
author thinks fit to mention as its last hero a

---

[1] Ecclus. iv. 7 :—

הַטֵּב נַפְשְׁךָ לַכְּנֶסֶת

וְלָרַב הַמֶּלֶךְ אֶת־רֹאשֶׁךָ

(cf. B. Baba Mezia, 87a.)

[2] Ecclus. xxxv. 9 :—

בֵּין רַבְרְבָנִים אַל תִּתְרַבְרַב

וּזְקֵנִים לֹא הַרְבֵּה תָשִׂיחַ

(Syr. חֶרְפָּה תִסְוַח).

certain Simon son of Onias, of whom unfortunately little is known; but his services to the community seem to have consisted in spending money on public buildings. Ben-Sira is fully conscious of the oppressed condition of the community of which he is a member; he prays for the renewal of the wonders of which he has read so much, and desires that some positive proof should be given of the grandeur of Israel; and it may be that that prayer helped to raise up Judas Maccabæus. But if we wish to find the parallel to the society which Ben-Sira addresses, we shall find it in the works of authors like Seadyah,[1] who writes as a member of a subject community at a time when the Caliphate of Baghdad was supreme in the Eastern world.

Thirdly, a word may be said about Ben-Sira's language. Jewish writers call him "one of our holy Rabbis,"[2] and the specimens which the oral tradition preserved of his verses bear this statement out. He writes the language of the

---

[1] The correct spelling of this name is given in a poem in MS. Bodl. Heb. d 65 (*Wâfir* metre) :—

כְּתָב בָּא מִפְּאַת צִעַן בְּשֵׁם אִישׁ
שְׁמוֹ חֶסֶד אֱלֵי דֹרוֹ סְעַדְיָה

[2] Nachmanides in his Preface to the Law at the end. R. Bachya, *Chobath Ha- Lebaboth* (Warsaw, 1875), i. 88, quotes him as "a certain sage"; the purpose of these periphrases is to conceal an error committed by Seadyah in his commentary on the "Book of the Creation."

Rabbis, not the language of any part of the Bible. An oral interpretation of large portions of the Old Testament was then current; and when his metre requires it, he substitutes the words used in that oral interpretation for those of the text of the Old Testament. The beginnings of the Mishnah can here and there be traced in his work, and even a few of the technical terms [1] which the Scribes evolved in the course of their study of the law. The name Mishnah itself was not yet in circulation, for that is apparently posterior to the Christian era.

That Ben-Sira knew and used the Wisdom of Solomon was suggested in the preceding chapter. This proposition must now be demonstrated.

In his account of Solomon he states that "the countries marvelled at his *Odes, Parables, Proverbs,* and *Commentaries.*" [2] Since the first three of these names clearly refer to the writings attributed to Solomon, it is probable that the fourth word " Commentaries " also refers to a book ; the alternate text of this verse substitutes " Prophecies " for " Commentaries," but this is probably a guess at an unusual word.[3] The first three are clearly identical with the Song

---

[1] *E.g., halachas,* i. 4*d.*

[2] xlvii. 17.

[3] The same text (the Syriac) curiously *introduces* the word פשר " commentary " by mistake for the Hebrew בשיר.

of Songs, Proverbs and Ecclesiastes; for
Ecclesiastes is certainly imitated by Ben-Sira;
and since the tradition which identified Kohe-
leth or "the Preacher" with Solomon is not
known to have sprung up after Ben-Sira's time,
we are justified in finding an allusion to it in
either "Proverbs" or "Parables." As is well
known, the ancient languages do not distinguish
very carefully between these two notions, and
which ever of these names does not belong to
"Proverbs" is intended to signify Ecclesiastes.

The only book ascribed to Solomon which
can with justice be called a Commentary is the
Wisdom of Solomon. A considerable portion
of it might be termed a Midrash on the Pentateuch. The purpose of this sort of commentary
is not linguistic, but edifying or homiletic; it
gives an insight into the deeper or more hidden
meaning of events or enactments; and Wisdom
not only reminds the reader of, but is occasionally identical with, the desultory comments on
passages of Scripture contained in the Mishnah
and Gemara. Ben-Sira's assertion that "the
first man had not completely understood the
Bible," [1] implies that such commentaries had
been tried by many persons.

Secondly, there are places in which Ben-Sira
has matter that is very similar to that contained
in Wisdom. And in such a case it is reasonable

---

[1] xxiv. 26 : לֹא כִלָּה הָרִאשׁוֹן לְדַעְתָּהּ

to assign the priority to Wisdom, on the ground
that Ben-Sira confesses himself an excerptor.[1]
Whether Solomon wrote Wisdom or any one
else, the book makes no similar *confession* to that
which Ben-Sira makes.   The writer of Wisdom
claims to have been naturally talented, and by
praying for Wisdom to have obtained it.   It at
any rate lays claim to originality, and in the
places where it bears a strong resemblance to
other books we shall presently have to inquire
into the justice of that claim.

The remarkable passage Wisdom iii. 16 to
iv. 6 is too strikingly like certain passages of
Ben-Sira's book to admit the possibility of
independence.   The treble doctrine that is
taught in these passages is that the offspring
of adultery will not thrive ; that even if they
live long, it will not avail them ; and that childlessness is better than an ill-doing progeny.
The corresponding passages of Ben-Sira are
xvi. 1–3, xxiii. 22–27, xli. 5–11.   If these
passages of Ben-Sira be read side by side with
those of Wisdom, it will, I think, seem clear
that the priority is with the latter.   In the first
place the verses form a single paragraph in
Wisdom, whereas they are scattered about
Ben-Sira.   Secondly, some things that are clear
in Wisdom are obscure in Ben-Sira.   "Such
fruit," says the author of Wisdom, speaking of
adulterous offspring, "is uneatable and gene-

[1] xxiv. 28.

rally useless, for such children are a witness to the wickedness of their parents." Compare with this the account of the adulteress in Ben-Sira xxiii. 25 : " Her children shall not take root, and her branches shall not give fruit " ; and xli. 7, " An impious father shall be reproached by his children, because on his account they shall suffer shame."

Wisdom iv. 1 : " Better is childlessness with virtue, for immortality is in the memory of it, since it is recognised by God and man ; whereas a prolific crowd of evildoers will not be of use." Ben-Sira xvi. 1 : " Desire not a multitude of *useless* children, neither rejoice over impious sons : if they be many, rejoice not over them, if the fear of the Lord be not with them. For one is better than a thousand, and to die childless than to have impious children."

Wisdom iii. 16 : " The children of adulterers shall be without result, and the offspring of unlawful union shall be destroyed. If they be long-lived, they shall not be accounted of : and their old age at the end shall be dishonoured. And if they die quickly, they shall have no hope, neither consolation in the day of discrimination."

Ben-Sira xli. 5 (after observations on the fact that death is appointed to all mankind) : " Abominable children are the children of sinners, and they that consort with the dwellings of the impious : woe unto you, impious

men, that have abandoned the law of the
Most High ; if ye are born, ye shall be born
unto cursing ; and if ye die, a curse shall be
your portion." "The grief of men is over
their bodies ; but the ill name of sinners shall
be blotted out. Have a care of your name,
for that will last longer than a thousand
myriad talents of coin.[1] A good life lasts a
few days, whereas a good name lasts for
ever."

I can only regard the verses of Ben-Sira as
a paraphrase of the doctrine of Wisdom.
Immortality may be interpreted in three
ways : either (1) as *continuity ;* and this interpretation we find in Plato. A man has a
share in immortality in so far as he has the
power of being a parent. Hence the high
importance attached to parenthood in many
religious systems. Each citizen is bound to
see that the honours of the gods do not lapse ;
and this can only be by a constant supply
of persons to maintain them. But if the offspring be either unlawfully born, or be of
bad character, this form of immortality is
undesirable. The curious thing is that neither
the author of Wisdom nor Ben-Sira can quite
distinguish between these two alternatives.
(2) As perpetuation of the *name*. Whereas,
says the author of Wisdom, the immortality

מֵאֶלֶף רִבּוֹת אוֹצְרוֹת הוֹן ‏[1]

which most men aim at consists in leaving
descendants (compare Ben-Sira xxx. 4), virtue
gives an immortal *name*. It is admired during
life, and mourned for after death. This doctrine
is found in Plato also, where the observation
is made that the immortality of a Homer or
Hesiod is a better thing than the immortality
which consists in being one of an infinite series.
The thought of this form of immortality is
what suggests to Ben-Sira the "praise of famous
men" (men of name) with which his book
closes. (3) As personal continuance after death.
This doctrine involves that of the resurrection
and the final judgment. Ben-Sira hopes to
be one of those who shall rise at the coming
of Elijah. "He of whom it is written in the
'Remonstrances,' that he shall come to turn
the hearts of the fathers to the children ; happy
he who, having seen thee, is cut off: how
much happier we who shall arise!"[1] The
author of Wisdom is far clearer on this subject.
The idea that early or even shameful death
is a misfortune is, he says, a mistake due to
superficiality. The certainty we have of God's
justice proves that the condition of things

---

[1] xlviii. 10 :— הַכָּתוּב בַּתּוֹכָחוֹת לְאֵתוֹת

לְהָשִׁיב לֵב אָבוֹת אֶל בָּנִים

אַשְׁרֵי רוֹאֲךָ וּמֵתחָרֶם

אַף כִּי אֲנַחְנוּ חָיֹה נִחְיֶה

must have been misunderstood. On the "day of discrimination" the wicked will find out their error—when it is too late to repair it. They will turn out to have forfeited all three sorts of immortality; for their children will not survive; their name, if it survives, will be ignominious; and finally, the next world has no consolation for them, but the very contrary.

Whereas, then, in Wisdom we have this (assuredly remarkable) doctrine worked out in a series of closely reasoned paragraphs, the ideas are scattered about Ben-Sira's book: nor is Ben-Sira sufficiently philosophical to banish from his work the commoner notions. It would seem to be characteristic of *proverbial* philosophy not to trouble itself to reconcile the often contradictory aphorisms which superficial examination of phenomena suggests. But what seems clear is that the paragraphs in Ben-Sira and those in Wisdom cannot be independent; the one writer must be adopting the ideas and even the phrases of the other. And since Ben-Sira acknowledges himself an imitator, and seems very clearly to mention Wisdom among Solomon's writings, we are justified in concluding that Ben-Sira imitates Wisdom. Hence we have shown that Wisdom was a Hebrew classic to Ben-Sira, who attributed it to Solomon. In the last chapter reasons were given for thinking Wisdom the first

Hebrew book translated into Greek. Hence
we have taken Wisdom back to about 350
B.C. Let us see whether we can take it back
still further.

The chief question that suggests itself is
connected with the passage in which the origin
of idolatry is explained (xiii. 10–19). Much
of this passage is also found in Isaiah xl.–xliv.
Is it the case that the verses in Wisdom are
taken from Isaiah, or that the verses in Isaiah
are taken from Wisdom?

The clue that we have to start with is the
same with which the above inquiry in the case
of Ben-Sira started. Isaiah is known to embody
in his prophecies matter that already existed ;
so in xvi. 13 he says, " This is the word which
the Lord spake against Moab aforetime " ; and
the prophecy with which chapter ii. starts is
also an old one. Wisdom, as we have seen,
acknowledges no obligations.

In the second place, the description in
Wisdom forms a closely reasoned paragraph,
whereas in Isaiah the verses are scattered and
mingled with other matter. Either, then, they
are scattered reminiscences of Wisdom utilized
by the Prophet, or the author of Wisdom has
gathered the disconnected verses of Isaiah.
The former is the more likely operation.

It is also a canon that the more intelligible
passage is likely to be the earlier. In Wisdom
everything is clear. After condemning other

5

forms of Paganism, the author proceeds to that
which consists in worshipping idols, which he
shows us means putting faith in the dead.
These idols are either of metal, or of stone,
or of wood. The process by which the last
is made is then described. Some carpenter
cuts down a tree, scrapes off the bark, and
first of all makes some utensil or piece of
furniture. The sawdust and chips he then uses
for cooking his food. Probably some knotty
and crooked stump remains, and of this in his
idle hours he makes a god. He carves it, that
is to say, into the resemblance of a man or
some animal, paints it red, raises for it a shrine
to which he nails it, so that it should not fall :
for, being an image, it cannot help itself.

If we compare this description with Isaiah's
(xliv. 13–16), we shall find some certain marks
of originality in the description given in Wisdom.
Isaiah in his indignation has *forgotten one
important detail* in the operation ; viz., the
original purpose of the carpenter in cutting
down the tree, which was of course to make
some article of furniture. The purpose of the
operations with gauge, rule, and pencil described in Isaiah xliv. 13 must surely be to
make a table or a chair ; but the writer has
simply *forgotten that it is so*. The place where
the furniture should be mentioned is xliv. 16 :
" The half thereof he burnt in fire ; on the
half thereof he eats flesh, he roasts him a

roast, and fills himself; yea, he warms himself
and says : I am warm, I have seen fire." It
is evident that the Prophet's idea of the use
of the second "half" does not differ materially
from the first. Perhaps we are to distinguish
the cooking fire from the warming fire, but
this distinction seems strange. Yet in verse
18, where the description is repeated, the real
distinction is still obscured. The further operations of fixing the image in the shrine are
mentioned by Isaiah xl. 20, where a clever
carpenter is sought in order to fix the statue
so that it should not fall. The cleverness
would seem rather to be required for *shaping
the image* out of the wood, as is described in
Wisdom xiii. 13.

In Wisdom xv. 7–10 another form of image
is described ; viz., that produced by the potter.
He, we are told, rivals the metal-workers, and
thinks it a great thing to counterfeit their work.
But it is his heart which is *dust*, and his hope
which is more worthless than *earth*, and his
life which is more dishonourable than *clay*.
For surely he must know how absurd his
practice is. Of all forms of image-maker, the
potter is the most contemptible. If we study
Isaiah xl.–xliv., two phrases will be found
that seem to come from the Solomonic description.

xliv. 20: " He feedeth on dust ;[1] a deceived

[1] For אפר=עפר see Rashi on B. *Taanith* 16a.

heart has made him to swerve," follows after
the account of the worker in wood. For the
words "he feedeth on dust" the LXX. substitutes what is clearly a reminiscence of the
passage of Wisdom, "know that his heart is
dust." This reminiscence is felicitous, but not
employed with sufficient dexterity; it should
rather have taught them to render the words
of Isaiah, "his thought is dust :[1] a deceived
heart has led him astray." Thus it appears
that both writers use the same phrase, the
author of Wisdom of the potter, Isaiah of the
worker in wood. But in Wisdom it is suggested
by the context. The potter is said to be the
most contemptible of the idol-makers, because
his material is *worthless*. Gold and silver are
at any rate precious metals; and wood is not
valueless, for a special kind of tree has to be
sought out for such a purpose; but *clay* is
worthless, so that to make a god of *it* is the
grossest form of Paganism. The brains of such
an idol-maker must be as worthless as his
material. And the writer repeats this thought
twice.

But in Isaiah, where the sort of idol described is one of *wood*, this thought is not
suggested by the context, since the Prophet
allows that the material is of some value. We
might, indeed, render the word translated

[1] Pointing רָעֶה for רֹעֶה.

"dust" by "ashes," and think of a reference
to the parts of the tree that have been *burned ;*
but we should have to supply in thought too
many premises, in addition to the fact that
it is unfair to identify the material (wood) in
the state in which an idol can be made of it
with the same material in a wholly different
state. Hence we have two writers employing
the same phrase, and one so remarkable in its
character that they cannot be employing it
independently. To one of these writers it is
suggested by his context, while to the other
it is not suggested by the context, though the
context may very well have *reminded* him of
it. Hence it must be the property of the former
writer, and borrowed by the latter.

Next we see that the author of Wisdom
taunts the potter with *rivalling* the workers
in more choice material. Compare with this
Isaiah xli. 6 : "Each man helps his neighbour
and says to his brother, Be strong." "So the
smith strengthened the smelter, the hammerer
the forger. Saying of the soldering, It is good,
and strengthening it with nails that it should
not fall." This "strengthening" would seem
to refer to the co-operation of various labourers
in making an idol ; it reminds us of the word
rivalling used in Wisdom of the potter, which
would probably be expressed in Hebrew by
a derivative of the same root.[1] Moreover we

[1] חזק.

have seen already that the operation of fixing with nails seems to belong rather to the case of the wooden idol with which Wisdom associates it.

A point noticed by the author of Wisdom, but not by Isaiah, is the painting of the wooden image with red chalk or red lead. The localization of this practice would require some archæological investigation.[1] The combination of this statement in Wisdom with the other about nailing the image to its place reminds us of a fragment quoted by Suidas,[2] which refers to the treatment of an image by the people of *Tyre*. At the time of the attack on their city by Alexander the Tyrians, fearing that one of their idols intended to desert to the enemy, " nailed it to its base, and scourged it with ropes steeped in red lead." I presume that the purpose of that substance was to make it seem as though the scourging had drawn blood.

Whereas then the supposition that the stray flashes in Isaiah were combined by the author of Wisdom into his orderly and closely reasoned paragraphs presents considerable difficulty, the hypothesis that Isaiah wove into his " remonstrances " various phrases taken from the passage in Wisdom suits all the facts that are before us.

[1] Pliny asserts that the gods of the Ethiopians were painted red.   [2] *s.v.* μίλτος.

Isaiah xxviii. 15 : " Ye have said, We have made a covenant with death and a treaty with the grave." The idea of making a covenant with death is not quite easy to grasp. People who thoughtlessly devote themselves to pleasure are sometimes said to act as though they had *immunity* from death ;[1] but to make a *covenant* with death implies giving and taking. What is it, then, that the drunkards reproved by Isaiah give death in order that they in turn may be delivered from the passing scourge? This is not stated by the Prophet, who only assures them that their covenant will be got rid of ; death will find a quibble by which to get out of it.[2] But in Wisdom i. 16, where the same phrase occurs, we again find ourselves in the middle of a closely reasoned paragraph, which tells us far more of the nature of the contract in question. Death had originally no part in the world. It is the conduct of the wicked that has summoned him. " Thinking him a friend, they melted (?) and made a treaty with him." Of what notion the word " melted " is a mistranslation it is not necessary now to inquire ;[3] we learn, however, that the treaty

---

[1] Hariri, ed. de Sacy, p. 108 : " 'Tis as though ye had put yourselves under the protection of death, and had procured a safe-conduct from destiny."

[2] The phrase in Isaiah is very near the Arabic usage.

[3] Perhaps חמיסו in Syriac, " they sought" (*Thes. Syr.*, col. 1021).

with death was to admit him into the world on condition that he spared them. This, then, seems to be the same phenomenon as before : what is a flash in Isaiah is part of a steady flame in Wisdom. And when this reminiscence has been identified, other points in Isaiah xxviii. are made more intelligible by the same clue. The coarse verse xxviii. 8 is the prophetic representation of Wisdom ii. 7 : "Let us leave everywhere signs of our merriment." The "crown of pride of the drunkards," which is the subject of verses 1, 3, and 4 in Isaiah, is the crown of rose-blossoms which the drunkards in Wisdom would put on before they fade.

Isaiah xl. 15 : "With whom took He counsel ? For the nations are like a drop *from a bucket*, and are accounted as the dust of the balance." Wisdom xi. 22 : "Who shall resist the might of Thy arm, seeing that the nations before Thee are like the dust of the balance, or like a drop of morning dew *descending* [1] to the earth ? " It is evident that either Isaiah is imitating Wisdom, or the author of Wisdom is imitating Isaiah. In the case of one of these

[1] The word מדלי (from a bucket) is used with the sense "ascending" of dust in B. *Taanith*, 9b. In Arabic it would mean "coming down," "descending," *Aghani* vii. 15, 3 a.f. This is the sense which the translator of Wisdom gave the word. Hence this passage may be added to the proofs that he is translating from Hebrew.

images the imitation is close, in that of the other it is remote. The context must decide with whom the originality lies. The author of Wisdom is dealing with the power of God as compared with that of *man*. He chooses to punish men in kind,[1] *i.e.*, in the same manner as they have sinned. And this must be designed; for owing to His almighty power he could punish them in any way He chose. For who can resist Him, seeing how infinitely great He is as compared with man? Here, therefore, the context requires that the infinite disproportion between man and God should be illustrated in some such way as is here given. But in the passage of Isaiah there is no such necessity. It is the *absolute* greatness of God with which the Prophet is occupied; he is explaining how utterly unworthy of Him is the idea which the idol represents. Hence the *nations* are only mentioned in a series of objects; they are followed by the *isles;* then by the forest and the herds of Lebanon, which together would not produce an adequate sacrifice. The context does not, therefore, necessitate an illustration of the triviality of the nations. If the author of the Wisdom of Solomon were consciously borrowing a phrase from either the original of Isaiah or from the LXX. version, his altering it would be surprising; but if he altered it in order to avoid the appearance of anachronism,

[1] Compare B. *Sotah*, 9*b*.

it is strange that he should not have altered it more completely. On the other hand, there would be nothing remarkable in Isaiah, while utilizing the phrases of a national classic, altering them arbitrarily.

What the two illustrations actually meant is another question. If the " dust of the balance " mean a weight so small that its addition or subtraction makes no appreciable difference, it is an appropriate concept, though the possibility of such an interpretation is doubtful. " The drop from the bucket" is picturesque, but suggests the disproportion less forcibly than we should have expected it to be expressed : in Wisdom the drop of morning dew is sufficiently forcible as well as picturesque, but scarcely natural. Probably the actual illustrations which lie at the base of both passages are lost.

The most remarkable parallel between Isaiah and Wisdom is, however, to be found in the celebrated fifty-third of Isaiah as compared with Wisdom ii.–v.

The chief differences between the scene presented in Wisdom and that in Isaiah are three : (1) In Wisdom the Sufferer is distinctly said to call Himself the *Son of God* (ii. 16, 18), whereas in Isaiah the words Righteous and Servant are applied to Him, but not Son.   (2) In Wisdom nothing is said of His intercessory function, on which so much stress is laid by Isaiah.   (3) In

Wisdom the oppressors of the Just One are identified with those who afterwards marvel at His deliverance, whereas in Isaiah there is not more than a passing allusion to this.

Otherwise the scene in Isaiah greatly resembles a reduction or abridgment of the scene in Wisdom. What is it at which the nations and kings, whose words are recorded in Isaiah liii., wonder? Wisdom tells us : "They shall wonder at His extraordinary deliverance" (v. 2). "We thought His life madness and His end dishonoured : how then is He reckoned among the Sons of God, and His lot among the Holy Ones?" Wisdom says, "His endurance must be put to the test" (ii. 19); Isaiah adds that this test was properly undergone. The dishonourable *death* is insisted on by Wisdom (ii. 20, v. 4), while the remarkable character of His *burial* strikes Isaiah (liii. 9). Even Isaiah's first phrase in this most remarkable passage seems to require Wisdom to interpret it : "Behold my Servant shall *be prudent*" (lii. 13). This must mean what we are told in Wisdom (iii. 9) : "They that trust in Him *shall understand the truth*, and those that are faithful in love shall wait for Him," *i.e.*, shall understand the Divine counsel in allowing apparent injustice to be perpetrated, whereas the wicked who interpret the facts superficially are absolutely deluded (ii. 22).

Although in these two passages there are

striking differences, as well as similarities, and the comparison between them by no means lessens the admiration which each of the writers may claim, it seems rather easier to think of Wisdom as utilized by Isaiah than of Isaiah as utilized by Wisdom. The phrase "Righteous, my Servant" (Isaiah liii. 11) implies familiarity on the Prophet's part with the identification of the typically Righteous One with the Servant of the Lord, and this identification needs Wisdom ii. 12, 13 to explain it : "Let us waylay the Righteous, for He is grievous unto us ; He professes to have knowledge of God, and calls Himself the Servant of God." 18 : "If the Righteous be the Son of God, He will help Him." v. 1 : "Then shall the Righteous stand with much boldness before the face of His oppressors." Here we see that the name whereby He is familiarly known to the author of Wisdom is "the Righteous," whereas to Isaiah He is best known as "the Servant of the Lord." But the name "Righteous" is so familiar to Isaiah that he can use it as a proper name without the article ; whereas in Wisdom (ii. 13), where the statement that the Righteous is God's servant is regarded as an arrogant assumption by the wicked, which they propose to put to the test, the latter is clearly not yet a familiar phrase in this context. Hence Isaiah implies Wisdom, but Wisdom does not imply Isaiah.

" By His knowledge shall Righteous, my
Servant, justify many." Here again the thought
is not sufficiently clear without the guidance of
Wisdom (ii. 13) : " He professes to have knowledge of God." His insight into God's purpose
is what, enabling Him to stand every trial,
justifies the human race, because Satan's
accusation against it is answered. In the
chapter on Job this will be more fully worked
out.

The last parallel to be noticed is between
Isaiah lvi. 4, 5 and Wisdom iii. 14. In Isaiah
the eunuchs are mentioned together with the
strangers ; neither are to despair, since the
former, if they keep the Sabbath, etc., shall be
given a monument in God's house that is better
than sons or daughters, while the strangers will
form an integral part of God's people. In
Wisdom the eunuchs are mentioned after the
virgins, which is assuredly the more natural
context for them. On the whole the mention
of the eunuchs in Isaiah is most naturally
explained as follows : In verse 2, " Keeping his
hand from doing any evil," which comes in the
context of the prophecy, reminds the Prophet of
Wisdom iii. 14, where this phrase is used of the
eunuch. Hence the Prophet, in verses 3-5,
repeats and enlarges the promise made to them
in Wisdom. Even here there seems to be the
same relation between the two books that has
several times been noticed : there is a steady

flame in Wisdom, flashes in Isaiah. "The eunuch who does no wrong and thinks no wrong shall be well rewarded for his faith, and given a fair allotment in God's temple ; for good deeds bear famous fruit, and the root of Wisdom is imperishable." Isaiah seems to take the temple literally ; but how in that material temple can the eunuch have a monument that is better than sons or daughters ? Wisdom clearly thinks of the House of God not made with hands—the community of righteous souls.

If, then, it has been shown that Isaiah made use of the Wisdom of Solomon, what inference are we to draw ? It makes no difference whether we regard the chapters quoted as the work of one writer or of a series, all earlier than the return from the Exile : in either case there will be a strong probability that the work which ascribes itself to Solomon is really Solomon's. There would be little likelihood of such a work being fabricated between the age of Solomon and that of Hezekiah.

For in the first place this book is either genuine or else a deliberate fabrication. It is not a work which from its philosophical character would be uncritically attributed to Solomon by those to whom the name and date of the real author were unknown. On the contrary, the writer claims to be Solomon. He tells us some facts about his own life, of his natural abilities, of his succeeding to his father's throne, of the command given him to build the Temple, of his scientific pursuits.

If we submit the work to some of the tests suggested above, it will not be found wanting. The author addresses the right audience—one of kings and judges of the earth. It is the audience to which the second Psalm is addressed. The language, owing to the paraphrastic nature of the translation which we have, cannot be restored in sufficient quantity to enable us to pass judgment on its character ; but it is evidently in the style of the Prophets, *i.e.*, unmetrical, but with a fairly regular observance of the antithesis. Finally, the author makes a statement about the treatment of Israel as compared with that of other nations, which, while exceedingly suitable for the time of Solomon, would be surprising in the mouth of any serious thinker who had witnessed or lived after the first exile. Israel, he says, is subjected by God to paternal discipline, but other nations are scourged ten thousand times as much ! [1] Now we know that the author of Psalm lxxxix. *quotes* this doctrine, but finds it impossible to reconcile the facts with it ; he offers up the same prayer for the renewal of God's wonders as is offered up by Ben-Sira some decades before the appearance of Judas Maccabæus. This sentence, therefore, reveals a period of high prosperity, in which the Israelites

[1] Wisdom xii. 22.

could look back with satisfaction on the discipline which they had undergone and from
which they thought they had issued trium-
phantly.

But supposing it to be a fabrication, what
purpose had the fabricator?   Certainly not to
prove to the Greeks that their philosophy had
been anticipated by the Hebrew sage : for, as
we have seen, the arguments by which this
book is shown to have been originally in
Hebrew cannot be eluded.   The *translator* may
well have had that object ; and for that he
probably not only omitted the proper names,
but introduced the very decided Platonism
which arouses so much suspicion : [1] for that
Solomon and Plato did not arrive independently
at the fourfold division of virtue may be granted,
and also that Plato did not borrow it from
Solomon.   The suspicion, however, that that
passage has been tampered with by the translator is confirmed by the fact that some confusion appears in the Greek, and that the old
Syriac version exhibits a threefold instead of a
fourfold division.   Moreover an *author* whose
purpose was to impress the Greeks with the
idea that Solomon anticipated Plato would not
produce a Midrashic commentary on portions of
the Pentateuch, with which a Greek audience
would probably be quite unfamiliar.   A Midrashic commentary must certainly have been

[1] Wisdom viii. 7.

intended for believing Israelites ; and a fabricator who wrote for their benefit would probably
have personated Solomon earlier than chapter
vii., where he first begins to speak of himself.
Further, the very high merit of most of the
book makes us look for the author among men
of renown. Solomon's reputation for Wisdom
must have been based on something : for he is
by no means a mythical personage, but one on
whom history sheds a strong light. In the continuous thinking, the lofty conceptions, and the
poetical images of this book, as well as the
scientific interest which it displays, we have a
full justification for the opinion of antiquity.

But how comes it that the very memory of
the work has disappeared among the Jews ?
In the time of Melito [1] they clearly had lost it,
for the Jewish informant of this writer identified
Proverbs with Wisdom [2]—a fact which seems to
imply that the title had been preserved, though
the book was lost, whence it was ignorantly
transferred to a book with a different title ; and
of this phenomenon literary history offers a
variety of illustrations. Yet of course the title
" Wisdom " may have been learned from Greek-
speaking Jews or Christians, and the utilization

---

[1] Ap. Cureton, *Spicilegium*, p. 35.

[2] This appears to be done by Hamzah of Ispahan,
who obtained a canon from a Jew named Zedekiah in
the year 920 A.D. at Baghdad (Hamzæ *Annales*, ed.
Gottwaldt, St. Petersburg, 1844, p. 84).

of the book in the New Testament by no means proves that its original still existed in Palestine.

Fragments of it were indeed retained in the traditional interpretation of the Pentateuch ; one striking case was noticed in the first article ; attention may here be called to some more. The statement in xvi. 21 that the Manna, to gratify the desire of the taster, turned to whatsoever he wanted, is repeated in the Midrash.[1] " The Manna," it says, " contained every sort of taste, and each Israelite tasted whatsoever he wished." But the author of Wisdom apparently asserts this on his own authority, for he gives it as a justification of his description of the Manna as "adequate to every pleasure and suited to every taste." It must therefore have drifted from Wisdom into the Midrash, certainly before the Book of Wisdom was appropriated by Christians. The comparison of the darkness of Egypt to a prison is also found in the Midrash.[2] From the account of the darkness given in the Midrash some light can be thrown on Wisdom xviii. 1, 2. " But thy holy ones had very great light, whose voice they hearing, but seeing not their form, that the others too had suffered, accounted blessed, but that having been injured they did no harm, rejoiced." Truly an involved sentence, wherein the translator's determination

---

[1] *Rabbah*, ii. 36a ; also B. *Yoma*, 75a.
[2] *Tanchuma*, i. 79b (Warsaw, 1879).

to omit all proper names, especially that of Egypt, has led him to talk in enigmas. Who were the others who had suffered (or "suffered not," if that be the right reading)? It is probable (though not certain) that all this is to be explained from the Midrash. "There were," says the Midrash *Rabbah*, "certain sinners in Israel, who were unwilling to leave Egypt. God said, If I bring a plague on them openly and they die, the Egyptians will say, The same things happen to Israel as to us. Therefore He brought three days' darkness upon the Egyptians, that the Israelites might bury their dead without being seen by the Egyptians, and might praise God on that account." The Midrash *Tanchuma* tells the same story, adding,[1] "Israel gave thanks and rejoiced, because their enemies did not see their punishment and rejoice thereat." From this we can interpret the passage in Wisdom. The Egyptians could hear the voices, though they could not see the forms of the Israelites; the suffering of the Israelites which the Egyptians accounted blessed was the loss of certain members of the Israelite community, who were buried while the Egyptians being in darkness could not see. The remaining clause, "rejoiced that having been injured they did no harm," appears from the Midrash to mean that the Egyptians were thankful that the Israelites who could have

[1] i. 84*b*.

taken advantage of the darkness to rob them,
did not do so ; and in consequence of this proof
of Israelitish honesty they were willing to lend
them vessels of gold, etc.   The sentence which
follows in Wisdom is so obscure as to be
untranslatable.   We can just see that the
Hebrew word for "lent"[1] has been mistrans-
lated "besought"; but it is scarcely possible
to restore the rest of it, though the sense must
be that supplied by the Midrash.

Let us, before basing any inference on so
paradoxical a result as the genuineness of the
Wisdom of Solomon, recapitulate the arguments
whereby it has been reached : we shall then be
able to see whether it is likely to hold its own
against opposition, or to collapse as soon as it is
assailed.   First, it was shown to be a translation
from Hebrew (a) by the fact that the true form
of one of its verses is preserved in the Hebrew
of the Midrash ; (b) by the fact that in several
cases by retranslating passages of Wisdom into
Hebrew we obtain a better sense than the Greek
offers; (c) by the fact that other passages of the
Midrash which preserve matter contained in the
Wisdom of Solomon do not appear to be based
on the Greek, but on an original which gave
either the same or a better sense.

Next we notice that Ben-Sira mentions this
work among the Solomonic writings, and

[1] Probably השאיל.

utilizes it for his anthology just as he utilizes the canonical Scriptures. Hence the work must have been classical by 200 B.C.

Next we find that the Greek translation of Wisdom was utilized by the LXX. translator of Isaiah, who is shown to have done his work before 260 B.C. The Greek translation of Wisdom is therefore little later than 270 B.C., and the original probably some generations earlier.

Next we compare a number of texts of Wisdom with a number of similar passages in Isaiah. In each case the phrase which is common to the two books appears to belong to the context of Wisdom rather than to that of Isaiah, and to be more specially appropriate in Wisdom, whereas in Isaiah it can most easily be understood as an allusion to the work of the earlier classic. In one case the prophetic terminology which is already familiar to Isaiah appears in Wisdom to be in course of formation.

Then we notice that the nature of the audience addressed, the style of composition, and the historical background, all agree with the theory of Solomonic authorship ; and to these may be added the general excellence of the work, and still more the grasp which it displays of the most important of the prophetic messages—the mission of Israel, the passion of the Messiah, and the hope of immortality.

Whatever in this book appears to be distinctly Greek may without audacity be attributed to the Greek translator, whom, from the fragment in the Midrash, we know to have treated his original with great licence.

In the chapter on the Bible of the Jews an attempt will be made to explain the nature of decanonization and its consequences for the book decanonized; and the question may be asked whether, if Job had been decanonized and in consequence preserved only in the Greek translation, we should have known more about it than we know about the Wisdom of Solomon.

The importance of this result is that it seriously damages the modern criticism of the Pentateuch. For that the Pentateuch known to the author of Wisdom was practically the same as our Pentateuch does not admit of question. The moderns assert that the Tabernacle was an imitation of Solomon's Temple; but if Solomon himself states that his Temple was an imitation of the Tabernacle, this theory must be dismissed. If, therefore, the criteria whereby documents are separated in the Pentateuch have any scientific value, it must be very different from that which is ordinarily assigned them; and indeed it may be doubted whether our critical instruments are sufficiently powerful to analyse documents of such remote antiquity in a language with which recent events have proved us to be so imperfectly acquainted.

The theory of Winckler, according to which the history of the Pentateuch is a fiction invented by David, is of course not overthrown by the fact of Solomon having commented on it, but it would require some very powerful evidence to make us believe that David's fiction could in so short a time have obtained such circulation and recognition.

That our Book of Genesis was known to Solomon may be inferred from the Song of Songs vii. 11, where the bride says, " Unto him is my desire," with an obvious reference to the familiar words said to Eve after the fall. But Wisdom without question contains references not only to Genesis, but to Exodus, Numbers, Deuteronomy, and Joshua, with whose work its history stops, whereas Isaiah is already familiar with the history of the Judges.

III

UNITY AGAINST PLURALITY

A. ISAIAH

ARISTOTLE tells us that a work of art should be so constructed that the removal of any part should cause the whole to fall to pieces. We can therefore easily tell whether such a work is a unity by seeing what will happen if we take any part away. If the experiment results in leaving two unities where we fancied there was one, there will have been no original unity of plan. But if the result of the first experiment leads to endless dissection, then it will have been shown that the work was originally an organized whole.

If this canon be applied to the results of modern criticism on Isaiah, we shall be disposed to find the unity of the works ascribed to that Prophet brilliantly vindicated. To bisect Isaiah at the end of chapter xxxix. might seem an easy and legitimate process ; but the result has been such as to justify Aristotle's worst fears. To speak of a theory of two Isaiahs is to intentionally mislead. Even the earliest dissectors of the Prophet were forced to turn him into three or four. If the newest Introduction to Isaiah be taken as representative of the newest criticism, the number of Isaiahs required is more than can be easily counted. The world, till about 1790, thought it had the works of a great Prophet, the productions of a mind sublimely, if not uniquely, gifted. But that was a childish mistake. What it really had was a patchwork made of scraps produced by a number of obscure individuals so insignificant that posterity thought their names unworthy of record, or so dishonest that they dared not avow them. It is a cento of scraps of that sort that humiliated the literature of Greece and Rome and won Europe for Christ!

Now it is the business of science to produce results that are either certain or probable. Either they have their place in the chain of experience, or they are in harmony with it. Where a style of literature is common to many races, the scientific method is to master the history of the case which is most perfectly recorded, and to use the results to provide a working hypothesis for the cases that are more obscure. Thus Greece has epics, India has epics, and Persia has epics. In the case of the Greek epics history is silent both before and for some time after their composition. The Indian epics can be located with rather more ease; for though India has no history, it is certain that Sanskrit literature does not begin with the epics. But in the case of the Epic Cycle of the Persians the whole history of the structure of the poems lies before us in faithful records. Therefore the working hypothesis for the cases of Greece and India should be supplied from the literary history of the Persians; for the inquiry will have been started in accordance with the principles of science.

In the case of *Prophecy* we have to deal with a class of literature unrepresented anywhere but in Israel. The Greek oracles bear some resemblance to the Prophecies as regards matter, but no collection of them ever formed a literary monument of consequence. They were moreover thought to be the actual compositions of the god, and Plutarch naïvely points out how extraordinary it seemed that the deity who inspired the poets should be so poor a composer himself. Therefore the only analogies that can guide us must be got from Hebrew literature. And, happily, we have one that is amply sufficient to serve as a touchstone for the twenty-Isaiah theory. By the side of the lengthy roll of Isaiah is the less lengthy roll of the twelve Minor Prophets. Few of these Prophets figure in history; and the judgment of mankind on their literary merits places none

of them in the first class. They neither thrill
as Isaiah thrills, nor have they influenced mankind as Isaiah has influenced it. How comes
it then, if it was really the fashion of the Israelites to lump the oracles of different Prophets
together, that the works of the whole series are
not ascribed to the first? Why are not the
prophecies of Haggai ascribed to Hosea? Some
of the Minor Prophets have produced one
chapter or thereabouts; but the tradition has
not forgotten their names. How then comes it
that the brilliant authors of the Isaianic oracles
are for the most part utterly forgotten and
neglected?

In order to give some colour to this paradox
one piece of external evidence is adduced:
"Rabbi Simon, quoted in the Midrash *Rabbah*,
states that the verses 19 and 20 of Isaiah viii.
were really by Hosea's father, but incorporated
with Isaiah for fear lest they should get lost."
The Midrash *Rabbah* appears not to have been
committed to writing before about 1000 A.D.;
and the Jews attach to it far less authority than
they attach to the legends recorded in the
Talmud. The Rabbi Simon referred to is
probably the pupil of Rabbi Joshua Ben Levi,
and his *floruit* may be placed about 250 A.D.[1]
We begin, then, by assuming that the oral

---

[1] See Kohut, *Aruch Completum;* Weiss, *Dor, Dor, we-
Dor'shāw*, vol. iii. ; Frankel, *Introduction to the Jerusalem Talmud* (all in Hebrew).

tradition by which this saying was assigned to
Rabbi Simon was faithfully preserved for some
750 years! Truly this is a large assumption.
Writers such as Weiss, who make no very great
pretensions to scepticism, place little faith in
the lemmata of the Midrash. But supposing
Rabbi Simon to have said it, how are we to
suppose he got his information? Either the
oral tradition preserved the correct account of
the authorship of the verses from Isaiah's time
to Rabbi Simon's—another 1,000 years—or he
discovered it himself. If he discovered it himself, his authority is simply worthless; a work
in which such an opinion is even alluded to
except for the purpose of ridicule may even be
branded as unscientific. Yet that Rabbi Simon
did discover this himself is perfectly clear. His
name figures fairly often in the Midrash and in
the Jerusalem Talmud, and he clearly is an
exegete of the Talmudic type. In the first
section of the Midrash on Leviticus he is cited
for the observation that the Books of Chronicles
were written to encourage allegorical interpretations. He proceeds to show that Jared
(1 Chron. iv. 18) means Moses, because Jared
means "command," and Moses was a king.
The word "Jewess" is applied to Jochebed, he
says, in the same passage, because she, though
of the tribe of Levi herself, gave the Jews a
footing in the world. Elsewhere,[1] he infers

[1] Jer. *Rosh ha-shanah,* i. 3.

from Genesis xxi. 17 that God judges men at
the time of their actions, though the verse has
no connection with the subject. To suppose,
therefore, that this precious comment on
Isaiah viii. has any other source than the
imagination of some Rabbi is to misunderstand
the Midrash. Rabbi Simon of course *inferred*
that those verses were written by Hosea's
father, and I will undertake to reproduce most
of the steps of his reasoning. One premise is
that when the father of a Prophet is mentioned
in the Bible, the father must have been a
Prophet as well as the son ; for this I may refer
to the ordinary commentary on the Midrash.
Therefore Beeri, father of Hosea, must have
been a Prophet. In Isaiah viii. 20 we read,
" Assuredly they shall say unto you like this
word which have no dawn." Stars can, it
is said, be seen at midday at the bottom of a
well [1] ; since the dawn in ordinary cases chases
the stars, one who lived at the bottom of a well
would have no dawn. But the name of Hosea's
father means " the man of the well." Therefore
" which have no dawn " means Hosea's father.
Hence Isaiah viii. 20 was written by Hosea's
father ; and since it contains the phrase " like
this word," which probably refers to the pre-

[1] The observation is made by Aristotle, *de An. Gen.*,
vol. i. p. 780 ; also by Pliny, *Nat. Hist.*, ii. § 58. It
must have drifted to " Rabbi Simon " from one of these
authors.

ceding verse, verse 19 was by the same author.
But has not the text, "*they* shall say unto you"?
Because the same prophecy was to be uttered
by Isaiah, the plural is used ; or "do not read
'they shall say,' but 'he shall say.'" That this
was the line of reasoning followed by Rabbi
Simon is practically beyond question [1] ; and
since the stream cannot rise above its source,
the Biblical criticism of the nineteenth century
apparently *approves* methods of reasoning which
a child of ten could confute.

But suppose that we have here not an absurd
inference, but a valuable fragment of history :
what follows ?   Place the value of Rabbi
Simon's statement as low as you like, provided
you allow it *some* value ; then remember that
the Isaianic authorship of Isaiah xl.–lxvi. is
assumed by all the Rabbis and attested by
many of them. The statement of an isolated
Rabbi, recorded in a work of no authority,
about a matter that happened 1,000 years before
his time, is worth something ; then shall the
evidence of *all* the Rabbis be worth nothing ?
However atomic the value assigned to Rabbi
Simon's statement, if it be once admitted as
evidence, the case for the dissection of Isaiah
is hopelessly lost.   For it must be observed
that the theory that Isaiah viii. 19, 20 were
written by Hosea's father does not conflict with

---

[1] Many passages of the Bab. Talmud will supply
examples of the method. *Yoma, 22b,* supplies several.

traditional views, for Isaiah himself confesses in
one case that he has incorporated an earlier
oracle with his prophecy : Rabbi Simon's statement adds to our knowledge, but does not alter
existing conceptions. Hence this argument, if
admitted, in no way helps the dissecting theory,
whereas it brings in a cloud of witnesses who
effectually ruin it.

But stay. Perhaps these Rabbis are better
friends of the dissecting theory than you think.
" The book of Isaiah in the Hebrew canon
seems to have stood after Jeremiah and Ezekiel." This is proved by a reference to the
Gemara of *Baba Bathra*, 14*b*, where reasons are
given for placing Isaiah after Ezekiel. The
terms " Hebrew canon " and " Gemara " are too
vague for science ; let us try to limit them more
closely. The Babylonian Talmud (Mishnah
and Gemara) was compiled and written down
about 800–850 A.D.[1] The best accredited traditions were given a place in the Mishnah, less
accredited ones in the Gemara. The " Hebrew
canon" is a less accredited tradition. And
justly so, for it is not regularly followed. In the
year 920 A.D. a Jew named Zedekiah provided a

[1] See chapter v. Probably the earliest notice of the
existence of the Jewish Tradition in a book is in Yakubi,
ed. Houtsma, i. 73 (circ. 890 A.D.). Jahiz (quoted by
Raghib of Ispahan, *Colloquies,* Cairo, 1287 A.H., ii. 248)
asserted that the Jews of his time had " neither wisdom
nor proverbs, nor poems " (before 868 A.D.).

canon for the historian Hamzah of Ispahan ;
his order is, Isaiah Jeremiah Ezekiel Daniel.
Seadyah Gaon (ob. 942 A.D.) won the case for
the Talmud, and a pupil of his provided a
canon for the Arabic *Fihrist*, compiled in
987 A.D.   His order is, Isaiah Jeremiah Ezekiel
Kings Minor Prophets.   In the fourteenth
century another Jew provided a canon for the
author of the *Irshad al-kasid*.   His order is,
Isaiah Jeremiah Ezekiel Minor Prophets.
Hence it appears that, in spite of the Babylonian Gemara, this order obtained no great
following after the Talmud was compiled.
Then had it any before the Talmud was compiled?   Melito made inquiries before 200 A.D.
of Palestinian Jews, and their order was, Isaiah
Jeremiah Minor Prophets Daniel Ezekiel.   The
order of the Syriac and Armenian versions is,
Isaiah Minor Prophets Jeremiah Ezekiel.   The
order of the LXX. is, Minor Prophets Isaiah
Jeremiah Ezekiel.

The date of the tradition in *Baba Bathra* can
be fixed not with certainty, but approximately,
as the seventh century of our era.[1]

Hence we have the following alternatives
before us.   The Babylonian Gemara may retain
a tradition of an ancient practice that goes
back earlier than any other authority.   About
270 B.C., when the LXX. translation of Isaiah

[1] The word מירכס, which it contains, seems to be
Armenian, *Korus*, " lose."

was made, uncritical people had already wrong notions about the order of the books, which were shared at the end of that century by Ben-Sira. But the critical historians through whose hands the Talmudic traditions passed kept up a vestige of the truth. What a splendid vindication we have here of the Talmud as a source of history! Authors many centuries earlier went wrong, and authors many centuries later went wrong; but the accurate and critical Talmud retains the truth! Unfortunately, when a conservative critic proceeds to quote the evidence of the Talmud for the *unity* of Isaiah, he is certain to be told that it is grossly uncritical to cite such an authority. The witnesses are to be believed only when their evidence favours a particular side.

How comes it, we may parenthetically ask, that the mediæval Rabbis were so much more critical in their Biblical studies than the scholars of the nineteenth century? for it is quite certain that neither Seadyah nor Ibn Ezra would have employed Talmudic evidence in this way. The reason is that they did not ordinarily comment with a particular interest in view. *Now* the interest is the ejection of the supernatural; and the desire to accomplish this leads at times to very curious results.

Secondly, we may suppose that the order was originally as one of the ancient authorities has it—was then altered, and altered again. In

7

this case the tradition is of no use for the
purpose for which it is cited.

Or, thirdly, we may suppose that there was
no order. The Bible was a collection of books,
which might be arranged according to the fancy
of the owner. The order mentioned in B. *Baba
Bathra* was the order of a casual copy. There
is an accommodation to common sense in this
view which I fear will render it unpopular.

Here, then, the impugners of the unity of
Isaiah call in a witness who is either useless, or
proves far more than can be desirable.

Before quitting the Introduction referred to,
we may notice what is, according to it, a *certain*
proof of non-Isaianic authorship. The mention
of Cyrus or the use of an Aramaic loan-word is,
we learn, flagrantly opposed to the possibility of
authorship by Isaiah.

Let us take the second test first. Aramaic
loan-words are found in hieratic documents
many centuries earlier than Isaiah. In
Deborah's song, which is assuredly a very
early specimen of Hebrew, there occurs an
Aramaism *yethannu*, " they shall celebrate " ;
for there is no ground for severing this from the
Aramaic. In the patera of Baal-Lebanon (800
B.C. ?) there occurs the Aramaic loan-word
reshīth. Then we know from 2 Kings xviii. 25
that the Aramaic language was learnt by court
officials in Isaiah's time; hence, if Isaiah's
oracles were full of Aramaic loan-words, we

should have no occasion for surprise. The only Aramaic loan-words that prove anything are words that we can date; and when words known to have been introduced into Aramaic later than 700 B.C. are found in any part of Isaiah, it will be proper to pay them due respect.

With regard to the mention of Cyrus, that involves questions concerning the power of God which are scarcely worth discussing, because agreement is not likely to be arrived at.

These few examples of arguments have been dealt with chiefly out of respect for the chief authority on Isaiah in this country. If science have an even balance, and deal in certainties and probabilities, we may safely brand both the methods and results which we have noticed as *unscientific*. Worse authorities than Rabbi Simon and the Babylonian Gemara we could not cite; when either is cited on the conservative side, the argument is received (and often rightly) with a burst of laughter. More inaccurate statements than that about Aramaic loan-words could not easily be made; let such a statement be made on the conservative side, and he who makes it will repent. Hence the arguments that are to be adduced cannot be less scientific than those in which " Biblical criticism " is wont to indulge. Let us hope that they may be found more so.

Our first reason, then, for assailing the theories

that split Isaiah is that the result to which they lead is uncritical, and even ludicrous. That two authors of stupendous merit might accidentally get bound up together, and so the works of the second get attributed to the first, is exceedingly unlikely, but not so unlikely as to be impossible; in the case of Isaiah, however, not only is the analogy of the Minor Prophets decidedly against it, but that of Ezra and Nehemiah still more so. Owing to the similarity of the subject of which these authors treat, they appear in several canons under the single head of Ezra; but the Jews, though they probably often bound them up together, never confused them. Still, if the division of Isaiah between two authors gave satisfaction, and further dissection did not immediately follow, this solution would not go so far outside the bounds of experience as to be called uncritical. But the fact that this first dissection leads to innumerable others renders it useless. The assumption that we can locate disjointed fragments of Hebrew is to be summarily rejected. Even if we knew the Hebrew language as well as we know, say, Greek, and Israelitish history as well as we know, say, Greek history, and if we could be sure that we were familiar with all the forces which go to the making of history, such an assumption would be arrogant. But the case is infinitely less favourable than that supposed. We know so little Hebrew that the simplest correction of a

Biblical text is a hazardous undertaking. Of
Israelitish history we know little in any case ;
on the showing of the Biblical critics that little
has been fraudulently altered over and over
again to suit religious prejudices current at
different epochs. Moreover, the world—and a
world including men like Bacon, Locke, and
Newton—has till very recently been convinced
that forces entered into the development of
Israelitish history, of which the history of other
nations exhibits but faint traces. What chance
is there, then, of any form of criticism that ven-
tures far from documents and monuments
finding its way ? There is none. And science
disdains all results that are neither certain nor
probable.

Next, it must be perceived that the author of
chapters xl.–lxvi. is either a Prophet, or a great
rogue and impostor. The mention by him of
the name of Cyrus (xlv. 4–6) is declared to be a
tremendous miracle wrought in order that the
whole world from East to West might know
that Jehovah was the only God. If the fact
was that the prophet of an unimportant and
oppressed community mentioned in the name
of his god a conqueror whose fame was filling
the world, what miracle was there in this ? The
world might as well ring with the fact that
Vergil mentioned Augustus. Yet the " second
Isaiah " claims foreknowledge so constantly and
so emphatically that he has left himself no

loophole. " Let the strange gods come forward
and tell us what is going to happen, and then
we shall know that they are gods (xli. 23).
See, the former things have come to pass, and
now I am telling you of the latter things
(xlii. 9). Who is there like Me, who can tell
things in their order, and proclaim coming
events and the future ? (xliv. 7). ˙ Be not afraid
—have I not told you of old and made you
hear and ye are my witnesses ? (*ibid.* 8). Let
all the nations be gathered together—which
among them can foretell this ? Let them tell
us the former things (*i.e.,* show that they have
foretold things that are now realized), and produce witnesses of good character who shall
assure us that they heard the prediction and
confirm the assertion. Ye are *my* witnesses
(xliii. 9, 10). I foretold the former things long
ago ; they went forth from my mouth so that I
could make them heard ; then suddenly I
wrought them and they came about. This was
because I knew that thou art obstinate ; thy
neck is like a bar of iron, and thy brow like
brass. Therefore I told thee of them long
before ; before they came about I announced
them to thee ; lest thou shouldst say ' my idol
wrought them, my image ordained them ' (xlviii.
3–5)."

These are not all the passages in which this
writer insists on the fact that he, as God's
spokesman, has foretold events with certainty,

whereas the representatives of other gods have been unable to predict. The author therefore speaks like a man of *science*, who is aware that the truth can submit itself to tests. God, who is the Author of phenomena, can also predict phenomena ; and in order that genuine inquirers may be able to test the truth of Israelitish monotheism, He has empowered His servant to predict events before their arrival, and in certain cases long before their arrival. The earlier predictions have been realized, therefore the later predictions will be realized. Care was taken to have the earlier predictions properly attested *before* the event, so that when the realization took place the fact of the prediction could not be doubted. The predictions have been *public* (xlv. 19 ; xlviii. 16), so that there can be no doubt of their genuineness. And in the case of the predictions which occupy chapters xl.–lxvi. all Israel is their witness.

The false gods, or rather their worshippers, are asked to produce similar cases of predictions. Such predictions must, says the Prophet, be attested by witnesses of good character ; if they can be produced, and be shown to have been realized, then the false gods have a claim to be regarded as true gods. But the Prophet declares that no such predictions and no such attestation can be produced.

It is undoubtedly providential that we have before us a record of some of the oracles of

false gods, preserved in the work of Herodotus.
Crœsus, who very rightly thinks the oracles
ought to be tested, finds the Delphic oracle
satisfy *his* test, viz., it can tell his messengers
what he (Crœsus) is doing many hundred miles
away.   But when he proceeds, after lavish gifts,
to ask the oracle what will be the result of his
war with Cyrus, the oracle *flinches ;* it devises
an answer which can have no other purpose
than to save its credit in any contingency.
Now, the " second Isaiah's " oracles about the
event of Cyrus's campaign against Babylon are
positive and uncompromising.   Either, then,
they were before the event, or they were after
the event.   If they were before the event, then
the Prophet has undergone his own test
satisfactorily ; but, in order to make it unques-
tionable, it ought to have been uttered before
the name of Cyrus was ever heard.   If, on the
other hand, it be after the event, then the
" second Isaiah " is a rogue of no common
order ; for the worst sort of impostor is one who
not only practises without authorization, but, in
addition, forges a certificate.

It is noticeable that the passages in which
the " second Isaiah " declares that he has foretold events begin very early in the second half
of Isaiah.   What then are the events which he
has predicted ?   " The former treatise have I
made, O Theophilus "—whoever reads these
words infers at once that the author of the Acts

must be the author of the Gospel ascribed to St. Luke ; for no one would commence a book with a reference to a former work that never existed, unless he meant to deceive. If, therefore, we regard chapters xl.–lxvi. as the *continuation* of the first half of Isaiah, the references to the former events which had come about as the Prophet had predicted are intelligible ; the failure of the invasion of Sennacherib, which his annals conceal, is attested by the Greek historian ; and we are justified in ascribing that failure to providential interference. That was, doubtless, the most striking of Isaiah's predictions, but in other cases he took the wise precaution of having his oracles properly attested (viii. 2 and 16 ; xxx. 8). Either, then, we are to suppose that the " second Isaiah " had foretold events successfully, but that his predictions attracted so little attention as to be lost ; or we are to suppose that this profession of his is a piece of imposture ; or, thirdly, there remains the old and traditional theory that the oracles on the fulfilment of which the " second Isaiah " bases his claim to credibility are the oracles of the " first Isaiah." Rejecting the first proposition as absurd, and the second on the ground that a claim so forcibly put forward would certainly have been challenged unless substantiated, we are driven to the third alternative ; the " former events " to which the passages quoted allude must be the events predicted by the "first Isaiah," and duly realized.

Either, then, the first Isaiah wrote the work ascribed to the second, or the "second Isaiah" wrote the work ascribed to the first; for the idea that the "second Isaiah" claimed falsely to have produced the oracles which were really by the first Isaiah may be excluded. Either the first Isaiah was gifted with astounding knowledge of the future, or a false prophet of the time of Cyrus forged a whole series of oracles, some of which corresponded well with past history, in order to attach to them an appendix of oracles referring to events in the then future. This latter supposition may be refuted when any serious writer maintains it.

Out of the oracles of the first Isaiah it seems impossible to banish certain leading ideas which perpetually recur. *A remnant shall return.* This is the name which the Prophet gives one of his sons. It is asserted in the middle of the very oracle in which the failure of Sennacherib is foretold (x. 21). It is the burden of the opening chapter; were it not for a *remnant*, Judah would be like Sodom or Gomorrah. The nation must undergo a process of purifying similar to that by which silver is extracted from lead. The *relics* of the nation will one day be gathered together from the four corners of the earth (xi. 11) by a miracle resembling that whereby Israel was in old times delivered from Egypt.

The children of Israel will be picked up one by
one from the nations whither they have been
banished (xxvii. 12, 13). If, then, the true and
genuine message of Isaiah is that a remnant
shall return, and yet that remnant is not to
return from Assyria, whence is it to return?
Chiefly from Babylon, as the historically attested
oracle in chapter xxxix. implies; and what is
clear is that the "second Isaiah," like the first,
knows little of Babylon but the names Babel
and Chasdees; and that except the name Cyrus
the second possesses no detailed foreknowledge
of later events that is not also at the command
of the first.

Leaving alone the references to Cyrus and
Babylon, let us see whether the date of chapters
xl.–lxvi. can be fixed by other considerations.
There is some geography in these chapters, and
there is also some in Jeremiah and in Ezekiel.
If the "second Isaiah" wrote in the time of
Cyrus, he must have had the works of these two
Prophets before him, and can scarcely have been
less familiar than Ezekiel with the geography
of the countries that entered into Babylonian
politics. But it is the fact that the "second
Isaiah" is ignorant of what was commonplace
to Ezekiel.

The races Meshech and Tubal, to the Assyrians
Muski and Tabali, to the Greeks Moschi and
Tibareni, formed a natural couple, like Holland
and Belgium, or Norway and Sweden. Ezekiel

mentions them together *five* times (xxvii. 13,
xxxii. 26, xxxviii. 2, 3, xxxix. 1); and they are
named together in the genealogical tables, which
couple Javan (the oriental name for Greece) with
them.   To Ezekiel, therefore, it was well known
that Moshech (as Meshech should be corrected)
was a *proper name*, belonging to a nation or
country.   But Isaiah thought it a Hebrew word,
meaning " drawer," and he interprets it "drawers
of the bow."   Thus the verse lxvi. 19 reads, " I
will send refugees of them to Tarshish, Pul, and
Lud, *drawers of the bow*, Tubal, and Javan."
But the Hebrew for " drawers " is *Mosh'che*.   If
we compare the lists in Ezekiel and in the genealogical tables, it will seem clear that " Drawers of
the bow " is not an epithet of Lud, but the name
of a race, viz., *Moshech.*

For in the first place there is no reason why
Lud only out of the whole list should have an
epithet, least of all an epithet which has no connexion with the operation in which the visit of
the refugees to them will result.   Moreover if the
fame of the Lydians as archers were such as to
justify the employment of " archers " as a perpetual epithet, irrespective of the context, the
ancient Greek writers ought to know something
of it.   But what Herodotus says (i. 79) is not
that they were archers, but that their mode of
fighting was on horseback, that they carried long
lances, and were clever in the management of
their steeds.   If the lance was the national

weapon of the Lydians, the bow was not so characteristic of their mode of warfare that a perpetual epithet could be taken from it.

What is remarkable is that Jeremiah had this passage of Isaiah before him, and stumbled over it curiously. In enumerating some warlike tribes (xlvi. 9) he mentions Cush and Put, bearers of shields, and *Ludim, bearers treaders of the bow.* This variation is highly interesting. In the first place his grammatical sense dislikes the coupling of a collective tribal name with the plural of the adjective ; therefore the plural of the individuals is substituted for the tribal collective. In the second place we have the ungrammatical " bearers treaders " in place of Isaiah's " drawers." [1] The verb *māshach* is so rarely used of " the bow " that the Prophet might well doubt whether Isaiah's phrase meant " draggers " of the bow or " pullers " of it ; *i.e.*, whether it referred to the carrying of the bow, or to the employment of it in actual warfare. The alternate suggestions, curiously enough, remain side by side in the text; but the reason of the association of the bow with the Lydian lancers is lost.

Jeremiah is, however, one step further than Isaiah in that he has the correct form *Put* for the incorrect *Pul*. The name Pul is probably due to a reminiscence of the name of an Assyrian king.

[1] The relation of this phrase to that in Psalm lxxviii. 9 is not clear.

How are we to suppose that the Israelites became acquainted with the names of these distant nations? Probably one of the chief sources of ancient geography was a source that is still highly productive—interest in the doings of the great. How many of us a year ago had ever heard the names of Mafeking and Magersfontein? But now they are household words, not only in England, where they have a terrible interest, but wherever there are newspapers in any language. Because the interest of England was focussed on those places, the interest of the whole world was focussed on them. We cannot doubt that the vicissitudes of Assyrian politics were closely followed by the inhabitants of those countries which stood in danger of depopulation from the freaks of Assyrian kings. Some rough translations of the Assyrian kings' despatches were probably circulated, at any rate orally, and from these the surrounding peoples would learn something of the names and localities of foreign nations. Now the Moshech figure repeatedly in the *Annals* of Sargon, in whose reign they played an important part. Their king entered into more than one coalition against the power of Sargon, and we at present have only Sargon's account of the issue of the campaigns. Like the Greek and Hebrew writers, Sargon mentions Moshech and Tubal together (*Annals*, ed. Winckler 9, 173–4). It is almost surprising that any Israelite, writing *after* 711 B.C., should have

mistaken the name *Moshech* for a Hebrew appel-
lative ; yet the report of Sargon's campaigns that
reached Jerusalem may have been sufficiently
inaccurate for this. Isaiah, moreover, does not
display anywhere the erudition that characterises
Ezekiel. The forms of the name that appear
most frequently in Sargon's *Annals* are Muski
and Mushki, and it is this latter form transliterated into Hebrew characters that Isaiah
knows. That word seemed to mean " drawers
of " to which the word " bow " formed a natural
supplement. It is not probable that Isaiah
meant it as an epithet of Lud ; he probably
regarded it as the name of a tribe, like the
" Man-eaters " of Herodotus. Jeremiah supposes it to be an epithet of Lud, and we have
seen his curious attempt at reproducing it.
Ezekiel is thoroughly familiar with the name
Moshech—it has been suggested that Ezekiel
could even read cuneiform—and hence we see
from this passage in the *last chapter* of the
" second Isaiah " a proof of priority to Jeremiah
and Ezekiel.

To see whether this argument will stand, let
us try to elude it. The simplest way is to emend
the text ; to speak more plainly, to falsify the
evidence. But as this method will be required
in order to meet the argument from the name
Pul, it must not be employed again in the same
verse. And indeed in order to bring Isaiah's
knowledge up to date we should have to strike

out " bow," and emend the preceding word. This
method is useless, because the even balance of
science requires that both parties should be
allowed to exercise the same rights ; the defender
of the second Isaiah will also be entitled to strike
out of the text whatever goes against him, and
so the whole affair be taken out of the hands of
science. Since, then, the words are genuine,
either they constitute an epithet of Lud, or they
do not. If the former be the case, how comes it
that the Lydians are made archers, whereas they
really were lancers ? If the latter be the case,
let a tribe of " Drawers of the bow " be localized.

If the passage of Jeremiah be not an imitation
of that in Isaiah, Jeremiah's mistake (in making
the Lydians archers) remains unaccounted for,
and also his hesitation between two possible
interpretations of the word *māshach* is still
obscure. But if we conjecture that the passage
of Jeremiah is also an interpolation, we are
making too many hypotheses.

Hence I believe the explanation given to be
the *only one* which will account for the phrases
in Isaiah and Jeremiah, and this explanation
makes Isaiah earlier than Jeremiah, and also
earlier than Ezekiel. But if the last chapter of
the prophecies of the " second Isaiah " is so much
earlier than Jeremiah that the latter *comments* on
it somewhat unintelligently, its genuineness is
practically demonstrated. And the last chapter
of a book is ordinarily the latest portion of it.

The next geographical argument is one from silence. The "second Isaiah" knows the name of Cyrus, but he does not know the name of Persia ; and if chapter xiii. be by him, then he knows the name of Media, and thinks that it is Media which will overthrow Babylon. If chapters xli.–xlvi. be by him, he only knows that the destroyer of Babylon will come from the north-east. But of course the real contemporaries of Cyrus were as familiar with the name of Persia as we are with that of Germany. And Ezekiel, who belongs to the captivity, is quite familiar with the name, though he does not seem to know the locality. He names it by the side of Lud and Put (xxvii. 10) or Cush and Put (xxxviii. 5). Ezekiel, therefore, knows more geography than Isaiah or Jeremiah, and probably more than the genealogical table. For the old suggestion that in that table (Gen. x. 2) *Tiras* stands for *Pāras*, "Persia," seems highly attractive. Since no copier of Genesis after the fall of Babylon would have made a mistake in transcribing the name Pāras, that table is earlier than the fall of Babylon. The error must, therefore, rest with the genealogist, who must be earlier than the time of Ezekiel. But if Ezekiel was familiar with the name of Persia, it is impossible that it could have been unfamiliar to a contemporary of Cyrus ; and though it would be no gross inaccuracy to speak of the Medes taking Babylon, it is unlikely that a contemporary who

hoped to derive priceless blessings from the
success of Cyrus would make the mistake of
calling him a Mede.   And it is practically impossible that a contemporary of reasonable
intelligence could describe Cyrus as God's
Messiah, and yet know no more about him than
that he came from somewhere in the north-east.
Hence the prophecy about Cyrus is earlier than
the time of Ezekiel.

A geographical name that is deserving of
keen attention is that of *Seba* (xliii. 3 and
xlv. 14).   This nation is mentioned in company
with Egypt and Ethiopia, and its eponymous
hero is called by the genealogist a son of Cush
(Genesis x. 7).   In Psalm lxxii., which is of the
same *spirit* as Isaiah xl.–lxvi., it is coupled with
Sheba, probably on account of similarity of
sound.   Isaiah, however, by no means confuses
the two nations, but rightly names Sheba (more
correctly Saba) in company with Arabian races.
He, then, is the only author who knows anything about the people Seba, beyond the fact
that they are connected with Ethiopia.   They
are a *tall* race, apparently employed as slaves,
and as such they are to be brought to Jerusalem.
There seem good grounds for identifying the
Sebans with a race mentioned in the oracle of
chapter xviii., where it is said that a nation
dwelling apparently far beyond the rivers of
Ethiopia, of lengthy stature and close-shaven,
shall be brought as an offering to the Temple

at Jerusalem. Now when could an Israelite
know anything of a race that dwelt beyond the
rivers of Ethiopia ?   Only when a Cushite
dynasty was reigning in Egypt. The Ethiopian
rule in Egypt came to an end in 662 B.C. or
thereabout. While lower Egypt was in Cushite
hands there would be opportunities for Israelites
to associate with Cushites, and learn something
of the geography of the interior of Africa.   I do
not assert that the weird description of chapter
xviii. is derived from anything but prophetic
second sight ; but the repetition of the description makes it likely that we have here a formula
perhaps borrowed from despatches.   The fact
that the passage about Seba in chapter xlv. and
the oracle of chapter xviii. fit together like
pieces of a puzzle, and a puzzle that can only
have been constructed before the fall of the
Cushite dynasty in Egypt, makes very strongly
for identity of authorship, and also for the
traditional date of the " second Isaiah."

The geographical names in chapter lx. are
also of some interest. Camels bred in Midian
and Aifah are to come from Sheba (Saba);
sheep from Kedar, and rams from Nebaioth.
Aifah is named after Midian in the genealogical
table (Gen. xxv. 4); since Isaiah knows something about Aifah, whereas the genealogical
table cannot be shown to know anything,
probably the name of Aifah is inserted in the
table from this passage. Kedar figures else-

where in Isaiah; xlii. 11: "Let the wilderness
and *its cities*, the *courts* wherein Kedar dwells,
lift up their voice." One would have thought
the wilderness had no cities: "that made the
world as a wilderness, and destroyed the cities
thereof" (xiv. 17); "they wandered in the
wilderness in a solitary way; they found no
city to dwell in" (Ps. cvii. 4). The Hebrew for
"its cities" is *'ārāv*. Now compare Ezekiel
xxvii. 21: "*Arabia* and all the princes of
Kedar." The Hebrew for Arabia is *'arābh*,
scarcely to be distinguished in pronunciation
from "its cities." Hence it would seem that
Ezekiel's geography shows the same advance
here on Isaiah's as we noticed above in the case
of Moshech. Arabia and Kedar are almost
synonymous in the annals of Assurbanipal;
but the name Arabia is not known to the
author of the genealogical table, whereas the
name Kedar is (Gen. xxv. 13). The word has
come to Isaiah's ears, but he thinks it means
"his cities," just as he thought Moshech meant
"drawer"; but in Ezekiel's time the name has
become thoroughly familiar to Hebrew writers.

That the mistake is the Prophet's and not
that of a copyist, is shown by the fact that the
genealogical table has not got Arabia, whereas
we have seen that it takes Aifah from Isaiah.

These are, I think, the only geographical
names whence any chronology can be obtained
that meet us in the "second Isaiah." From

them we gather that the author was earlier than
Jeremiah and Ezekiel, and was utilized for the
last edition of the genealogical table, which,
however, is further advanced in geographical
knowledge. That it takes no notice of *Pul*
may be due to its identifying this land with
Put; that it does not mention the mysterious
Sinim (xlix. 12) is probably due to the supposition that this referred to the wilderness of Sin,
mentioned in the Pentateuch, or Sinai. The
indication of date got from the Prophet's mistaking *Moshech* and *Arab* for Hebrew words
seems convincing. We learn from it, moreover,
that the Prophet cannot have been acquainted
with the cuneiform script, in which it would
have been impossible to commit such errors.

Before quitting this "line of defence," we may
first see whether it would lead to sound results
if applied to books of which the date is certain.
In the Koran it seems clear that the author
thinks the Arabic name for "Christians,"
Nasārā, is derived from the verb *nasara*, "to
help" (*Sura* iii. 45); but the geographer Yakut
is aware that it means *Nazarenes*, *i.e.*, the followers of Jesus of Nazareth; hence we infer
that Yakut is later than the Koran—as he is
indeed by more than six hundred years.

Secondly, are we saving the unity of Isaiah
at the expense of his intelligence? Since this
is a scientific inquiry, that question cannot be
asked; however, in the case of Vergil, who is

not only a great poet but a man of learning also, errors worse than those noticed have to be condoned. The island Inarima is acknowledged to be due to an erroneous reading of Homer's "in Arima." The wish, "let everything be the middle of the sea," is a *Verballhornung* of "may the whole course of nature be changed." Isaiah's geographical errors will have sufficient justification if they serve to save his date.

Thirdly, is the mention of the Lydians by Isaiah consistent with the statement of Assurbanipal (Rm. i. col. 2 line 96) that Lydia was "a far-off country, the mention of whose name the kings my fathers had never heard"—a formula which, it must be confessed, seems to be the basis of the phrase which follows in Isaiah—"the distant islands which have never heard the rumour of me"? Assyria, it must be remembered, was very much farther from Lydia than Palestine. The style in which Lydia is mentioned in that most interesting passage is not inconsistent with the supposition that the fame of Lydia may have reached Palestine a half-century before.

Of the archæological notices contained in Isaiah xl.–lxvi., some have already been seen to be based on the Wisdom of Solomon. There are besides some of great importance in chapters lvii., lxv., and lxvi. The abominations described in chapter lvii. include (verse 5) the worship of *elim* under green trees; the only other place in

which this technical term appears is Isaiah i. 29
("Men shall be ashamed of the *elim* which ye
have desired"). The ceremonies rebuked in
chapter lxv. include sacrifices in *gannoth* (verse
3), and the same technical term figures in
chapter lxvi. (verse 17); the only other place
in which it is found is also Isaiah i. 29 ("Ye
shall be ashamed of the *gannoth* which ye have
chosen"). That *gannoth* here does not mean
ordinary gardens, but is a technical term,
appears from the threat in i. 30, where the
votaries of these *gannoth* are told that they
shall become like a *garden* that has no water.
For this threat evidently derives its suitability
from a play on words, and resembles that of
lxv. 11, 12, "Those who fill a libation to Mina;[1]
and I shall *commit* you (*manithi*) to the sword":
a similarly contemptuous jest being found in
lvii. 6, "Thy lot is in the stones of the wadi,"
where the words for "lot" and "stone" are
almost identical. If the word *gannoth* were not
technical, the play on the words would be point-
less; and we may observe that the threat of i. 30
is matched by the promise of lviii. 11, "Thou
shalt be like a well-watered garden," where
(owing to the absence of any other allusion)

---

[1] The Massoretic pointing *Mānī* agrees with *Al-Mānī*,
"the Dispenser," which is used as a name of God in a
verse quoted by Yakut; but as the word in Isaiah has
not the article, the vocalization of the local name *Mina*
seems more likely to be right.

the ordinary form of the word for "garden" is used. As we shall soon see, the worship with which these terms *gannoth* and *elim* are connected was exceedingly elaborate, and therefore characteristic of a period. We learn, therefore, that the authors of Isaiah i. and of Isaiah lvii. and lxv., lxvi. were contemporaries. That the first chapter of a great classic could be attributed to any one but its right author is too wild a surmise to deserve consideration. We start, then, with the remarkable fact that the "first Isaiah" uses two technical terms with which the "second Isaiah" and no other Hebrew author is familiar. And the "second Isaiah" acts as interpreter to the "first Isaiah," by enabling us to locate, and to some extent comprehend, the nature of the cults to which these technical terms belonged. And from this observation a very easy step leads to the identification of the two authors.

The description of chapter lxv. would seem to apply particularly to the worship of the gods Mina and Gad. The former name seems identical with that of a place that still figures in the ceremonies of the pilgrimage to Mecca ; but the feminine form *Manāt* is better known as an actual object of worship. Owing to this idol having been named in the Koran (*Sura* liii. 20) the Arabic antiquarians [1] have preserved some

[1] Azraki in Wüstenfeld's *Chroniken der Stadt Mekka,* i. 78–84 ; Al-Baghawi's *Commentary on the Koran* (litho-

useful notices of its character. According to one authority this feminine form merely means "*a* stone," whereas the masculine would mean "stones," or "rocks"; and that the idol named Manāt was not an image, but a rock or stone, appears from some of the stories which the antiquarians preserve. According to one account it was a flat stone on which a man clarified butter; when he died, some people appropriated the stone and made a god of it. Clearly the clarified butter must have been an offering to the stone, similar to the milk which, according to Azraki, was offered to another idol. According to several authorities, Manāt was set up on the seashore—perhaps was a rock on the coast.

"The full libation," which, Isaiah tells us, was offered to Mina, was therefore an idolatrous practice common to Israel with the Arabian tribes, and the "table spread for Gad" was doubtless of the same order. We notice that just as Manāt was a rock by the sea, so in Isaiah lvii. it is the stones of the torrents that are objects of worship, while other hideous rites are performed under "rocky crags." An authority, followed by the geographer Yakut, who states that idols were brought into Arabia first in the form of ordinary stones, adds that the worshippers gave as their reason for propitiating the stones the fact that they could be petitioned for *rain*. This notice

graphed at Bombay); Yakut, *Geographical Lexicon, s.v.* Mina.

seems to give us the light we require. The sea
and the rivers were personified as gods from
whom water might be sought ; and the propi-
tiatory rites were chiefly for the purpose of
securing rain or water, the constant need for
which permeates all Arabic poetry, and the
poetry of Isaiah even more. Sacrifices by lakes,
rivers, and rocks were common among American
races, *e.g.*, the Chibchas ;[1] and even Horace, in a
familiar ode, describes a sacrifice to a spring.

Isaiah (lxvi. 17) informs us that the worshippers in these cases claimed a special sort of
sanctity. This was apparently in virtue of their
being houseless and eating weird food, such as
the ordinary law forbade. The notices of the
Arabic antiquarians illustrate this. At certain
periods the worshippers of these stone idols
thought it improper to come under a roof, and
we learn from the Koran that they prided
themselves greatly on this form of asceticism.
To some similar custom the Prophet alludes
(lxv. 4) when he speaks of those who dwell in
holes (?) and graves, and who, owing to their
superior sanctity, refuse to let others come near
them. To the custom mentioned in this text
we can easily see a reference in Isaiah ii., where
it is said that men will have to retreat into holes
in order to escape the Divine vengeance. There

[1] Waitz, *Anthropologie der Naturvölker*, iv. 363 ; for
Africa, see ii. 175 ; and for human sacrifices to appease
water-gods, ii. 198.

will then be a reason for the practice, which is at
present an idolatrous caprice.

The customs described in lvii. 5–10 may also
be identified with the practice of the Arabian
idolaters : "those who heat themselves with *elim*
under every green tree." The commentator on
the passage of the Koran that has been quoted
tells a story of a man who took three stones, set
them up under a tree, and then told his tribe
that this was their god, to be propitiated by
circuits. The ceremony to which the word
"heating themselves" refers will then be a
circuit of this kind, in which the worshipper
ran round the object of his worship. The circuit of the Kaabah is probably the only relic
of the practice in Arabia. "Slaughtering the
children in the wadis under the rocky crags."
This reminds us of the offerings of children
to water-gods practised by African negroes.[1]
Among the Chibchas a young man captured
from the enemy was dedicated to the sun,
beheaded in the open air on a mountain, and
his blood sprinkled on a rock.[2] The sacrifice
of children, especially of the first son, was
observed as a practice of the Peruvians.[3] The
Greek custom of presenting a lock of hair to the
river-god is probably a relic of a more barbarous
form of propitiation ; while the Roman anti-

---

[1] Waitz, *Anthropologie der Naturvölker,* ii. 198.
[2] *Ibid.* iv. 461.
[3] *Ibid.* iv. 461. Compare iii. 207 for Florida.

quarians, doubtless with justice, regard the practice of throwing straw figures to the Tiber as a relic of human sacrifice. But this form of infanticide also reminds us of that which was practised by the pre - Mohammedan Arabs, which Mohammed has the credit of having abolished. The antiquarians confine the custom to the burying alive of female infants; and this, they say, was done by only a few tribes. There is, however, some ground for thinking that it was carried on on a larger scale. One of the women of Mecca, who, after the city had yielded to the Prophet, was asked to accept the conditions of Islam, being told that she must not kill her children, replied, " We reared them when they were small, you killed them when they were grown." [1] This answer would be off the point if the slaughter of male children was unknown.

That the offerings recorded by Isaiah were originally intended to procure rain seems most likely. The " stones of the brook" would represent the river-god, where, as is the case with the torrents mentioned in Scripture, the river has water only at special seasons. Where the rivers are deep, the victim can be thrown in,[2] and this is a common practice. But where the water is insufficient for that purpose, the victim has to be dispatched as in the scene recorded by Isaiah.

[1] *Al-Fachri*, ed. Ahlwardt, p. 126.   [2] Waitz, l.c. iv. 363.

A remarkable suggestion that has been made
to account for infanticide is worth repeating.
The soul of the newborn child, being absolutely
pure, is thought to be best able to act as intercessor with the god. This theory seems to
group several of the notions current in Arabia
together. That a son is the natural intercessor
for his father is asserted even by Mohammedan
writers.[1] The old theory is said to have been
that the idols were God's daughters, and carried
on intercession, and these ideas Mohammed
seemed at one time willing to adopt. If,
therefore, the superior sanctity of which we
read in chapter lxv. and lxvi. were claimed
by those who had tried this method of acquiring
it, we can understand both the tenacity with
which the claim was maintained and also the
indignation which it provoked.

Verse 6 proceeds to describe the offerings of
food and drink to the stones of the torrent,
which have already been illustrated. In verse
7 he adds, "On a high and lofty mountain thou
hast set thy bed." This worship on mountain-
tops is attested for the Arabs by Azraki; it
belongs to a very early form of Paganism.
The mountain-top is thought to be nearer God
than any lower part of the earth. The description that follows seems to refer to licentious
rites, but in the language of the Prophets on the
subject of idolatry it is difficult to distinguish

[1] *Letters* of Abu 'l-'Ala, p. 131.

simile from realism.   In the declaration of
chapter ii. that every high mountain shall feel the
wrath of God and be brought low, we recognise
an allusion to the rites described in this verse.

Verse 8 continues, " And behind the door and
the doorpost thou hast set thy remembrance that
thou hast gone away from me."   This seems to
be an allusion to a custom whereby a woman
who left her husband's house for good put some
mark indicating that she had done so.   In
Exodus xxi. 6 we read that permanent adop-
tion by a family was indicated by a ceremonial
in which the door and the doorpost figured ;
whence it seems natural that permanent emanci-
pation from a family should be indicated by a
ceremony in which they figured also.   The verb
here employed for " to emigrate," or " to run
away," is ordinarily used of forcible expulsion ;
but the earlier sense, " to migrate," is known to
Isaiah in v. 13, and also appears in 2 Samuel xv.
19.   When this word had once become indissolu-
bly connected with the melancholy exile of the
Jews, it is unlikely that the earlier sense could
remain ; whence these passages must be pre-
exilian.   " Thy remembrance " probably refers
to some article specially characteristic of the
mistress of the house, which would be hung
"behind the door and the doorpost" as a sign
that the position was abandoned.[1]

[1] Compare the custom of the southern Kaffirs, among
whom the bride was presented with "ein Besen, ein

The rest of the verse is too realistic for discussion. Verse 9 begins, "And thou didst . . .
for Molech with oil." The figures here, and in
what follows, are taken from the practice of
courtesans, who employed unguents and per-
fumes to render their persons charming; the
sense, therefore, will be correctly represented
by "thou didst anoint thyself," though the
actual meaning of the verb used is lost. There
follows, "And thou didst send thy messengers
unto a distance, and didst send them down even
unto Sheol." In the first of these phrases we
recognise the author of xviii. 2; and in the
second, the author of vii. 10. The practice
referred to would appear to be that of seeking
foreign alliances, whereas, in the opinion of the
Prophet, the Jewish kings should have trusted
entirely to Divine aid; of course, such a charge
would be ridiculous after the exile. " If sending
down into hell " is to be taken literally, the
reference is to the necromancy suggested by
viii. 19.

The purpose of the illustrations of these ceremonies is to prove that the latter were relics of
extreme antiquity. Some of the closest parallels
come from the American savages; while in some
cases we are able to identify the rites with those
current in Arabia from time immemorial, and
finally abolished by Mohammed. The source,
Napf und ein Mühlstein" on the wedding-day (Waitz,
l.c. ii. 388).

then, of these practices in Palestine must have
been ancient and undisturbed custom ; they had
been brought by the Canaanites with them from
Arabia, and the Israelites had learned them
from the Canaanites.   They were kept alive
by attachment to particular mountains and
particular rivers, and in part were based on
the system which connected and even identified
the gods with particular localities.   The cultiva-
tion of them involved an insult to the Temple
(lxv. 11), which, therefore, must have been standing at the time of the rebuke.   These passages
are in consequence so clearly pre-exilian, that
even some of those who were in favour of the
dissecting theory have been unable to place them
any later.   While, then, the "first Isaiah" is
supposed to be interpolated with post-exilian
matter, the "second Isaiah" is supposed to be
interpolated with pre-exilian matter.   Naturally,
a theory that involves so much complication can
make little claim to probability.

   The author of chapter lxv. 8, 9, takes the same
view of the purpose of the exile which is taken
throughout the book, and indeed, throughout
the Bible.   Attachment to these savage and
primitive rites could only be dissolved by
removing the worshippers from the soil on
which they were practised ; hence, the exile
was not only a punishment but also a correc-
tive.   From it there returned those whose
progenitors had not bowed the knee to Baal,

while those whose interests were far removed from the objects which Israel was destined to accomplish lost their nationality. Those who came back were cured, or rather purified, from this particular form of evil. That they were not faultless we know from the Prophets of the return ; but, to attribute to them fetish worship of a primitive sort is a gross anachronism. One might as well accuse the English of the 19th century of burning heretics or using ordeals as evidence.

That the rites described in chapters lxv. and lxvi. are of the same sort as those so vividly depicted in chapter lvii. need not be doubted ; indeed, it was from chapter lxv. that the clue was obtained which led to the search for parallels in the works of the Arabic antiquarians. The phrase "behind one in the midst" of lxvi. 17 reminds us of the Arabic *imām*, or leader of ceremonies, who does not face the congregation, but goes through the performance in the front place while the congregation do the same behind him. That word is certainly taken over into Mohammedanism from the earlier cult.

Next after the idolatrous rites rebuked by the "second Isaiah," we may consider some other crimes which he condemns. One of the most serious impeachments is to be found in lix. 2–9. The Prophet there states that the sins of his countrymen have been a bar between them and God ; they have caused God to hide

His face and prevented Him from hearing.
This is the same message as that in i. 14, 15,
with a slight difference in the tense and the
expression.   He then proceeds : " for your
hands are polluted with blood."   This also is
identical with the accusation in i. 15, " your
hands are full of blood " ; or, perhaps, "tainted
with blood."   Now this is as grave an accusation as can be made ; to what it precisely
refers our slight knowledge of Israelitish history
does not enable us to say; the Prophet may
have in mind either judicial murders (such as
that in old times of Naboth), or recklessness
of human life among loose livers, or the infanticide just discussed.   Whichever of these
it be—supposing it does not refer, as many
have thought, to a judicial murder in the distant future—the two "remonstrances" must
clearly belong to the same period.   And that
period can only be pre-exilic ; the mere notion
of such a remonstrance being addressed to the
returned exiles seems to involve anachronism.
Indeed, the Prophet's idea is clearly that the
exile was a sort of sea in which these offences
were to be washed out.

The terrible impeachment of his contemporaries which follows strongly resembles that
contained in chapters i. and v.   It is illustrated
by similes taken from natural history, in which
words otherwise only used by the "first Isaiah"
are employed.   Verses 9 and 11 contain a free

paraphrase of v. 7 ; but the play on the words
in the earlier chapter is intentionally altered ;
an imitator would probably have reproduced it.
In lvi. 10–12 the impeachment is confined to
the rulers ; they are accused of drunkenness,
corruption, and incompetence, just as they are
in v. 22, 23, iii. 12, and ix. 15. That the same
impeachment could be made with justice at
such different periods as the time of the " first
Isaiah," and the close of the exile or commencement of the return, seems unthinkable ;
but to deny the authenticity of the early
chapters of the book is uncritical. How could
such a forgery have remained undetected ?

In chapter lix. the people are accused of lip
service ; they ask why their punctilious performance of ceremonies is unproductive of
results, and are told that it is owing to the
fact that their service is not accompanied by
a corresponding reform in their conduct. The
same is the burden of chapter i. and of xxix. 13.
Surely the remonstrances addressed to the
Jews before and after the great crisis in their
national existence cannot have been so similar.

Let us now see whether the second half of
Isaiah tells us anything about the Prophet's
person. Ewald seems to have rightly interpreted viii. 18, " Verily I and the children
which the Lord hath given me are for signs
and tokens in Israel," of the names Isaiah,
Shear - yashub, and Maher - shalal - hash - baz.

Clearly the names "A remnant shall return, and "Hasten the spoil, hurry the plunder," were too full of meaning to escape notice; therefore the Prophet's own name, "The salvation of the Lord," must also have been of notable significance; and, indeed, that theme, "the salvation of the Lord," pervades the whole book.

But it follows that the Prophet must have taken this name himself. Thus only would its significance be forced on the minds of his contemporaries. It was thus that at the time of the French Revolution men took such names as Publicola, Timoleon, Harmodius, to be able to exhibit their republicanism to the whole world. Similarly at the time of the Civil War in England Puritans took verses of Scripture for their names. Such designations were significant only if they were intentionally taken or given. Hence the name "Salvation of the Lord" must have been adopted by the Prophet with prophetic intent. What then was his original name?

This appears to be given in xlii. 18–21. The way to translate these verses seems to me the following: "Hear, ye deaf; and look, ye blind, so as to see. Who was blind but my servant, or deaf as my messenger whom I send? Who was blind as *Meshullam*, and blind as the servant of the Lord? Seeing much without noticing; open-eared without hearing. The

Lord was pleased of His grace to make a great
and notable example." The name Meshullam,
as will be seen by consulting the Concordance,
is by no means uncommon; it belongs to a
root which gives a great number of proper
names both in Hebrew and Arabic; they all
mean "safe and sound," and are names of good
omen; Salim, Selim, Shallum, Salman, Sulai-
man, Solomon, Maslamah, Musailimah, Salma,
Sulma, Salama, Musallam, mean all practically
the same. The "great and notable example"
then lay in the fact that he, Meshullam, had
been enabled to see; why then should not
others?

Let us compare this with the most auto-
biographical chapter in Isaiah—chapter vi. In
the first place, the vision there justifies the
description of himself in the above passage as
"My messenger whom I send." For there he
heard the question asked by God, "Whom shall
I send, and who shall go for us?" And he
answered, "Here am I; send me." And he
was told to go and say to the people, "Hear,
but understand not; see, and know not"—the
very condition wherein, according to xlii. 20,
the messenger himself had been.

Then we see that in verse 5 he identifies his
condition with that of his countrymen until
the live coal had touched his lips. The immediate result of that was to be the removal
of sin; but assuredly the image is meant to

suggest " the scholar's tongue," which in l. 4, he says, was given him by the Lord, to utter the words which (as Ben-Sira says) blaze like a fire, and, indeed, however inadequately they are translated, thrill the reader and hearer more probably than any other form of utterance. Hence it would seem that the verses xlii. 18–21 give us a very needful supplement to the biographical notice of the chapter vi.

But is the supposition that Meshullam is a proper name a wild conjecture, or an observation that is likely sooner or later to be generally accepted? I trust the latter, because modern scholars see the necessity of correcting the text, owing to the fact that taken as a substantive, the word gives no satisfactory meaning. Now we have already seen that the correction of the text in the case of Hebrew writers is an operation which is very unlikely to lead to satisfactory results. It is only in rare cases that such a proceeding is dictated by the canons of science. On the other hand, I can imagine no reason grammatical or other which stands in the way of the interpretation given above. And seeing how deeply this Prophet is imbued with the feeling that a new condition calls for a new name (cf. lxii. 2), the conjecture of Ewald that the name Isaiah was meant to mark the Prophet's new condition seems highly probable.

Whether the Prophet was accurate in de-

scribing his own state as equally forlorn with
that of the blindest it is difficult to determine.
There are many cases of men called to humbler
stages of the same vocation who have painted
their former lives in colours which those who
knew them would not have recognised. But
surely the verses in chapter xlii. must proceed
from him who saw the vision of chapter vi.

We learn, then, from chapter vi. that the
mission undertaken by the Prophet was without
hope of brilliant success; it was only when
Jerusalem was reduced to a ruin that it was
to begin to be heard. In l. 6–10 we hear the
Prophet complain of its ineffectual character;
the reception of his message was just what had
been promised; it was greeted with contempt
and ridicule, with blows and buffets. The consolation that he had was the same as that which
nerves all those who are defending the cause of
science against tremendous odds, viz., that the
truth is permanent, and must slowly approve
itself, whereas the opponent is transitory.
Naturally it might be said that this was too
often the fate of those who interpreted the
purposes or work of God aright for the first
time to serve for scientific identification; but
then it must be observed that we have no other
justification save this passage for the oracle of
chapter vi. For the personal narrative in
chapter xx. refers to a symbolic act, such as
other prophets, both true and false, practised;

from the remainder of the personal notices in chapters i.–xxxix. we should gather that Isaiah had the enviable post of court Prophet, particularly enviable in the case of one who had to announce good news ; for the office was ordinarily connected with announcements of the contrary import.   According to current notions he would, in the scene recorded in chapter vii., have had the good fortune to have uttered with impunity a foolhardy challenge. Many of his oracles, moreover, were concerned with the fate of foreign nations, whose disasters were not likely to cause the Prophet's fellow-countrymen very acute suffering.   But if these oracles were only occasional, whereas the Prophet's constant message was that sketched in chapter vi., of frequent recurrence in chapters i.–xxxix., and thoroughly elucidated in chapters xl.–lxvi., then the contempt and scorn which he had to endure are easily intelligible, and consonant with experience.   The occasions on which he was called in were occasions on which desperate remedies were required ; Ahab calls in the services of Micaiah, and the murderers of Gedaliah those of Jeremiah under somewhat similar circumstances.   The bulk of his time was spent in remonstrances which were ridiculed, and uttering predictions to which few attached any significance.

That we should not know the name of an author who has told us in verses 4–11 so much

of his personal history would be remarkable;
what could have put it into any one's mind to
attribute them to the successful court Prophet
of chapters xxxvi.–xxxix. ? Jeremiah would
be the author with whose fate they would
apparently correspond best. The valuable
notice in xlii. 19 of the author's former name
Meshullam seems intelligible only on the hypothesis stated above. Had it not been known
that the author of that chapter bore the name
Isaiah, the chapter (and the collection in which
it occurred) would be of course attributed to
Meshullam. Any one who has ever catalogued
MSS. is aware that the first expedient adopted
for finding out the name of an author is to
search through his book for some proper name
that may from the context be his. To those
with whom classical Hebrew was a living
language a proper name would be as easily
distinguishable as to us in reading English ; in
such a sentence as " who is so pathetic as gray,"
the absence of the capital would confuse no
intelligent reader ; and hence, had not the
readers of these oracles from the time they
were first issued in a roll been convinced that
the author's name was Isaiah, it would never
have occurred to them to render Meshullam as
" perfect," or " requited," or " devoted." But
since the fact of the Prophet having changed
his name was only recorded in the allusion of
chapter viii. 18, his former name was forgotten

That "who so blind as Meshullam?" meant
"who so blind as Isaiah before his mission?"
was not perceived by those who only knew of
Isaiah. Even in this country, where a change
of name is usually preceded by the most important work in a man's life, the name by
which a peer was known before his elevation
is constantly forgotten by the majority of the
public. But where the change is preceded by
no important work the original name is likely
to be lost altogether. How many educated
persons could say offhand what was the original
name of Voltaire or Neander or Lagarde?

The arguments that can be drawn from language and style are ordinarily too inconclusive
to have scientific value. The same writer, in
different works or at different periods of his
life, may employ wholly different sets of words
and phrases; just as on the same day (as
S. Ephraim well observes) he may hold contradictory opinions. On the other hand, admiration
for a model may lead an imitator to employ
with preference words and phrases found in that
model; in which case what might at first sight
seem to be an indication of identity is in reality
an indication of the contrary. Still less can
be built on those more subtle nuances which
scholars profess to perceive without being able
to state precisely what they mean. When a
scholar of even the greatest eminence declares
that he can tell by intuition that such-and-such

an ode is not by Horace, or such-and-such
a play is not by Shakespeare, it is best to
attach no value whatever to the statement. For
if such intuitions had scientific value, it is clear
that every scholar who had acquired a certain
degree of proficiency would feel the same ; for
that is the case with all intuitions that are
really the result of skill. Those, *e.g.*, who have
acquired a certain proficiency in photography
know by intuition the right exposure to give
in order to obtain a particular effect ; and,
therefore, they all give the same exposure. The
intuition in such a case merely means extreme
velocity in conducting an operation, which, in
the case of less skilful operators, has to be
gone through in detail. That in the case of
literary criticism these supposed intuitions are
valueless is shown by the extraordinary diver-
gence of the opinions of the highest experts.
Of the Satires of Juvenal the tenth has won the
poet the most lasting fame ; it is more often
quoted, and has been more frequently imitated
than the others. But the foremost Latinist in
Germany in recent times assured the world that
it was not by Juvenal. The writings of Horace
are supposed to be marked by so strong an
individuality as to be inimitable ; but there has
during this century been a school in Holland
and Germany which denies the Horatian
authorship of every other ode ; and that school
contains some names of first-rate eminence.

Bentley, whose fame to some extent rests on his exposure of ancient forgeries, held that the Epistles of Plato were genuine; but the majority of Greek scholarship is against him. What one expert thinks the finest line in Vergil is condemned by another as a silly interpolation.   Hence to adduce arguments from any of these regions is to take the question out of the region of science.

A scientific argument can be drawn from the use of words only when they can be dated either before or after.   By the latter method of dating I mean the case in which we can show that by a certain date the sense of a word had been entirely forgotten in a community; for then whoever is found using it in the old sense will almost certainly be earlier than that date. The discovery of this scientific principle is the service rendered the world by the Greek critic Aristarchus; let us see whether it will help us to determine the date of the "second Isaiah."

1. There is a verb *nāshath* used by Isaiah once in the first half of the book (xix. 5), and once in the second (xli. 17).   In both those passages it clearly means "to be dry"; "the waters shall dry up from the Nile," and "their tongue is dry with thirst."   It is well to know the etymology of a word before we base any argument upon it : and here the surest source of Hebrew etymology, classical Arabic, does not fail us.   The verb *nashifa* has from time

immemorial been used by the Arabs precisely
as Isaiah uses this. Thus the excellent native
dictionary called " The Arabic Tongue" begins
its article on this word as follows : *nashifa*, used
of water, *to dry up :* also used of the earth,
sucking it in." After other illustrations we are
told that it may be used of the udders of camels
drying up, *i.e.*, being without milk. Dozy, in
his Supplement to the Arabic dictionaries,
quotes from mediæval writers phrases in which
this verb is used of the eyes being dry from
tears, and of the saliva being dried by long
talking. The sense, therefore, of this Arabic
verb is precisely what is required in the passages of Isaiah. The change from *th* to *f* is
certified in the case of some Arabic words.[1]
The Arabic *sh* ought to be represented by
Hebrew *s ;* but this rule is not invariable, and
in the present case the pointing may be to
blame. What, therefore, appears is that the
authors of both parts of Isaiah are acquainted
with a verb *nashath* or *nasath*, meaning "to be
dry," and in all probability identical with a very
familiar Arabic verb meaning the same.

Now let us examine two passages of Jeremiah.
The first is li. 30. " The champions of Babylon
have ceased to fight; they sit in their fortresses :
their manhood is *nashath :* they have become
women" (*nashim*). The second clause is here
evidently in explanation of the first; it tells

[1] *Lisān al-'arab*, xv. 356.

us what *nashath* means, viz., "to become effe-
minate." The author regards it as a denominative from *nāshim* "women," probably through
an abstract *nāshūth* "womanhood." Hence
between the time when Isaiah II. wrote and
the time of the composition of Jeremiah li. 30
the meaning of the verb *nashath* must have
been forgotten. Therefore the author of Isaiah
xli. is earlier than the author of Jeremiah li.
by some generations.

That this observation is correct is shown by
Jeremiah xviii. 14. "Can the cool flowing
waters be *destroyed*" (*nathash*)? That men do
not speak of water being destroyed or plucked
up is evident ; the author must mean "can they
dry up?" The phrase, then, is modelled on
Isaiah xix. 5, but the later Prophet being no
longer familiar with the old verb *nashath*,
"to dry up," substitutes *by conjecture* the more
familiar *nathash*. By the time li. 30 is written
he has remembered that Isaiah uses not *nathash*,
but *nashath*, in connection with waters drying ;
hence he gives it a special application, adding
an etymological explanation. The process is
very similar to that which was traced in the
last article in reference to "the Lydians,
drawers of the bow." Just as Isaiah utilized
the lost book of Wisdom, so Jeremiah utilizes
the language of the existing classic Isaiah.
In the case of obsolete phrases he makes
guesses, which, as philology is not the purpose

of Holy Scripture, by the fact that they are unfortunate, give us valuable clues of date.

To show that this account of the passages in Jeremiah is in accordance with experience, I may produce a parallel from an author who has already been of help—Theocritus. The ancients were in doubt as to the meaning of a difficult word in Homer—ἔκηλος. Some thought it meant "peaceful, undisturbed," others thought it meant "idle." When Theocritus wrote Idyll xvii., he took the former view, and said (v. 97), "the people work at their business ἔκηλοι undisturbed." But when he wrote Idyll xxv., he had changed his opinion, and, speaking of the labourers on a farm, says, "there was no man ἔκηλος idle" (verse 100), but in order to show that he means this, he adds in the next line "in want of employment." So in Jeremiah xviii. 14 the view represented is that Isaiah's word for "to be dry" is a transposition of a verb meaning "to extirpate"; but by li. 30 he has changed his opinion and connects it with the word for "women." Whence we may infer that Isaiah's works were to Jeremiah somewhat as Homer's were to Theocritus.

2. The book of Isaiah is rich in words for "sorcery" and "witchcraft." One of these, *shachar*, is homonymous with a word meaning "dawn." It is familiar in Arabic, where, indeed, it habitually stands for the "black art."

The Armenian *skhareli*, "wonderful," "bewitch-
ing," cannot very well be separated from it ;
but to which language it of right belongs is not
so clear.   The word occurs first in a text of
Isaiah which we have already had before us :
"assuredly they shall say unto you thus : 'there
is no witchcraft for it'" (viii. 20).   The corresponding verb is used in the second half of
Isaiah (xlvii. 11), "there shall come upon thee
an evil which thou canst not charm away."
The fact that among the various synonyms for
enchantment that occur in the Old Testament,
this (which is so familiar in Arabic) is found
only in the first half of Isaiah and in the second
half of Isaiah, seems to me to be a striking
mark of identity of period.   Moreover, if the
second Isaiah had borrowed the phrase from
the first, we could scarcely imagine him handling it so freely as to make a denominative
verb from it.   There is, therefore, ground for
supposing that this particular synonym for
"sorcery" fell out of use shortly after Isaiah's
time ; probably because of its identity in form
with the ordinary word for "the dawn," whence
these two passages were wrongly explained till
the methodical application of the study of
Arabic to the explanation of the Hebrew
text.

   This seems to me a case of extreme interest
as supplying an argument which cannot easily
be eluded.   For it is the phrase of Isaiah II.

which supplies us with the right, though not
the obvious, explanation of that in Isaiah I.
As we have already seen, the explanations
given by a later writer of first-class competence,
Jeremiah, are by no means philologically correct; therefore a *later* writer would almost
certainly have supposed Isaiah I. to mean "there
is no dawn for it," as indeed we have seen that
" Rabbi Simon " interpreted it. The amount
of skill required to see that the words meant
"there is no witchcraft for it," and freedom
in handling the language requisite for the
alteration of the phrase as it appears in Isaiah
xlvii. 11, seem to me far beyond what any
imitator could possess. On the other hand, if
we consider the number of words used to
denote things connected with witchcraft, and
the frequency with which references to it
occur in the Old Testament, it seems right to
regard the equivalent of the Arabic *sihr* as
a mark of date. This makes the authors of
Isaiah viii. and xlvii. contemporary and probably identical.

Let us, as before, take some example nearer
home than the Hebrew of the Old Testament
to see whether this reasoning is correct. In
a familiar passage of *Sartor Resartus* Carlyle
speaks of a Baphometic Fire-Baptism, a phrase
which occasioned his earliest reviewers some
difficulty. But he who reads the *Miscellaneous
Essays* will find in the Essay on the Life and

10

Writings of Werner a passage that will completely explain the phrase. It came from a German play to which Carlyle had access, but which very likely no other English writer of the time had read. We have seen that the word for "sorcery" used by Isaiah may be Armenian, in which case it may have been learned from some Hittite. Isaiah would then have been familiar with a name for "sorcery" which was not in ordinary use.

3. In Isaiah x. 18 there occurs a difficult phrase, rendered in our Authorized Version "as when a standard-bearer fainteth." The meaning of this expression is probably lost ; but it must have been known to the author of Isaiah lix. 19, "the Spirit of the Lord shall lift up a standard against him." For the same word (*nōsēs*) is here used, but in an entirely different context. There can, therefore, be no question of imitation ; the Prophet must have known the meaning of the word though we do not know it, and the argument is unaffected by the question of the meaning which should be assigned it.

These three words would appear to be of real importance, because the argument drawn from them is of a sort that science recognises. The manner in which identity can best be proved in a court of law (where there has been no continuous residence) is by finding, if possible, some facts known only to a few persons, of whom the person with whom the claimant seeks to identify himself must be one; if, then, the claimant knows those facts, he gives fair presumption of the justice of his claim. The argument in this paper is of the same sort. No one save Isaiah appears to know anything of the worship connected with *gannoth* and *elim*, or to know the meaning of the words *nashath, shachar*, or *nōsēs*. Jeremiah, as we have seen, if he had claimed to be Isaiah I., would have had his claim disproved by the third of these words. Now the author of Isaiah xl.–lxvi. makes the same claim, and, when questioned on these five matters, turns out to know all about them. Whence it would appear that his claim is just.

The second class of examples are not as valuable, but still they seem deserving of consideration. Agriculture and natural history seem clearly to interest the author (or authors) of these oracles very much; and allusions to these subjects lead to the employment of a considerable number of technicalities. Whether a member of the exiled community would have had the opportunity of becoming so familiar with these subjects seems doubtful; but documents illustrating the life of the exiles may some day be discovered, which will enable us to speak positively on this matter. There are some facts about the use of these terms in the two parts of the book which seem to me scarcely explicable on the hypothesis of divided authorship.

In the Parable of the Vineyard (v. 1–6) there occurs a word for " to hoe " (*adar*, verse 6), and also a word for " to stone," meaning " to remove stones " (*sikkel*, verse 2).   Both these verbs have other meanings, which are more familiar ; but in the case of the vineyard there could be no mistaking their import, whence they are used without any explanation.   However in vii. 25 the Prophet has occasion to use the word for " to hoe " in a less technical context, so this time he adds "with the hoe " that there may be no error.   The author of lxii. 10 has occasion to use the word for " to stone " of a road, where it would be ambiguous ; for " to stone a road " might mean to put stones on it or to remove them from it. Hence he adds " from stones " that there may be no error.   Now either there never was an Isaiah, or the oracles of chapters v. and vii. are Isaianic. Therefore lxii. is also Isaianic.   For it must be remembered that these words in their technical sense only occur in these two places. The theory that another author felt the same scruple about the second as Isaiah had felt about the first scarcely commends itself ; a later imitator would have thought Isaiah's authority sufficient to justify him in using " to stone" for "to remove stones."

In xxxiv. 15, and twice in lix. 5, a verb (meaning literally " to split ") is used of hatching serpents' eggs ; it does not occur elsewhere in this sense.   In xxxiv. 15 a special verb is used for "to be delivered of," " produce," which only occurs in lxvi. 7 besides.[1] Jeremiah (xvii. 11) is apparently acquainted with part of this scientific vocabulary, but not with the word for " produce." Now the author of xxxiv. seems on other grounds identical with the " second Isaiah "; the reference to Edom and Bosrah in verse 5 cannot with any probability be separated from that in lxiii. 1, and the address to the " nations and peoples " in xxxiv. 1 is evidently in the style of the author of xli. 1. The threat in xxxiv. 3 closely resembles that with which the book of Isaiah closes. Chapter xxxv. also cannot with any probability be separated from chapters xl.–lxvi.; both the thought and the language are closely akin to, and in part identical with, those of the " second Isaiah." On the other hand, it is by no means easy to separate xxxv. from what precedes; verse 5 takes us back to xxix. 18, and verse 4 to xxxii. 4. Now this fact hits the splitting theory very hard, for the apparent simplicity of the assumption that the prophecies of B being anonymous were tacked on to those of A is lost. Instead of the analysis A + B, or A + C + B, we get A + B + C + B, which has no probability; for why should B have got divided in two? And yet this order is really far simpler than any which a serious critic of the dissecting school could adopt.

A word for "a rush" (*agmōn*) occurs twice in

[1] Job xxi. 10 employs a synonym.

the early chapters of Isaiah which seems also to have been known to the author of Job. As before, however, it is the "second Isaiah" who can tell us something definite about it: "to bow thy head as a rush" is a scornful utterance in lviii. 5. A word for a "branch" or "sucker" (*neser*) is found in both parts of the book, but is only used besides by Daniel. A word for a "tree trunk" occurs in xi. 1 ; this is also known to the author of Job, but it is from Isaiah xl. 24 that we are able to be sure of its signification.

These seem to be sufficient as additional illustrations of the fact that the "second Isaiah" is the best interpreter of the language of the "first Isaiah"; the limits of the ancient Hebrew vocabulary are unfortunately too little known to us to justify us in building much on identity of diction, except in the cases in which we can prove the words used to have been lost to the later language. If any ordinary book were divided near the middle, we should assuredly find that a certain proportion of the words used in the first half recurred in the second ; but the nature of that proportion would vary so very much with a variety of conditions that science has at present no use for calculations of this kind. It is clear that the employment of precisely the same vocabulary and entirely different vocabularies would be due to design ; but probably no other inference of value could be drawn. Although, therefore, the tabulation of the Isaianic vocabulary gives the sort of proportion of identity and of diversity which would harmonize with the theory of a single author, it is best not to use arguments which science cannot recognise.

We may now arrange in order what seem scientific grounds for believing in the Unity of Isaiah.

1. The external evidence, so far as it can be traced, is unanimously in favour of it ; and, since the second part of Isaiah has enjoyed exceptional popularity, it is improbable that the name of the author would have been forgotten within 200 years of the time when he wrote, and his work merged in that of a writer of a few scraps of 150 years before.

2. The theory which bisects Isaiah leads by a logical necessity to further and further dissection, and so to results which are absurd.

3. The geography of chapters xl.–lxvi. is earlier than the geography of Jeremiah and Ezekiel, and a geographical notice in the last chapter of Isaiah was mistaken by Jeremiah.

4. The idolatrous practices rebuked by the second Isaiah are pre-exilian rites, such as we cannot, without anachronism, attribute to the Israelites either during or after the exile. They can only be explained as relics of a very primitive fetish-worship, connected with particular localities.

5. Other crimes rebuked by the second Isaiah

are identical with crimes rebuked by the first
Isaiah, and are of a sort which imply the existence of an independent community long established on the soil.

6. The "second Isaiah" gives us some personal details which enable us to identify him
with the Prophet of chapter vi., and, what is
most important, tells us the name borne by the
Prophet before he took the name Isaiah.

7. The second Isaiah employs words only
known otherwise to the first Isaiah, of which the
meaning was lost by Jeremiah's time.

8. The second Isaiah shows himself otherwise
possessed of a scientific and technical vocabulary
which the first Isaiah only shares with him.

Is there, then, nothing in the splitting
theories? To my mind nothing at all. The
phenomenon of prophecy is one which is at
present scarcely understood; it belongs to a
class of experiences which are not yet brought
into the region of science, though it is conceivable that they may be. The words used by the
prophets to describe their experiences imply that
they were not ordinary; that they were bestowed
only on particular individuals; and that they
were often falsely claimed by persons who did
not really entertain them. The process, therefore, by which the ostensible results of these
experiences are denuded of their supernatural
character and treated as ordinary utterances is

only scientific if the profession of the prophets be shown to be false, *e.g.*, if the scene described in chapter vi. be shown to have been either a delusion or a dishonest invention. How this can be demonstrated is not obvious; but until it is demonstrated, the assumption that such experiences must be delusions is to be classed with the theory that nature abhors a vacuum, or with the belief that the orbits of the planets must of necessity be circular. Such assumption may lead to the writing of books, but they are not *science.*

Interpreting as commonplace that which is ostensibly extraordinary is unlikely to lead to a sound result. It is a process decidedly analogous to that of assuming that the colours of objects will affect the photographic plate precisely as they affect the eye, or that the tinting of the photographic plate will affect all colours equally. Nothing would seem more natural than such assumptions; but nothing would in reality be falser. When the laws of chemistry and optics are correctly made out, the picture seen by the eye can be interpreted in terms of the photographic plate; but before they are made out, such a process is impossible. It would appear that either the photograph must be incorrect or the eyesight must be defective. Science shows that neither is correct; the eye is correct and the plate is correct. But the optics of prophecy is a science that has not yet been started; and though such a science may never make much progress, nothing of value will result from the substitution of arbitrary assumptions for scientific deductions.   Hence we have within the last few years seen a writer of eminence start a theory of Maccabean Psalms on a series of arbitrary assumptions and modify it on the faith of a forgery of the eleventh century A.D., which he grossly misdated ; but had the former results been based on sound premises, nothing could have ever shaken them.   It is on that ground that science is worth pursuing.   The deductions which it produces may be important or they may be trifling ; but once produced they last as long as this world shall last.

B. JOB.

IT is an acknowledged principle of criticism that texts should be regarded as sound and entire, unless there is reason for supposing them unsound and imperfect.   Real difficulties may be dealt with by trenchant methods, but unless there is an obvious ulcer, the knife should not be applied.   Any explanation of a book which requires no secondary hypothesis to shore it up has therefore an advantage over explanations that are based on a number of unproved assumptions.   Before what are called critical methods came in vogue the unity of the book of Job was assumed, although different explanations were given of the lesson to be derived from it. The modern process of dissection has scarcely led to any greater agreement on this latter point, and has besides introduced a subjective element which renders the chance of ultimate agreement infinitesimal. For, as Homer says, " the steel possesses an attraction of its own "; if all the critics whom you respect use the knife, you will be unable to resist the temptation to use it on your own account.

As a whole the book of Job is intelligible, and indeed, easily intelligible ; as a piece of patchwork it defies explanation. Supposing that it could be shown to contradict itself seriously, we should have to show that other works on the same subject do not contradict themselves seriously before we could derive from that fact any proof of composite authorship. And the argument to be derived from inconsistency is of the least possible value where the subjects discussed are those whereon scarcely any one has a fixed opinion—indeed, if there be any truth in Kant's antinomies, on which every man almost of necessity holds contradictory opinions.

The explanation of the book would naturally be sought in the prologue, and it is there given with the utmost precision. Does man do work in order to take wages, or does he take wages in order that he may do work ? God's intention is the latter ; the view of the accuser of the

human race is the former. Job is to be the
test case. Job is called God's servant, or rather,
slave. A servant is clearly one who has to do
work; whether he receives wages or not is a
secondary question. In the case of a slave the
master scarcely professes to give him more than
will enable him to do his work : but if the
performance of the work be the important
matter, and the wage be defined as the amount
of material comfort which will enable the worker
to perform it with the greatest efficiency, the
takings of the slave and of the free labourer
will be identical, supposing the master in both
cases to understand his interests. The prospect
of wages may have been the inducement which
at the commencement caused the labourer to
enter the service; but if he be a true worker,
it will be the prospect of doing the work which
will induce him to continue in it, even though
the wages be diminished, or practically cease.
Love of God in any practical system has always
meant anxiety to carry out God's commands,
irrespective of any reward present or future ;
and the only way of proving whether any man
really love God is to subject him to the test to
which Job is subjected in the Hebrew book
that bears his name, and the just man is sub-
mitted in Plato's *Republic*. If any man pass
the whole of it, then Satan may be told
that God has a servant upon earth ; if the
best man fail to pass it, then the book may

be regarded as a prophecy of ONE who will pass it.

The fact that Satan appears in the prologue and is afterwards not mentioned has given rise to some very superficial criticism. Clearly there is no difficulty about it. We are not dualists, who believe in a Power of Good and a Power of Evil. But the accusation of the human race has to be put in some one's mouth; there can be no trial without an accuser. What accuses the human race must be the difficulties before which they recoil, just as what commends them would be the record of difficulties overcome. Now, the difficulties that are to be thrown in Job's way cannot be brought on the stage and made to speak before they exist; that would violate all dramatic propriety. Satan, whose name is a general term for them all, speaks in their stead. But when his pleading is over, his presence is of no further use. The author does not make Satan himself produce any effect beyond the striking of Job with disease; and this he does as God's minister. For the other misfortunes he is responsible only so far as it is at his instigation that the experiment is being tried.

We therefore dismiss at the outset all theories that make the book of Job resemble a Platonic dialogue, as exhibiting the process whereby an opinion formed itself in the mind of the author. The author *assumes* that the purpose of evil is probation. In the process whereby chaos is turned into order it has pleased God to give man a share; as a servant he must do work. Is he to be a beginner who complains because the work set him is too hard, or an expert who grumbles if it is too easy? Is he to be an infant who fancies that his parents wish him to work in order that he may get a prize, or a scholar who is aware that he is given prizes only because it is desirable that the best worker should possess the best tools? Now to distinguish between different sorts of obstacles is difficult, if not impossible. For each sort science has either precaution or remedy: in the worst case alleviation. A sudden change of fortune is therefore parallel to a sudden transference from one form of service to another. *Faith* will suggest that such transference is designed, and due to the ascertained fact that the victim of the change will discharge the second service well as he has discharged the first well. Since a cheerful demeanour under such changes will certainly be one test of a servant's competence, it will be easy to tell whether Job can stand his trial or not. If he abandons God's service, we shall know that Satan was right.

Meanwhile the author of the book is standing *his* test. He professes to take us behind the scenes, and he has to prove that he has been there himself. The account which he gives of evil is that whereon the best writers are probably agreed. His view is in accordance with experience to a nicety. That good conduct ordinarily produces prosperity follows from the working of economic and physical laws; but to say that it always produces it is to run counter to experience. That morality is suggested by the desire for physical comfort may be true ; that it always needs that support is grossly untrue. Hence the writer of the book of Job proves his competence to compose a work in which men are represented as discussing the problem of evil by showing that he has himself solved it so far as its solution is practicable or desirable.

In the second place he shows himself fit to write a drama by representing men acting as they normally act. The author of a martyrology would probably have represented Job's family as employed in religious exercises ; our author makes them occupy themselves as the young normally occupy themselves—in sport. Job's own time, we presently learn, is far too valuable to be passed in the same way ; but while he countenances his children's gaiety, he takes pains to see that they do no harm. The point, however of verses 4–6 of the first chapter is evidently to provide a probable occasion for the misfortune which happened to Job's children, while showing that it cannot have been earned by any actual offence.

The order in which the misfortunes come is that of magnitude—loss of wealth is the lightest, loss of children next. Job's faith is equal to these two trials, and apparently his wife's faith is equal to them also. To have made Job's wife greatly inferior to Job would have been undramatic—an eccentricity only to be justified by the author's dealing with historical matter which he could not seriously alter. But in making her succumb at the third trial, while Job himself does not succumb till the fourth, the author agrees with the opinion of most ancient writers, who regard the male sex as more patient than the female. That Clytemnestra can hope for ten years that Troy will fall proves, according to Æschylus, that she has the soul of a man. Had Job's wife been produced on an actual stage, she would doubtless have been of smaller stature and physically weaker than her husband ; similarly, in her power of endurance, she is made unusually strong, but not so strong as Job. Those who judge her fairly will admire her patience under loss of property and children, instead of finding fault with her for giving advice like that of the " foolish women " at the third trial.

After these three losses, what has Job left that he can lose ? *His good name.* Plato and our author are agreed that if we would test the really just man, we must deprive him of this also. Other tests will scarcely be greater than those which the common soldier and sailor have to face, which the fear of losing their good name ordinarily enables them to bear cheerfully. The just man must not only bear losses and afflictions, but must be thought, while doing so, to be worse than his neighbours, and to deserve no sympathy. Here, then, we have a matter for which the dialogue is the appropriate vehicle; for reputation lives on men's mouths. The other afflictions could best be told by a narrator. The loss of Job's good name can be most powerfully portrayed if Job's traducers are themselves brought on the stage; and the blow will be heaviest if those traducers are men of note and honour themselves, and Job's familiar friends. It is time, then, for the narrator to withdraw, and for the *dramatis personæ* to appear.

Moreover, since a reputation is not blasted at once, the length of the dialogue will give the hearer time to mark the stages whereby confidence in Job is shaken, and his guilt supposed to be proved. If he stand this last test—if, in spite of loss of fame, he continue to speak reverently of God, then Satan will be answered; it will be clear that Job will have recognised that reputation, like other goods, is an instrument to help certain forms of work for God, whereas for others it is not required, so that he will no more repine at the loss of it than a drummer who was made captain would repine at the loss of his drum.   Whereas if in this last case he prove unfaithful, we shall know that his former conduct was not based on the right principle, but rather on instinct or habit ; and if the best man in the world be so insufficiently armed, what must be the case with the others ?

The persons who are first introduced are representatives of the best wisdom and morality of the time.   The LXX. translator, who makes them princes, though his intention is to give what is sometimes called a social lift to the characters, does not seriously violate the author's intention.   They are learned, one of them professes himself a prophet, and they are all observers of the order of nature ; only, like the vast majority of mankind, they have no moral courage.   They have a certain theory of the ways of God, viz., that moral conduct is a coin wherewith prosperity is purchased from God. Prosperity is the end, and virtue the means ; and God must of course be just in His dealings. Whereas then the right and scientific method is at all times to start from facts and only arrive at principles from them, with the probability that the principles will have to be corrected or modified by fresh experience, Job's friends are unable to see more than a part of experience. From the fact that Job and his children were certainly innocent, they dare not reconsider their principle ; the only course before them is to deny the evidence of their senses and do an injustice, in the idea that God will be pleased thereby. Any one who has ever had to argue with persons who have a strong interest in believing something, can prophesy that the argument will not advance, because the opponent will throw up everything rather than acknowledge that his principle is wrong. And, in Job's case, Job is not more enlightened about principles than his friends ; he is personally conscious of his innocence, but is so immeshed in the false principle that it is clear he would have judged as they judged. So far, then, as the three friends argue, the parties become more and more embittered, and the belief in Job's guilt, which was at first faintly whispered, becomes, by the third round, a matter of conviction. But where people meet facts with theories there is no chance of their arriving at the truth, for that can only be got at through the facts.

The question whether Job's friends represent different theories has sometimes been discussed ; it is clear that if they did so, such a subject would never have given rise to discussion. Reputation is a thing that requires a number of votes. One man is not sufficient to stand for public opinion ; hence the more nearly the friends agree in their notions, the more dramatically will they stand for the world in general. If Job could have got one of the three to see his side of the question, his reputation would not have appeared hopelessly lost ; since by defending himself he makes each one of them think worse of him than the last, the reader feels that Job's good name is gone with his other possessions.

By the fact that the third speaker is silent at the third round, the failure of the friends in their capacity of consolers is indicated ; and, in the monologue, Job tells the hearer more calmly than he could do in the dialogue some of his convictions. We learn that he has a very good opinion of himself ; he goes through the whole list of offences and is certain of his complete innocence. He tells the hearer how keenly he misses the place of honour and the approval of the crowd, and pities the world for the loss of such a man as himself. He forgets himself in chapter xxvii. sufficiently to deliver a discourse which would have been suitable in the mouth of one of the friends.

The last speaker introduced is quite a different person from the sheikhs. He is young, verbose, and conceited ; but, like the young, he has a certain amount of candour and readiness to acknowledge facts which is wanting in his seniors. The difficulty of his language is so great that we cannot as yet interpret him with certainty. What is certain is, that he finds fault with Job, not for imaginary offences, but for actual blasphemy committed since the change in his fortunes, and that he contributes in chapter xxxiii. some very new ideas to the discussion.

Lastly, God Himself is introduced speaking. This is contrary to experience, for the speakers have several times distinctly asserted that it is impossible to arraign the Deity before a human tribunal. The voice of God is doubtless the light thrown on the matter by physical science. That reveals an amount of wisdom and power which makes it absurd for any human being to doubt God's justice ; for only he who comprehends the whole plan has a right to criticise any part of it. But it by no means gives the solution of Job's difficulty directly. He only learns that what happens to him must have its place in the gigantic plan. What its place is he does not yet know. The doctrine that the hardest problem is set to the aptest scholar must be discovered by man's own wit ; Job, though the most devout of mankind, has no notion of it.

Hence it would seem that there need be little about the *main thought* of Job that is un-intelligible. It is a drama in so far as it exhibits men acting as they normally act. If it were the custom for men to draw correct inferences from phenomena, and to abandon their prejudices so soon as they find them inconsistent with experience, then Job's friends would be violating dramatic probability in doing the reverse of this. It is clear that they have the materials for the study of the problem. Why do they come to console him at the start? Certainly not because of the wealth that he has lost nor the power which he is no longer able to exercise, but because of his virtue. That then being in their eyes as well as in Job's the important matter, how could externals stand in any causal connection with virtue, so that absence of fortune could imply absence of virtue? Hence the real relation of virtue to prosperity forms a profitable subject of discussion, but no one thinks of discussing it. That God is just is a self-evident proposition, which Job thinks fit to deny; the friends all assert it loudly; but it does not occur to them to try and define justice. Job himself can only think of what it *denotes*, not of its actual significance. And since the methods of moral science do not differ from those of physical science, but the latter is more easily started, nature recommends men to acquire their method over the latter. And indeed it is historically true that the physical philosophy of the Ionians preceded the moral philosophy of Socrates and Plato.

The tame ending to the story is what we should have expected from the experiment having failed. The friends are compelled to atone for having accused the innocent, in the idea that such advocacy was pleasing to the Divine Being; Job has also to make atonement

for having meddled with things that are too
high for him. The chance that he had was to
be God's *argument* against the Accuser of the
human race ; what he chooses is to be a worthy
paterfamilias and a man of wealth and station.
The human race has therefore to wait a series
of centuries ere ONE arise who shall beat down
Satan under His feet. Had Job known that
the worth of the human race was being tested
by his conduct, probably he would have stood
the fourth trial as he stood the first three. But
nature does not tell us when we are being
tested; and what we are to learn from Job's
failure at the fourth trial is that his passing
successfully through the earlier trials was in
part accidental. Had his conduct been based
on the right principle, he would have found the
fourth trial no harder than the former three.

But while the general plan and purpose of
the book and also its place in the Divine revelation are clear, it must be confessed that in
numerous cases whole verses are unintelligible,
sometimes indeed owing to our ignorance of the
meaning of particular words, but more often
in spite of our acquaintance with the signification of all the words employed. Occasionally this
difficulty can be dealt with on the supposition
that the text is corrupt ; but in most cases the
amount of correction required in order to produce a satisfactory sense is too great for critical
probability. Hence we have to look about for

a more likely solution of the problem, and there is one suggested by the local colouring of the book.

The scene is laid in Arabia. The home of Job may be identified with Al-'Iss, of which the valuable geography of Hamdani gives a description. It is, he says, the name of the country between Wadi Al-Kura and Al-Hijr.[1] The name figures several times on Mr. Doughty's excellent map. Job's home in Hamdani's time gave its name to a particular kind of dates;[2] and since we learn that from Al-Hijr to Tayma, the home of Eliphaz, was three days' journey, the length of time spent on the road by Eliphaz can be calculated. Both Hamdani and the author of the *Geographical Lexicon* mention Al-'Iss as being in the neighbourhood of *mines* —a fact which we might have suspected from chapter xxviii. If the name of Nejd include Al-'Iss (as, from Hamdani, seems to be the case), then it is observable that Job in xxix. 1–4 speaks of the sunny days of his life as his *autumn ;* for an Arabic meteorologer[3] observes that in Nejd it does not rain in the autumn, whereas in other regions of Arabia rain falls at that season of the year.

The life of the inhabitants of these wadis is known to us from the brilliant descriptions of W. G. Palgrave and others. The people are at

[1] Hamdani, ed. Müller, p. 131, 15.
[2] *Ibid.*   [3] *Lisān al-'arab*, x. 410.

times in danger of losing everything through
the torrents which pour down the mid hollow in
the rainy season, when the houses that are built
too low down are ruined.[1] Of the torrents
which ravaged Mecca a chronicle was at one
time kept.[2] On one occasion the stone called
" Abraham's Station " was swept away. Such
events are deeply impressed on the minds of
the speakers in Job. " A pouring river was
their foundation " (xxii. 16); " Why do you not
ask the travellers, and make sure of their landmarks ? how the wicked is reserved for the day
of trouble, the day when the torrents rush down "
(xxi. 30).[3] The landmarks of which the speaker
is thinking are probably the erections put up in
the Dahna by philanthropic travellers to guide
their successors.[4]

A remarkable piece of description is contained
in vi. 15–20. We are told there that the
caravans of Tayma and Saba had often to
return owing to the failure of the torrents on
which they had counted for replenishing their
waterskins. " My brethren," says Job, " have
betrayed me like a torrent (we seem to hear
the play on the Arabic words for " pool " and
" treachery ")[5]—like a channel wherein torrents

---

[1] Palgrave, *Travels*, i. 342.
[2] Azraki, p. 394.
[3] Cp. xxii. 11, xxvii. 20.
[4] Palgrave, *Travels*, ii. 131.
[5] *Letters* of Abu 'l-'Ala, p. 5, 11

pass, such as are turbid with ice, and whereon the snow is conspicuous. At what time they are ——, they disappear; when it is hot, they vanish from their bed. Their courses become tortuous; they 'mount into the desert' (here again we recognise an Arabic phrase,[1] of which the use in this context is perhaps wanting in felicity) and are lost. The caravans of Tayma were on the look-out, the companies of Saba hoped for them; they are ashamed because they ——(have sunk into the ground?); they come up to them and are disappointed." Compare with this what Palgrave tells us repeatedly. " The pools and torrents which form during the winter on the plateaus or furrow the valleys are soon reabsorbed in the marly or sandy soil."[2] " Rain fell abundantly and sent torrents down the dry watercourses of the valley, changing its large hollows into temporary tanks. None of the streams, however, showed any disposition to reach the sea, nor indeed could they, for this part of Nejd is entirely hemmed in to the east by the Towaik range."[3]   " None of these winter torrents finds its way unbroken to the sea : some are at once reabsorbed, while a few, so the natives of the country told me, make their way right through Toweyk to the Nefud on the west, or to the Dahna on the east and south, and *are there speedily lost in the deep sands*, where a

[1] Farazdak, first poem, line 2.
[2] *Travels*, ii. 176.   [3] *Ibid.* ii. 115.

Rhine or a Euphrates could hardly avoid a similar fate." [1]

Since the Arabic language would seem to have been spoken in Arabia from time immemorial, we should expect the speakers to have Arabic names ; and we are not disappointed. *Zofar* is felicitously identified by Al-Baghawi [2] with the name *Zāfir*, "conqueror," which is probably still in use, An Ibn Zafir figures in the list of Arabic authors ; [3] but the form Muzaffar is more common. *Elifaz* means " my God has won "—in the arrow game, the classical sport of the pre-Mohammedan Arabs. Winning in that game is typical of the grandest form of success ; Paradise itself is spoken of as the *grand prix*, or *gros lot*. *Bildad* cannot be separated from Baldud, " the name of a place near Medinah." [4] Both apparently belong to a dialect in which an M at the beginning of a word turns into B, and they mean respectively " the stubborn antagonist," [5] and " the place of the stubborn encounter." The name Job or *Iyyob* is easily identified with the Arabic *hayub*, " reverent " or " reverend " ; the authorities are doubtful which the word means. A tradition " faith is *hayub* " may mean either that the faith-

[1] *Travels*, i. 339.
[2] *Commentary on the Koran*, p. 593.
[3] *Matali' al-budūr* (Cairo, 1299, A.H.), i. 123.
[4] Yakut, *Geographical Dictionary*, s.v.
[5] Cf. Zamakhshari's *Mufassal*, § 4.

ful fear God and avoid transgression, or that they are objects of reverence.[1]   The description of Job as fearing God and keeping clear of evil favours the former explanation ; whereas Job's description of his life in chapter xxix. might favour the latter.   Among Job's daughters, one, Jemimah, has an Arabic name (*yumaimatu,* " little dove," diminutive of *yamamatu,* the name of a lady who played an important part in the legends of the Arabs) ; while the names of the others might be translations.   The last proper name, Elihu, might be either Arabic or Hebrew.

Possibly the most characteristically Arabic notion in the work is the author's idea of a book as a slab of stone.   In the well-known verses in the nineteenth chapter, " Would that my words were written, would that they were engraved in a book, with a style of iron and lead (?), dug in the rock for ever," it would seem clear that the book whereof he is thinking is a page of stone.   This takes us into Arabia.   The Arabic word [2] whence the Hebrew for " book " is derived means properly " a stone," and the verb taken from it means " to stone."   An early poet compares the effect of rain on the sand to the process whereby the composition is committed to the stones.[3]   In xxxi. 36 Job says that if he could get hold of the affidavit of his opponent (" the book written by mine adversary "), he

---

[1] *Nihayah* of Ibn Al-Athir.   [2] *Zubr.*
[3] Lebid, *Muallakah,* at the beginning.

would carry it on his shoulder! This would seem to imply that it would be a heavy weight, not a light slip of parchment or papyrus. The phrase that follows, " I should bind it on me as a crown," refers to a practice sometimes mentioned by ancient writers of carrying objects of special value on the head.[1] The weight in Job's opinion would be no obstacle in the way of his flaunting an accusation of which he could answer every word. The stone slab of Arabia therefore corresponds to the Assyrian clay tablet, or the scroll of the Canaanites. From a " stone slab," which is the meaning the word still has in Job, *sefer* came to mean " writing " generally, and afterwards " book " in the familiar sense.

The references to " sealing " are not inconsistent with the theory of stone books. Sealing is done with clay (xxxviii. 14) according to the Arab practice. The verb " to seal " is used with the sense of obstructing (xxxvii. 7). The clay employed for this purpose was a sort of mortar, which permeated interstices like light (xxxviii. 14). The process of instruction is pictured as boring a hole in the ear, and *sealing* it, *i.e.* filling it up, with knowledge (xxxiii. 16). When the sealing clay dries, it becomes abnormally hard (xli. 7).[2]

[1] Cobet, *Novæ Lectiones*, p. 394.
[2] The word in xxiv. 16 seems to mean " destined," and is from a different root.

The Arabs were great astronomers, and the references to Arabic astronomy in the book of Job are very curious. Very early poets [1] show themselves acquainted with the elaborate system of star-naming which the writers on astronomy explain to us. In Job xxxviii. 31 the sufferer is asked if he can (or did) tie the bonds of the Pleiads, and in the following verse if he can console [2] the Great Bear over her children ? These questions would be easily understood by an Arab. To him the Pleiads are typical of union, the stars of the Great Bear of separation. A writer begins a letter : [3] " I am to-night united with my companions like the Pleiads, but if you do not encourage our union by a present of wine we shall separate again like the daughters of Na'sh (the stars of the Great Bear)." " I pray God," says an elegant writer,[4] " that we may meet in a way that will resemble the union of the Pleiads in constancy." The same author says in a poem,[5] " The Pleiads have stretched westwards a hand in whose fingers the wager is locked," on which we are told that according to the Arabs the Pleiads consist of two hands, called respectively the

[1] *Jamharah* of Abu Zaid, p. 154.

[2] I assume in these articles that the Massoretic pointing is of little authority.

[3] *Matali' al-budūr*, i. 158.

[4] *Letters* of Abu 'l-'Ala, p. 54, 6.

[5] *Sakt al-zand* (Cairo, 1286 A.H.), i. 50.

Painted Hand and the Amputated Hand, the former appearing to be spread out, and the latter closed.   In Job iv. 9 it is said of mankind that they dwell in houses of clay, and are destroyed " before the Great Bear "—a phrase which the next verse shows to be equivalent to " constantly," " incessantly."   This reminds us of another verse of the same poet,[1] where he complains, " Thou hast left me, albeit I am constant like the Great Bear " ; and our commentator tells us that this constellation does not rise and set like the others, but " merely revolves round the North Pole without crossing the sky."   Hence the qualities of constancy and stationariness are attributed to it, as when a poet says (in illustration of the fact that a large family hinders promotion), " See the sun who is solitary can cross the height of heaven, whereas the father of the ' daughters of Na'sh ' remains low down."   Of the stars which constitute the constellation three were called Na'sh and four Na'sh's sons.[2]   A German scholar has rightly remarked that the name Na'sh is the same as the word in Job with the article prefixed.

In xxxviii. 15 among the effects of the dawn we read that " the wicked are precluded from their light, and the lofty arm is broken."   The second clause is easily intelligible.   There is

[1] *Sakt al-zand,* ii. 32.
[2] So in old poetry ; the alteration of "sons" to " daughters" is due to a grammatical theory.

a constellation called "the Arm," *i.e.* the Lion's Arm.[1] The word "broken" for "dulled" is chosen in order to suit the subject. "The wicked" must of course mean some stars or constellations ; the text indicates that both here and in verse 13, "and the wicked are shaken thereat," the first letter of the word for "wicked" is either corrupt or misplaced. Perhaps therefore we should read the *'Arshes*, *i.e.* two constellations called *'Arsh* or "the Throne." The verb "to be shaken" is perhaps as natural with this name as "to be broken" with the "Arm." There is a famous line in which a poet declares that the Throne of God shook the day his uncle died.[2]

With the style of the above verses we may compare some lines [3] of a poet who has already been cited. "The country," he says, "has been watered by the Lion's Arm with all his might, till not one finger's breadth is left. The *Simak* ('Spica') has thrust it through with its javelin, and the ropes that hold the Watering-pot have been cut over the country whereon the Pleiads shed copious tears." The old theory is said to have been that rain was due to the "Mansions of the Moon."

Job xxxviii. 31 *b :* "Canst thou undo the ropes of K'sil?" is in the same style. There

---

[1] Kazwini, *Wonders of Creation* (Cairo, 1309 A.H.), i. 78.

[2] *Letters* of Abu 'l-'Ala, p. 92, 10.

[3] *Sakt al-zand*, ii. 106.

is a constellation called "the Holder of the reins,"[1] and the author of the verse in Job seems to count on his readers being familiar with this appellation. The next question, "Canst thou bring out Mazaroth at his time?" must imply some similar knowledge; the name that resembles this most is the Arabic *Majarrat*, ordinarily used for the Milky Way. There is an old proverb, "Take the middle, O Majarrat, and the dates of Hajar will ripen."[2] The time then at which Mazaroth should come out was probably an important epoch of this sort. The dates of Hajar were famous throughout Arabia. Perhaps, then, the time referred to in this verse is the time when they should ripen.

In vii. 12 Job asks of God, "Am I a sea or a sea-monster that Thou dost set a guard upon me?" Certain stars or constellations were regarded as the *watchers* of others;[3] the theory appears not only in the Arabic astrology, but also in Homer. The "Sea-monster" is actually the name of a constellation; and in the case of one called "Sea-monster's belly" we are told the name of its "watcher."[4] The "Sea" is probably the constellation called by the Arabs "the River."

---

[1] *Wonders of Creation*, i. 57. It is not certain that this name is old.

[2] *Lisan al-Arab*, s.v. "majarrah."

[3] *Wonders of Creation*, passim.

[4] *Ibid*. i. 87.

The same source illustrates some mythological allusions in the book. In xxvi. 12 and 13, some of the deeds of God are enumerated : " By His wisdom He crushed Rahab, by His breath the heavens are cleared, and His hand transfixed *Nachash Bariach*." These words are often rendered " crooked serpent "; but it is more likely that they are to be regarded as proper names, taken from the old mythology. Indeed they seem fairly easy to identify. The term *nahs* (the equivalent of the Hebrew *nachash*) is applied to two planets, both supposed to bring ill luck, Saturn and Mars ; and the latter of these is called in Arabic *Mirrikh*, which, by the alteration of the first letter to B (a change noticed above in the case of Bildad) becomes Bariach. The word *nahs* is said to mean darkness, and especially that caused by particles of dust in the air. The brightness of the heavens is therefore in this myth attributed to a wound dealt to Nahs Mirrikh, who would have darkened them. Those who curse the day, according to Job iii. 8, do it by rousing Leviathan, whom Isaiah (xxvii. 1) identifies with Nachash Bariach. The prefixing of the name Nachash to the proper name of the planet is precisely similar to the prefixing of the word *Sa'd* (which means " of good omen ") to a number of other stars.[1] The identity of the names Nahs Mirrikh and Nachash Bariach,

[1] *Wonders of Creation, Index.*

together with the ascription of darkness to
the influence of the latter, seems sufficient to
justify us in thinking we have here the solution
of the difficulty. Hence it is an admissible conjecture that Rahab signifies the other Nahs,
i.e. Saturn; and indeed the Arabic name for
Saturn (*Zuhal*) seems to mean the same as
Rahab.

Among the primitive superstitions of the
Arabs were those connected with the Jinn,
whose name implies that they were hidden
from mortal view. To them both poets and
prophets owed their information. Apparently
the same Jinn ordinarily inspired the same
individual throughout his life, and at the death
of one favourite migrated into another. To
those favourites they sometimes appeared in
dreams. Their information was not always
trustworthy, and it was obtained in a dishonourable way. "Certain persons" we read
in Sura lxxvii. of the Koran "used to rely on
certain Jinn," who, however, only increased their
uncertainty with regard to God's purposes.
They used to station themselves somewhere
whence they could listen to the divine councils;
but in future, according to the Sura, any Jinn
who tried to do this would find a shooting-star
on the look out for him. This strange theory
is represented by Eliphaz in the book of Job.
"Hast thou listened at the council of God, and
got thyself wisdom?" he asks of Job in xv. 8.

This would be the natural way of acquiring knowledge of God's plans according to him, and indeed he owed his own acquaintance with them to a similar operation. "Unto me was a word *stolen*," he boasts in iv. 12, "and my ear took in a rumour [1] thereof." Doubtless a Jinn had stolen it, and indeed this Jinn communicated it to Eliphaz in the visions of the night. Eliphaz was unable to scan the features of the Jinn closely; one who appeared to Ibn Duraid [2] (according to his statement) and communicated some verses, was "tall, yellow-faced, and grey-haired"; another, who communicated certain poems and tunes to Ibrahim of Mausil, took the form of a richly clad sheikh, but afterwards became invisible.[3] It would seem that part of Elihu's polemic is directed against Eliphaz's theory of inspiration by Jinn. Job, he says, speaks not truly when he says God is too proud to communicate with man (xxxiii. 12). It is God Himself (not the Jinn) who speaks in the dream when he opens man's ear and fills it up with instruction.

To the same class of notions belongs the idea of the dead man's ghost watching over his grave, to which there is an allusion in xxi. 32: "And he is brought to the burial place, and watches over a grave." The Arabic name for

---

[1] שמע=שמע.
[2] Ibn Khallikan (Cairo, 1299 A.H.), i. 631.
[3] *Aghani*, v. 37.

the ghost is *hamah*, and the soul was "supposed to be a bird which escaped from the body when a man died or was slain, and cried over his grave."[1] One theory was that in the case of a murdered man it cried over his grave "give me drink" till the slayer was slain. The meaning of the next words (rendered "the clods of the valley shall be sweet unto him") is exceedingly obscure. It is very remarkable that the words for "clods of the valley" in *Arabic* signify a particular sort of date-tree or date.[2] The exact process implied by the first word was a matter of dispute among the old grammarians; "it means," says a good authority,[3] "supporting a valuable date-tree with an erection of stone or wood, if there is any danger of it falling owing to its height or the weight of its fruit." Another suggestion is that it means "hedging it round to prevent access to it." This is, I think, what the passage originally signified: the date-tree to which he no longer has access is sweet to him: he would fain return to the world, but cannot get back.

It is probable that the accounts of the Parias which are to be found in chapters xxiv. and xxx. can be best illustrated from Arabia. Von

---

[1] *Taj al-arus*, s.v. I think a line of Farazdak (p. 39, 1.) must refer to this.

[2] *Rujabiyyu 'l-nakhli. Lisān al-Arab*, i. 397.

[3] *Nihāyah* of Ibn Al-Athir.

Maltzan, in his *Travels*,[1] tells us of two sorts of
Parias existing in Yemen; and there are reasons
for thinking this institution a part of early
Arabian culture. Those to whom reference is
made in chapter xxiv. perform a variety of
menial duties, including forms of agricultural
labour, which an Israelite would certainly not
have thought degrading. With the Arabs
apparently it was otherwise. The poet Farazdak,
who is one of our best representatives of early
Arabian ideas, taunts one of his enemies [2] with
the fact that his *relations press oil in the Hauran*.
This is also regarded by the speaker in Job
xxiv. 11 as a humiliating labour, which, owing
to injustice, certain persons have to perform.
To the humbler class of Paria described by Von
Maltzan the account given in chapter xxx.
almost exactly corresponds. These persons are
not allowed to dwell near the rest of the nation ;
they are driven from the public places, and
howled after like thieves.

If we look at Al-'Iss on the map, and see
how vast a desert separates it from Palestine,
surely we shall be inclined to wonder whether
any Israelite could have interested himself in
this locality sufficiently to produce such a work
as the book of Job. Much of it, from the scanty
information preserved by Arabic archæologists
and poets, would, we see, have been intelligible
to an Arab, without, so far as we know, being

[1] *Reisen in Arabien*, i. 182–192.   [2] Page 74.

intelligible to a Canaanite. If any Israelite had taken the trouble to study Arabic in such a way as to enable him to create an Eliphaz, it is at least probable that his name would not have been forgotten by his countrymen.

Hence it was long ago suggested that the book must originally have been written in Arabic. The earliest Arabic which we possess is of about the year 600 A.D. It is, however, a canon of science that nature never deceives. That Hebrew, or Canaanitish, is a vulgar dialect of Arabic is as certain as if the best Canaanite writers themselves had told us so. And it is also certain that the Arabic whence Canaanitish was derived must have been a literary language, for the *orthography of Hebrew is etymological.* That fact postulates the existence of an Arabic literature earlier than the beginnings of Canaanitish. How long an interval elapsed between its decay and the renaissance of Arabic under the auspices of Mohammedanism is at present unknown. But the fact that the early Arabs wrote on stone gives us good hope that, sooner or later, their literature may be restored to us, just as those of ancient Egypt and Assyria have been restored.

This then gives us a likely clue to the difficulties of Job. The work is probably a translation, and translators are irresponsible. The original language was not the Sabæan, which we can now trace back to an early period, because Saba was a power hostile to the nation to which Job belonged. The character of the names of the speakers, no less than that of many of the institutions, makes it likely that it was classical Arabic. By following the clue, we may possibly recover in time the meaning of many passages in which the Hebrew conceals it ; and even if the process be slow, and more accurate *thesauri* of the Arabic language required than those which we now possess, it will be something to be on the right track. And it will also be evident that the process of dissection is excessively premature.

One or two fairly clear cases of mistranslation may be noticed here.

In xxxvii. 7 it is said of the snow that "it places an obstruction before every man (or, "ties the hand of every man") that all the men of his work may know," or "to know all the men of his work." Neither of these expressions seems intelligible, or to represent a possible effect of a snowstorm. The verb which in Hebrew means "know," in Arabic means "abandon" or "neglect." The sense required by the passage, which is surely "so that every man must neglect his work" [1] (where work is in the open air this is the certain result of a snowstorm) suits the Arabic meaning of the verb, and also suits the peculiarities of

----

[1] In Arabic חתי ידע כל רגל עמלה. The *elif* of prolongation was unknown in ancient Arabic.

Arabic orthography. A suggestion that this could be a trace of the older sense of the verb "to know" in *Hebrew* would have no probability; and even so, only half the difficulties would be solved.

xxxiii. 6, "Behold I am according to thy mouth unto God" is unlikely to be correct. The word "according to thy mouth" in Arabic letters would mean either "according to thy mouth" or "thy peer," "thy match." The same ambiguity would not, so far as we know, be found in Canaanitish. Yet it is evident that the sense "thy peer" is what is required. In an early chapter of Islamic history some champions refuse to fight with any but their "peers"; and the same word is used of equality for the purpose of marriage. "I am thy peer in God's eyes," is said by Elihu to Job, by way of affirming his claim to dispute with Job.

xv. 24, "Trouble and anguish shall suddenly overtake him; they shall prevail against him as a king ready to the battle," shows signs of mistranslation in the second clause. The word rendered "battle" is unknown. The figure of a king ready for battle seems inappropriate here, whether we think of the king as the attacking party or the attacked. The Arabic word for "ready"[1] (to the antiquity of which the Hebrew

[1] See Abu 'l-Walid's *Dictionary* (ed. Neubauer), col. 555.

word is witness) is identical in form with the proper name Ma'add, an early name for a nation in Arabia, often used as equivalent to "Arab." Hence the words rendered " a king ready" are likely to have meant " the king of Ma'add." The word Kidur ("battle") would in that case be also a proper name ; and, indeed, there are not a few proper names which resemble it, *e.g.*, Kaudur, king of the Himyarites.[1]   The allusion will then be to some sudden onslaught made by the king of Ma'add, which became typical of sudden and successful attacks.   If we could imagine any ground for calling Abram "king of Ma'add," we might suppose his onslaught on Kudur-Laghomer the event to which reference is made.

In some other cases it is not clear whether we have a mistranslation from Arabic, or a unique employment of a Hebrew root.   In xxi. 27, "Behold, I know your thoughts and your imaginations which ye *mutter* against me," it is possible that the Hebrew root (ordinarily " to do violence ") may have had the sense " mutter," but it seems more probable that we have a case of an Arabic word[2] represented by the Hebrew word that seemed to resemble it most.   The Arabic verb is used of people saying something to themselves, because they are afraid to say it out loud.   "When I say what is absurd," says a poet, " I raise my voice ;

---

[1] *Taj al-arus*, s.v.   [2] חמס.

but when I speak the truth, I *mutter* it long,"
i.e., " I say it under my breath long before I
venture to say it out loud." " Do you not see
that the days of youth give warning in a
whisper, or something gentler still ? " the same
poet asks in another place ; the young would
resent anything louder. " Our age cries aloud
what the ages that only *muttered* concealed
from us " gives a third illustration of this word.[1]
In Syriac the word means simply " to think."
It is clear that the verse of Job preserves an
early example of this word, for which, had it
been Hebrew in this sense, we should at least
have been likely to find some parallels in the
Bible.

It is not necessary for our purpose to pursue
this subject any further. It has, I think, been
shown that the probability is in favour of Job
having been originally in the language spoken
in the heart of Arabia : and this gives us the
prospect of solving many difficulties which are
at present unsolved, and, perhaps, of defining
the place of Elihu in the dialogue better than
it has hitherto been defined. There are, moreover, some other conclusions which are by no
means devoid of interest. We have seen that
the myth of Nahs Mirrikh is in Job part of a
system of astronomy which belongs to Arabia ;
and the myth of Rahab is similar. But elsewhere in the Bible we find these powers

[1] *Luzumiyyat* of Al-Ma'arri (Cairo, 1895), ii. 6, 25, 36.

identified with Egypt. This being so, it would
appear that Isaiah must have consciously
adapted the myths of Job to Israelitish history. The wounds inflicted on Nahs Mirrikh
and Zuhal had no meaning when the old
mythology had been forgotten or abandoned ;
what they must represent, it was now thought,
must be the great exploits of which the
Israelites cherished the memory ; and the
defeat of Egypt being the chief of these, Egypt
is identified with Nahs Mirrikh. It follows
thence that the translation of Job was classical
in Isaiah's time, and must have been made at a
very early period of Israelitish history. Where,
therefore, we find in Isaiah parallels to Job
(and these are very frequent), this must be
explained by Isaiah's style being modelled on
this old classic.

In the literatures of which the growth can
most easily be traced one generation is constantly found to instruct the next. The earliest
Greek writers imitate Homer, the next generation imitates *them*, and presently the earliest
Latin writers translate Greek works before they
are able to produce works of their own. Ennius
serves as a model to Lucretius, Lucretius to
Vergil, Vergil to all that follow. Since then it
is certain that the literature of Canaan was preceded by a literature in the language known to
us as classical Arabic, it would be natural if
Canaanitish literature commenced with transla-

tions from those old classics into the vernacular which now aspired to become a literary language.

The other possibility is that the translation of Job was made at the suggestion of some literary king, who may have played in Canaan the part afterwards played by Al-Ma'mun in the Mohammedan Empire. Since the difficulty of Job does not seem due to archaism so much as to mistranslation and, possibly, corruption, this latter hypothesis is the more probable ; and it is confirmed by the fact that in xxxiv. 15 there appears to be a reference to the text of Genesis. When Israelitish writers speak with respect of the wisdom of the " Children of the East," they most likely refer to the book of Job. That in the course of time the character of many of the speeches contained in it became modified is exceedingly likely ; thus it seems clear that Job's answer in chapter xxvi. is by no means justified by the address of Bildad in chapter xxv. Since Bildad's speech is, moreover, abnormally short, it is probable that a considerable amount of objectionable matter has been omitted. In the case of a translation, where the work was originally non-Israelitish in character, such omissions are easily explicable ; those of us who have to translate from the Sanskrit or Arabic, or even from the Greek or Latin, have constantly to omit matter which our taste rejects : and repeated handling of a book often reveals violations of taste which escape the notice of the first student. But that the general import of the Book of Job was sufficiently profound and prophetic to justify its admission into the canon has, I hope, been shown—by no means for the first time.

IV

THE ARGUMENT FROM SILENCE

THE argument from silence represents the following series of syllogisms. Had B existed in the time of an author A, A must have known of B. Had A known of B, he must have mentioned or cited B. But A neither mentions nor cites B. Therefore B did not exist in A's time.

It is clear that this argument involves two assumptions which are not always capable of demonstration. Human action is characterized by fitfulness, whence it is not absolutely certain that a man will perform an act which he may be well expected to perform. Hence, while knowing of B, he may for some unknown reason fail to mention B. Or, though the chance of his having failed to hear of B may be exceedingly small, it is often difficult to deny the admissibility of such a chance.

The most powerful argument from silence known to me is that urged against the genuine-

ness of the document called the Cairene Ecclesiasticus, a copy of Ecclesiasticus in Hebrew of
the eleventh century.   Hai Gaon, the most
learned Jew of the tenth century,[1] expressly
declared [2] that Ben-Sira's was not a "written
book"; and Rashi, whose work on the Talmud
embodies the whole of the Jewish learning of
the eleventh century, did the same.   There
seems, therefore, no chance that the Hebrew
could have been preserved among the Jews and
Hai Gaon and Rashi never have heard of it.   In
the same centuries dictionaries were written of
both Biblical and post-Biblical Hebrew; and
the lexicographers, who did their utmost to
illustrate their vocabularies from the sources at
their disposal, take no notice of the supposed
original of Ben-Sira.   In the tenth century a
Mohammedan of Baghdad got a learned
Christian and a learned Jew to give him lists
of their literature for his bibliography; and
Ecclesiasticus figures in the Christian list of
books translated into Arabic, but not in the
Jewish list.   If, then, there be an argument
from silence, we have here a case of one.   A
sufficient number of persons are involved to
eliminate the element of personal caprice; some
of them must have known of the book had it
existed; and most of them would have had an
interest in citing it.   Since they do not cite it,

[1] Neubauer, *Chronicles*, i. 66.
[2] *Teshuboth Ha-Geonim* (Lyck, 1864), No. xxvii.

we may justly infer that the book did not exist.

The argument from silence that is used to discredit Daniel is of a very different order. Ben-Sira, writing about 200 B.C., enumerates the famous men of the chosen line. In this list the name of Daniel does not appear. Had Daniel formed part of Ben-Sira's canon, the latter must have known of the work; and had he known of it, he must have mentioned Daniel among the famous men of Israel. This is how the argument runs. But the last premise is false, since he does not mention Ezra, although he mentions Nehemiah (xlix. 13). And the destruction of one link destroys the whole chain.

But let us question this witness rather more closely. Of Ezekiel, before or after whom Daniel would naturally be mentioned, he says (xlix. 9), "He also mentioned the enemies in rain, and set right those who walk straight." The Hebrew for "enemies" is scarcely distinguishable from the name *Job*, and our second source for Ben-Sira's verses, the old Syriac translation, here gives *Job* for "enemies." It seems marvellous that any one seeing this should doubt that the Syriac version was made from the original, and here preserved a valuable trace of it; but to German commentators this sort of argument apparently "does not appeal." No one now is likely to doubt that the Hebrew

meant "Ezekiel also made mention of Job";
and by the aid of the instruments which we
ordinarily employ for the restoration of Ecclesiasticus we elicit verses giving the following
sense : " He also mentioned Job, by a hint,
and declared happy those who walk straight." [1]
Ezekiel mentions Job in chapter xiv. (verses 14
and 20) as one of a trio of perfect men—Noah,
Daniel, and Job.   Ben-Sira is struck by his
mention of *Job*, and infers something from it.

But if he was surprised by the mention of
Job in this list, he evidently *was not surprised
by the mention of Daniel.*[2]   And what surprised
him about the mention of Job was the fact of a
non-Israelite being given a place in such a trio.
Hence he must have been aware that Daniel
was an Israelite.   Now whatever may have been
the case with Ezekiel, it is very certain that the
only Israelitish Daniel known to Ben-Sira who
could be mentioned in a trio of perfect men
must have been the Daniel known to us.   Ben-
Sira shows no sign whatever of acquaintance with

[1]

גַּם הִזְכִּיר אֶת־אִיּוֹב בְּרֶמֶז

וְאִשֵּׁר אֶת־מַיְשִׁירֵי דָרֶךְ

ברמז is an emendation for בזרם.   If the latter word be
rendered "among strangers," the argument will not be
seriously affected ; and indeed the word "Job" is all it
requires.   For רמז, cf. *B. Nedarim*, 39*b*.

[2] The author of *Chobath Ha-Lebaboth* (11th century :
Warsaw, 1875, ii. 158) is similarly struck by the mention
of Job here.

pre-exilic history going beyond our own. But if it seemed to Ben-Sira quite in order that Daniel should be mentioned in such a way, he must have had our book of Daniel in his canon.

And now let us examine Ben-Sira's inference. A clue to its import is given in a note appended by the LXX. translator to the Book of Job.[1] "And it is written that he, Job, shall rise up again with those whom the Lord raises." From this mention of Job then Ben-Sira infers that those who do good, irrespective of their nationality, shall have a share in the future world. Truly it is interesting to find this question discussed so early as Ben-Sira's time. Rabbi Seadyah in his religious philosophy, and a later Rabbi in his unpublished eschatology,[2] both incline to the view that the future life is for Israel only. Ben-Sira took the more liberal view, and assigned a share in it to all who walk straight, and this he inferred from the mention of Job in Ezekiel's list.

But how does the mention of Job by the side of Noah and Daniel prove this? The method of reasoning is an exceedingly familiar one in the Talmud, and resembles the "identical category."[3] In a list of terms whatever applies

[1] Compare also Justin, *Dialogue,* § 45, where the Jew utilizes the passage of Ezekiel (with some of the names altered) for the same purpose.

[2] *Megillath ha-megalleh* (Bodleian MS.).

[3] *Gezerah Shawah.*

to one applies to all. If, therefore, in the list Noah, Daniel, Job, we can find that *one* will be raised to life we are justified in inferring that all will enjoy the same privilege.

That one is Daniel, who is promised the future life in the last verse of the book that bears his name.[1] "Thou shalt rest, and stand in thy lot at the end of the days." No one could be promised resurrection more distinctly than thus. Since Job is mentioned side by side with Daniel, he too will have a share in the future life. Since he has it in virtue of his good conduct, therefore the same will apply to others, be they Israelites or not. A "beatitude" then as early as this means a promise of the future life.

If we examine the argument thus far, it will be seen that the provision made against doubts concerning the Divine revelation is worthy of attention. Had Ben-Sira's grandson translated the word *Job* correctly, it might have been condemned as an interpolation; the fact that he rendered it wrongly proves its genuineness beyond any question. Had Ben-Sira referred to an early chapter of Daniel, we should have been told that no argument could be drawn therefrom for the authenticity of the latter half; as it is, Ben-Sira refers to the *last verse*, a verse which implies all that has preceded. Had the LXX. translator of Job not gone out of his way

[1] The verse is used for this purpose in B. *Sanhedrin*, 92a.

to account for the introduction of Job into the canon, we should not have been able to evolve Ben-Sira's argument with certainty ; that little supplement guides us with precision.

But if Daniel formed part of Ben-Sira's canon, he ought to borrow phrases from Daniel as he borrows them from other parts of the Bible. And so he does. In xxxvi. 7 he asks the question, "Why, when the light of all the days of the year is from the sun, is one day superior to another?" And he answers, "By the sentence of God they were separated, and *He changed times and feasts*." [1] Here, as so often, the error of the Greek translator enables us to restore the original with certainty : he should have rendered the words, "He changed times and seasons." [2] These words are a quotation of Daniel ii. 21, "He changeth the times and seasons"; [3] and, indeed, it may be doubted whether Ben-Sira would have assigned this act to God without some warrant for Holy writ, such as this text of Daniel gives. In the same chapter of Daniel (ii. 9) occurs the similar phrase "until the time be changed"; [4] the meaning is not very clear : the wise men are charged by Nebuchadnezzar with having con-

---

[1] וְשִׁנָּה עִתִּים וּמוֹעֲדִים.

[2] ἑορτή = מוֹעֵד. The Syriac has this right.

[3] LXX. and Th. ἀλλοιοῖ καιροὺς καὶ χρόνους. Compare also Daniel xii. 7 with vii. 25, showing that עִדָּן = מוֹעֵד. [4] See also vii. 25.

spired to put the king off with some fabrication until the time changed, probably meaning "until some fresh interest diverted the king's attention." The phrase is in any case identical with that used by Ben-Sira xviii. 25, "from morning to evening *time changes*,"[1] which seems to signify "the weather changes." He supposed then that the king used the phrase metaphorically of his own state of mind, as might be done colloquially in our own language.

Is this sufficient to prove Daniel genuine? Probably not, but it is quite sufficient to wreck the theories that are at present dominant. Those theories require Daniel to be Maccabean; and it has now been shown that a pre-Maccabean writer bases a theological argument on the *last* verse of Daniel, and borrows phrases from the earlier part of the book. Hence the attack on Daniel has been for the moment repulsed, and any hypothesis which regards it as spurious will be confronted with the fact that Ben-Sira identified the Daniel mentioned by Ezekiel with the Daniel of the book that bears his name.

Let us now try to use the argument from silence on our own account. In the Biblical revelation an important place is occupied by the *Psalms*. The Arabs use for a collection of poems the term *divan*, and it is so useful that

---

[1] מִבֹּקֶר עַד עֶרֶב שׁוֹנָה עֵת. The Syriac משנא is intransitive.

we shall borrow it. Divans are of several sorts.
Sometimes the poetry of a tribe is collected
into a divan ; such a book contains the works
of all the poets whom the tribe produced. Only
one such seems to have been handed down to
us; but we can trace the existence of others,
and in one case can almost name the year in
which it perished.[1]   More often the divan
contains the works of a single poet; and where
the same author wrote on a variety of subjects,
his verses on each subject constitute a separate
divan.   There are also cases in which the poetry
produced by the members of one family is put
together.   In such a case the work of one gifted
member is likely to occupy a prominent position
in the divan, whereas the others only follow in
his train.

What sort of divan is represented by the
Psalter?

It is clear that the divan before us exhibits
selection.   It does not contain all David's
poems ; for out of four which his biography
preserves, the Psalter contains only one.   Since
three of these poems are dirges, we infer that
the dirge, a most important style, is not admitted.   Thence we may infer that the Psalter
is confined to one style, the religious ode, or
hymn, for the absence of the dirge gives us an
a fortiori argument.   If songs of that solemn
and semi-religious character are not admitted,

[1] *Letters* of Abu 'l-Ala, p. xiii. note 4.

still less can the encomium find a place. As for the epithalamium, it would seem to have no place in the Semitic divan. It would probably be regarded as a personal insult.[1]

Secondly, the divan must be exclusive not only *quâ* subjects, but also *quâ* authors. Hezekiah's thanksgiving after recovery resembles many of the Psalms in style. Since it is excluded, we infer that the productions of remote descendants of David are excluded. The Psalm of Habakkuk exhibits the technique of the Psalms. It is not admitted into the Psalter; we infer that the hymns of the prophets are not admitted. Jonah's psalm is a cento from the existing Psalter; therefore, the Psalter was complete before it was composed. If Jonah be historical, this will be before the fall of Nineveh.

The relation of the hymns of Hezekiah and Habakkuk to the Psalter is indeed of a sort which gives occasion for reflection. It is clear that both of them are modelled on the Psalms, so closely modelled that the room left for the author's originality is in parts exceedingly small. This fact is not of itself surprising. In the Arabic divans the subjects introduced, their order in a poem, as well as great numbers of similes and expressions, are "tralaticious," borrowed by one

[1] In *Aghani*, ix. 33, there is an allusion to a poem of the sort.

generation from another, in so long a series
that it is now impossible to name or locate their
originator with approximate correctness. Hence
the employment by these authors of whole verses
already found in the Psalter is not unintelligible.
But whereas the verse which is numbered 34
in Psalm xviii. is exceedingly suitable in the
mouth of a "man of war from his youth," in
that of a seer its appropriateness is far more
doubtful. We should be inclined to explain it
in the latter case as we explain the verses in
which the Arabic poets of the Abbasid period
describe their journeys through the desert, their
feats of prowess, their loves and the ruins of the
dwellings of their friends—as matter which the
laws of the art required to be introduced in a
poem, although there was no longer any reality
to which any part of it corresponded. In the
case of Hezekiah's hymn there is the same
peculiarity as in Jonah's, viz., a tendency to
apply to actual personal experiences words
which in the Psalms seem used rather more
vaguely and metaphorically. And there seems
in both cases a considerable likelihood that the
technical terms of the music of the Psalter are
misunderstood by the authors. Hezekiah's hymn
is called *Miktab*, "a letter." It at once suggests
itself that this word is intended to be the same
as the *Miktam* of the Psalms, and indeed bears
to it the same relation as Spenser's *Æglogue*
bears to the Vergilian *Eclogue*. In the latter

case it was not apparent what an *Eclogue* had to do with pastoral affairs ; a very slight alteration made it quite clear. Similarly the word *Miktam* is decidedly a puzzle ; by a very slight alteration a thoroughly familiar word is produced. The words with which Habakkuk's hymn closes seem to bear a similar relation to the title, " By Menasseach," of so many of the Psalms. One who read these hymns and, without prejudice, compared them with the Psalter, would probably conclude that they were not incorporated with the latter, on the same ground which would forbid our incorporating any other late imitation with its model. But the assumption of the spuriousness of all these hymns is somewhat complicated, and, in the case of the hymn of Habakkuk, clearly improbable.

Let us now see whether we can discover any means of dating the Psalter. Since the Psalms sometimes recount at length and frequently make allusions to the national history, they will probably mention (1) all events of primary importance down to their arrangement in the form of a divan ; (2) all the prominent individuals who took part in forming the national history down to that time, these persons being considered special objects of the Divine favour. This canon is based on the analogy of similar works in other languages,[1] and especially on the

---

[1] *E.g.* Horace, *Ode* i. 12.

Praise of the Fathers by Ben-Sira. He brings the history down to its last name—Simon son of Onias, whom he had known as a child. The name of Nehemiah is to him of supreme importance, and also that of Zerubbabel. " How," he asks, " can we adequately praise Zerubbabel ? He was like a seal-ring on the right hand." [1] Then of the Jewish kings he selects those for mention who did right in the sight of the Lord. Besides these he mentions the great prophets, including those of the northern kingdom.

He does not mention Joseph where he would naturally come, because with the captivity of Ephraim, which was not followed by a return, Joseph *drops out of the chosen line.* Since we are justified in regarding Ben-Sira as an adequate exponent of the theories current between the Return and the time of the Maccabees, stress may be laid on this point. The disappearance of Joseph from the list of patriarchs is characteristic of the time of the Return ; during the divided kingdom he was doubtless the patriarch of the northern nation, while during the united kingdom he was the patriarch of the larger and more important part of it.

Of the events which followed the Exodus, the most notable was the establishment of the monarchy ; after that the division of the nation.

[1] xlix. 11 :   אֵיכָה נְגַדֵּל זְרֻבָּבֶל
וְהוּא כְחוֹתָם עַל יַד יָמִין

Hence the number of considerations whereby
we can date the Psalter is not small.

Who is the last person mentioned in the
Psalms? Except David (the notices of whom
shall be considered presently), the last is
Samuel (xcix. 6). With him the catalogue of
saints stops. This is precisely what we should
expect if David were the author of the divan.
Samuel was to him as Simon son of Onias to
Ben-Sira. The difference in their ages was sufficient to give Samuel in David's eyes the rank
of an ancient saint.

The name *Joseph* is used as the equivalent of
Israel (Psa. lxxxi. 6, lxxx. 2). He is preferred
to Judah as the chief patriarch after Jacob
(lxxvii. 16). It is only where the fact of the
royalty being in Judah has stress laid on it, that
Joseph is made less than Jacob, and even the
verse in which this occurs points to a united
kingdom (lxxviii. 67). To the splitting of the
nation there appears to be no allusion. Jerusalem still "a city is securely built together;
thither the tribes of God go up, the tribes, they
go up thither" (cxxii. 4). They ceased to go
up in the days of Jeroboam, and this decen-
tralization of Jerusalem was commemorated by
a fast in the ancient calendar of the synagogue.
Ephraim, Benjamin, and Manasseh are mentioned together as equally integral parts of the
nation (lxxx. 3). Ephraim is God's pillow, and
Judah His staff (cviii. 9). Other tribes are

mentioned in the archaic Psalm lxviii. (28). Psalm lxxviii. brings the history down to the choice of David. Psalm cvi. leaps from the judges to the Exile. Psalm cv. stops with the entry into Canaan. Psalm lxxxix. stops with David. Psalm cxxxvi. becomes vague after the conquest of Canaan. Thus the assignation of the bulk of the Psalter to any late period is confronted with the argument from silence. The Psalmists who versify the sacred history must have known of the glories of the Salomonic era and of the splitting of the nation, if they lived after the close of the monarchical period ; why then do they become vague after the accession of David, or earlier ? If they belong to the period of the divided kingdom, why do we find no trace of the hostility which ordinarily prevailed between the two divisions of Israel, and no aspirations after re-union ? Why are Ephraim and Manasseh given an honourable place beside Judah and Benjamin ? The later we place the collection the stronger does the argument from silence become. For Ben-Sira's Praise of the Fathers must be our norm for the sense of the concept " sacred history " in the time between the Return and the Maccabees. And we find that with him the names of Nehemiah and Zerubbabel are as honourable as that of Samuel.

Of the theory of the prophets that the miracle of the restoration would outshine the miracle of the Exodus we find no trace. The Exodus is

the great marvel which the Psalms seem never
wearied of recounting. The "turning of the
captivity of Sion," on the other hand, is an
event still in the uncertain future (Psa. cxxvi. 4,
liii. 7, lxxix. 11, cvi. 47). Into details concerning the Captivity no Psalm save cxxxvii.
enters; but even there the scene is a wholly
ideal one. All that we can gather is that the
Psalm was composed before the fall of Babylon.
For after its fall there would be no occasion for
the curse with which it closes.

If the general spirit of the Psalms be considered, it is assuredly that of a fighting
community—one in which the hero has the
praises of God on his tongue, and a two-edged
sword in his hand. The forces of nature are
regarded as the warrior's allies; for since his
cause is identical with God's, he may reasonably
expect that God's weapons, the thunder and
hail, will be enlisted on his side. Sanskrit
scholars have called attention to the same
phenomenon in the Vedas; the primeval an-
cestors of the mild Hindu could fight as well
as sing. The spirit of the Psalms is in this
respect similar to that of the Vedas. If it be
true that in the Chronicles David, the king and
hero, has become a "book-bosomed priest," in
the Psalms he by no means appears in that
light. The devoutness of the Psalmists does
not interfere with their power of striking hard
blows. The spirit of Psalm xviii., in which the

singer declares that God teaches him to fight,
and makes him strong and agile, is also that of
Psalm cxliv. The martial instinct is exceedingly
strong in Psalms lx. and cx.

Psalm cxliv. is of interest because the author
tells us about himself. " God, who gives salvation to kings, teaches his hands to war and
his fingers to fight, subdues his people under
him, and saves His servant David from the evil
sword." It is evident that either David himself
is speaking, or that some one else has put the
words into David's mouth. If the former is the
case, his mentioning his own name may be
paralleled from the lyrics of many nations.
Imru'ul-Kais, our oldest Arabic poet, in his
famous Mu'allakah makes a woman call him
by his name. Horace hopes that a future
bride will remember how she sung the verses
of the bard Horace. Sa'di in his *Bustan*
mentions his own name very frequently. On
the other hand, one who chose to personate
David would have no difficulty in putting his
name in a line. Only what is there in the Psalm
that suggests such personation ?

In Psalm lxxxix. the author, assuming the
character of David, narrates a vision that had
been vouchsafed him, and complains that it has
not altogether been corroborated by the event.
He styles himself the Lord's Anointed (*v.* 39),
and declares that he carries in his bosom the
whole of many nations—a phrase something

like *l'état, c'est moi.* Some of the verses might
indeed be said in the name of Israel generally
(39–44); but the author has done his best to
render this interpretation impossible, by pleading
in verses 48 and 49 that, *his life being of limited
duration,*[1] the fulfilment of God's promise would
presently be despaired of. If David be personated, the transition from the real David to
the figurative is almost unintelligible. If, on
the other hand, David himself be speaking, then
the gloomy tone of the ode seems the natural
counterpart of the cheerful tone of others. To
those who study human nature the statements
in verses 39–47 offer no difficulty. The lake
which seems clear and calm at a distance is all
ruffled when seen close by. Newspapers that
are famed for common sense have repeatedly
within the last ten years declared that the glory
of England is departed. Even a slight reverse
or disappointment plunges the most confident
in gloom. Hence from odes of this sort it is
difficult to obtain historical details. We cannot
reproduce in thought the state of mind of the
composer.

Psalm cxxxii. repeats part of the same matter
as that contained in Psalm lxxxix., but finds no
contradiction between promise and fulfilment.
A particular act of devoutness on the part of
David is urged as meritorious, somewhat as
Nehemiah (v. 19, etc.) urges his merits.

[1] Cf. Ecclus. xxxvii. 25.

Verse 10 : " For the sake of David Thy servant refuse not the request of Thine Anointed "
would certainly seem to imply that the Anointed
and David are not the same ; but the service
mentioned, that of " finding a place for the
Lord," would seem to have been superseded by
the building of the Temple in the next reign,
and it is probable that fewer difficulties attend
the assumption of Davidic authorship than any
other.

The fact that these Psalms, wherein the name
of David occurs, are not placed near the beginning of the collection, but distributed about it,
implies that the collector interpreted the " I " of
the Psalms as David.   Had he cherished any
doubts   on   that   subject,   surely   any   Psalm
of   which   the   Davidic   origin   was   ostensible
would   have   been   put   near   the   beginning.   In
some   other   Psalms   the   phrase   " the   king "   or
" king " is used without any further specification
(xxi. 2, 8, lxiii. 12, lxi. 7, lxxii. 1).   In some of
these   the   phrase   is   clearly   identical   with   the
personal   pronoun   " I,"   and   the   wish   which   the
Psalm contains is of a sort that could only apply
to   an   individual.   These   Psalms   strike   chords
which   more   or   less   pervade   the   Psalter,   and
form   the   substance   of   Psalms   which   contain
no reference to David or to a king.

Of personal matters mentioned in the Psalms
perhaps the most curious is that the Psalmist
cannot write.   This is asserted in lxxi. 15, " My

mouth shall recount Thy righteousness, all day long Thy salvation, for I know not how to write." The phrase there employed is clearly identical with that used by Isaiah xxix. 12, where the context renders the sense certain. In Psalm cxix. 13, "With my lips have I recounted all the judgments of my mouth," the point seems to be the same. And in xlv. 2, "My tongue is the pen of a skilful scribe," the same is implied. The use of writing is still connected with the idea of rendering something permanent. Constant repetition is with the Psalmist a substitute for it.

Elsewhere the detail is less clear. We have notices of persecution undergone, of fierce battles, of calumny, of treachery and deceit, of disease and recovery, of variations between triumph and despair, confidence and doubt. The author is a fierce enemy, and a zealous worshipper and patriot. His cause is to him absolutely identical with that of God.

Is this series of meditations consonant with the character exhibited by the David of the books of Samuel? Let us try to find another example of a man who at different periods of his life was outlaw and prince, warrior and saint, sinner and penitent, who committed his devotions to verse. Such a character may be found in the author of a volume of as yet unpublished verse [1] — the Zaidite prince Abdallah Ibn

[1] Bodleian MS. (Arab. e. 6).

Hamzah. Like David this personage founded
a dynasty, indentified his own cause with that
of religion and patriotism, and cherished ambi-
tions which went beyond anything he was
himself permitted to realize.[1] When the
Caliphate of Baghdad was nearing its close,
Abdallah Ibn Hamzah, who was descended
from the Alid branch of the Prophet's house,
bethought him of raising the Alid banner in
South Arabia. It would seem that his first
efforts were due to real oppression of the
Arabs by the Ghuzz and other "barbarians,"
of whose conquests in South Arabia we read
in contemporary chronicles. Against them he
defended a fort or two with success ; thence he
began to be regarded as a champion who might
be summoned to lead in cases of emergency.
In the field he was frequently successful ; but
the allegiance sworn to him was repeatedly
violated, and he was often driven from home
and property. The poems in which he gives
vent to his feelings cover a period of over sixty
years ; and during that time he underwent a
number of experiences similar to those which
David in his day had to endure. Of the eight
books of which his divan consists one contains
moral reflections which in their tone bear some
resemblance to the homiletic Psalms. In those
which are more immediately devoted to recounting his own history there are not a few notes which

[1] The life of him by Safadi is also unpublished.

remind the reader of other parts of the Psalter.
He fancies God has secret favours towards him,
enabling him to see his desire on his enemies.
God, he thinks, has commanded him to cleanse
the countries from pollution, and wash the soil
clean of all evildoers. God bade him do this,
and he will command his sons after him to
continue the work.

What Jerusalem is to the author of the
Psalms such is San'a to Abdallah Ibn Hamzah.
" Thou, O San'a, art my greatest care, and
Dhamar, when it is mentioned, is my chief
desire." The barbarous tribes play with him
the rôle of the enemies whom the author of the
Psalms promises to circumcise (cxviii. 10). He
stood in the breach, what time the lions were
grinning round him with their terrible teeth.
The sword and spear, the shield and buckler,
have for him the same attraction as they had
for the old hero. The mail that sparkles like a
pond, while elastic as a serpent, and the spear-
points that flash like lightning from a cloud, are
the objects of his affection. What troubles his
mind is not such a disaster as the rout of his
army, but the wonder how a nation could be so
backsliding and perverse as to betray him after
they had invoked his championship. What
excuse will they be able to allege when on
the day of judgment God confronts them with
him ? The complaints which appear in several
of the poems of being *satirized* and lampooned

throw a curious light on such passages as Psalm xxxv. 16. The lampoon was, in Arabian antiquity, a weapon which was not always distinguished with sufficient precision from material weapons, and which was thought to have a very deadly effect.

The divan of Abdallah Ibn Hamzah is very far removed from the excellence of the Psalter, but its author believed in himself sufficiently to write repeatedly to the Caliph at Baghdad, demanding abdication in his favour, and to aspire to universal empire ; he also addresses his enemies with extravagant confidence in his ultimate success. The part of Arabia where his career was passed has rarely been subjected to foreign influence : its civilization in Abdallah Ibn Hamzah's time was not unlike that of Canaan in the time of David. David has to be pictured as far more earnest, far more conscious of his mission, and far more devout. The life of Abdallah Ibn Hamzah is probably no-where described so minutely and impartially as that of David in the books of Samuel. But the parallel will, perhaps, serve to remove the incongruity that might be felt in ascribing a devotional book to a man who lived the same sort of life. The ode is to such persons a faithful friend to which they can commit their emotions ; the interest which attaches to their persons induces some one or other in the immediate neighbourhood to claim to participate

in the solace of these effusions. So they come
to be perpetuated. Moreover, in the ode, as we
shall presently see, music is in certain cases of
great importance. And though men compose
poetry for themselves, music is for an audience.

A portion of the divan of Abdallah Ibn
Hamzah, which some day will interest students
of the Oriental character, is a series of odes
addressed by him to his wife, or rather his chief
wife, since the man was evidently a polygamist.
That delicacy, and even chivalry, should exist
amid the domestic institutions of primitive
times is strange ; but these odes bear witness
to it.

From the analogy of the divan we have just
left and others we should expect that "I" everywhere meant a definite individual, and, indeed,
the author of the poem in which it occurs.
Whole divans are devoted to the penitential or
ascetic style, of which the Psalter exhibits so
many specimens. That of Abu 'l-Atahiyah, a
poet of the eighth century,[1] contains some
hundreds of odes in which the author confesses
and preaches. The first personal pronoun is
common enough therein, but there is never any
doubt concerning its meaning. "I am tried
with a world whose cares never end ; and I see
nothing for it but faith and patience. When the
day's business is over, and I fancy myself secure
from mischief, night brings something fresh.

[1] Published at Beyrut.

How many an offence I have committed, of how many a crime have I been guilty! How many a friend has given me warning, but I would have none of it. Tempting passions called me to worldly things, so I let go my religion and went after them." " I have tried to give up the world, but still hanker thereafter. My hankering is blended with asceticism. And I find it hard to free my soul from habits that it fosters." These are all personal experiences, the value of which, indeed, lies in the fact that they are the confessions of an individual ; the " I " is the poet Abu 'l-Atahiyah, who thinks it worth while versifying his experiences for the benefit of his fellows. We open another ascetic divan, about a couple of centuries later. " My afternoon," says the poet, " is come, and soon my sun will be setting. I have been on no pilgrimage, but many a calamity goes on pilgrimage to me." The poet's biographers infer from this verse that he actually never went on pilgrimage, and, doubtless, their inference is correct. Indeed it would be a safe generalization that whatever may be the case with " Thou " and " He," by " I " the speaker himself is invariably intended.

We may now consider the evidence of the headings. These may be illustrated from Arabic literature in a double manner. On the one hand the fact strikes us that some of the Psalms have headings, whereas others have none. Some of them are tolerably precise, e.g. xxxiv. " by

David, when he feigned madness before Abimelech, who drove him out, so that he went."
Abimelech is an error for *Achish;* whence it
follows that this heading was not made by a
compiler, who would have got the right name
from 1 Samuel, but must have been a traditional
title attached to the poem. The same inference
is to be drawn from the title of Psalm vii. "sung
by David to the Lord concerning Cush the
Benjamite." Cush, the Benjamite, is otherwise
unknown, whence the heading must follow a
tradition that has perished ; for this name could
not be inferred from the content of the Psalm.
Therefore, if we examine the headings without
unreasonable credulity or scepticism, we should
infer that the compiler stated the occasion of
the Psalm where there was any tradition on
which he could rely ; that this tradition was
independent of the existing Bible ; and that
there was no intentional deception practised.
For in a life so fully told as that of David any
one who amused himself by discovering occasions for the Psalms would have no difficulty.
One who intended to deceive would therefore
either assign occasions to all the Psalms, or, if he
found the game tedious, would assign them, say,
to the first third. But the rarity of the specific
occasions, combined with the fact that, few as
they are, they embody some matter not otherwise known to us, would appear to be a striking
proof of good faith.

Most of the Arabic divans, whether published or still in MS., exhibit the same phenomenon. In writing the life of Abu 'l-Ala, of Ma'arrah, I found the headings of his poems preserve several traditions which the very full biographies of him that we possess had overlooked. And yet in the case of many of his poems there is no heading. The collection we possess seems to have been edited by a pupil, who probably asked the poet for some information about the occasions of all the poems ; in some cases this could be given fully, in others it had either been forgotten or was intentionally concealed. The biography in his case also preserves some verses which the divans do not contain, while illustrating his life from the divans. A principle of arrangement is not always to be looked for in these divans. Where it is alphabetical, the poems arranged under each rhyming letter are put together haphazard. Chronological arrangement is occasionally found, but is not very common. There is often a tendency to group together poems that bear on the same subject, but it is an error to regard as a principle what is merely a tendency.

An illustration of the nature of the headings in an ordinary divan may be taken by opening one of them at random, and the resemblance to the headings of the Psalms will be found sufficiently striking. We will glance at a series in the divan of the Sherif Al-Radi, a poet of the

end of the tenth century. First a dirge on a
man who died in 387 A.H., name and date being
given. Next poem one of consolation to the
Caliph on the loss of a son in the year 377, name
and month being given. The next an ode
describing the deposition of the Caliph in the
year 381. The next a lament over the ex-
Caliph's death in 393. The next a lament over
a famous vizier in 385, names and dates being
accurately recorded. The next a lament over
an eminent lady about whom some details are
given, of the year 399. The next " a lament
over one of his friends." Then come eight poems
with no details in the headings. Then one of
the year 383, "when the author was twenty-
three years of age, and saw some white hairs
appearing among the black." If we compare
this series, which could be paralleled from most
of the divans known to me, with a series of
Psalms, the chief difference will be found to
consist in the greater rarity with which the
headings of the Psalms give details and dates.
It seems almost impossible to lay too great
stress on the fact that in the great majority of
cases the compiler of the Psalter says nothing
of the occasion ; for this compels us to attach
importance to the cases wherein he breaks
silence on this subject.

But the headings apparently ascribe Psalms
not only to David, but to a variety of persons,
and sometimes to several at once. Psalm

lxxxix. contains, as we have seen, information which can only have come from David himself; but it bears the title "*Maschil*, by Ethan the Ezrachite." Psalm lxxxviii. has the title "Song for the lyre, by the sons of Korach. By Menasseach to 'Commencing to sing.' *Maschil* by Heman the Ezrachite." (Menasseach is evidently from this passage a proper name, meaning "Victor," like Zafir; the "chief musician" may therefore be deposed.) How can the same poem be by the Sons of Korach, Heman the Ezrachite, and Menasseach? No Arabic scholar would be puzzled by these headings for many minutes; the analogy of the titles in the *Kitab Al-Aghani* is too striking. What we learn from that work is that a poem might be the joint property of many persons; for the air to which it was sung was at least as important as the words of which it consisted. Hence we have only to read a few titles in the *Kitab Al-Aghani* to recognise, if not the exact equivalent, at any rate the precise analogy of *Maschil*, *Miktam*, Menasseach, etc. One or two specimens out of hundreds will suffice. "The poem is by Ja'far the Harithite; the air by Ma'bad; Amr Ibn Banah states that Ibn Suraij performed it to another tune; Hammad states that the Hudhalite performed it to another." "The poem is by Mansur Al-Namiri; the air (*ramal*) by Abdallah Ibn Tahir; also another (*ramal*) by Al-Raff; also another (*thakil*, no. i.) which

Habash also ascribes to Al-Raff." " The poem
is by Al-Akhtal, the air by Amr al-wadi (*hazaj*
with the first finger); also another (*ramal*) said
to be by Ibn Jami'; also another (*khafif ramal*
with the middle finger); also another (*khafif
thakil* with the middle finger) by Ibrahim."
We need have no further difficulty about the
words *Maschil*, *Miktam*, etc., or the names Asaf,
Menasseach, Heman the Ezrachite, etc.   To the
compiler of the Psalm-book, as to the compiler
of the *Kitab Al-Aghani*, the air is the important
matter ; for that, he probably had as imperfect a
notation as the author of the *Kitab Al-Aghani*
has.   *Maschil* and *Miktam*, which are so unintelligible to us now, had some definite meaning
in the old musical science of the Hebrews—a
science which very likely had the name *Kesheth*,
" the bow," since in 2 Samuel i. David's dirge
has prefixed to it the notice that David ordered
the children of Judah to be taught *Kesheth*.   To
David's poems airs had in some cases been
attached by himself, in other cases by famous
musicians ; hence the tradition of the airs is
what is preserved in the headings, and there is
nothing surprising in the same poem having
been set to music by a number of persons.   And
since the Psalms are unmetrical, the analogy
which should be before us is that of the modern
anthem rather than that of the hymn ; in the
former case it is clear that the name of the
musician is far more important than that of

the writer of the words, since the *artistic* part is
the musician's. As we have already seen, " the
word of the Lord is tried " by the fact that
owing to its power and profundity metre would
only fetter it needlessly ; but when the Psalms
were composed, the Hebrews doubtless thought
of the poem as the words belonging to a tune,
rather than of the tune as belonging to the
words.

The antiquity of the Psalms may therefore
be gauged by the following facts : when the
Chronicles were composed, the meaning of the
headings had been forgotten, and *Menasseach*
already regarded as a participle ; of the persons
who are mentioned as setting them to music
Solomon appears to be the latest ; for from
1 Kings v. 11 we learn that Ethan the Ezrachite
was earlier than he. Whether in the case of
Psalm xc. we are to suppose the air (*Tefillah*)
ascribed to Moses, and the words to David, or
conversely, is not clear ; nor is the matter of
much importance.

We should misunderstand the effect of music
on the Oriental, if we supposed the words of an
ode to have anything like the same importance
as the air. The great work to which reference
has been made is a mine of anecdotes illustrating
the power of music. Poetry, when recited, wins
admiration, if sufficiently brilliant ; but when
sung, it maddens. Often we read of the
capacity for drinking bearing a definite ratio

to the power of the music; "the Caliph drank so many quarts over an air" is a fairly constant formula, by which we can gauge its beauty. Another writer has collected verses, the sound of which, when set to music, caused the hearers to fall down dead;[1] fainting fits are by no means rare effects of verses sung to thrilling airs. At different periods of the Caliphate two singers are able to stop all the traffic between the regions of Baghdad. The art is ordinarily considered unworthy of a gentleman, but, nevertheless, members of the imperial family were found to cultivate it, and a minister who endeavours to suppress the talent in his son is rebuked. Sometimes the author of the poetry is also the composer of the air; but this was apparently not common. Owing to the imperfect musical notation of the time, the composer of the air had always to sing it himself in the first case; but often he would instruct some professional singer, male or female, who would then be employed to perform it in public, or in the patron's presence. The composer of the music counts in such cases as the chief author; for often the verses sung are common property, the name of the author having been forgotten.

We should not be justified in identifying the music of the Arabs with that of the Canaanites, and indeed the history of the former is so well recorded that such a proceeding would be im-

[1] *Al-'Ikd Al-Farid,* iii. 198.

possible. A fairly close resemblance is all that need be assumed. On two occasions in Israelitish history we hear of the lyre being employed to rouse and calm ecstasy. We should probably think of the procedure not as of the playing of pieces of instrumental music, but as the performance by a singer of some verses, that he had either composed or learned, with the voice and instrument at once.

That David was a musical expert is a historical certainty if anything connected with David be certain. He entitles himself "tuner of the airs of Israel," [1] and that title implies that in his mind also the music was the primary concern. It seems difficult to think of the work of the founder of the Judaic dynasty being either forgotten and neglected during the reign of his successor, or being mixed up haphazard with a whole pile of anonymous performances.

What, moreover, seems clear is that the collection was made before the technical language of the Davidic music had been forgotten, and this had evidently been forgotten not only when the LXX. translation was made, but even when the Chronicles were compiled. The loss of this science must have been occasioned by some break in the national history, and this is most probably the Exile.

The omission from the Psalter of odes which

---

[1] 2 Sam. xxiii. 1 ; נעים = *Naghgham* (*Taj al-'arus*, ix. 86).

should naturally have been given a place in it, had it been intended to include the works of others besides David, or had it been intended to include poems which were not religious, suggests the inference that the compiler only inserted hymns of which the words were supposed to be by David, though the airs were frequently by others.

The fact that the national history, as it appears in the Psalms, closes with David, makes the Salomonic age the most likely period for the compilation of the book. That some of the references to the Exile are inserted by editors who had no intention of letting them count as the work of David, is obvious ; but whether the references which are found in the body of the Psalms are necessarily signs of post-exilic origin cannot be determined till the whole phenomenon of prophecy has been brought within the domain of science.

When the Old Testament revelation was consummated in the New Testament, the Messianic Psalms formed, next after Isaiah, the foundation on which the Messiah's claims were based. David's words were regarded as authoritative ; the words of the 16th, the 22nd, the 110th, and other Psalms were given a new and thrilling interpretation. With the events foretold with fateful clearness in the Wisdom of Solomon and the latter part of Isaiah obscure passages of the Psalter harmonized ; it was seen

that the author of the Psalter was one of those
to whom the vision had been granted in which
God's purposes and plans were revealed. Such
a vision was a privilege accorded to the friends
of God ; and was not God *compromised* (the
word has been repeatedly used in this context)
by such a friend as the David of the Books of
Samuel ? Much of the conduct of David that
may with justice be impugned is excused on
the ground that morality is progressive, and
conduct, like scholarship, must be judged according to the standard of its age. But if the
worst act of David's life, the painful story of
Bathsheba, be considered, the underlying character which David exhibits is much better than
that displayed by most men in any age. Max
Duncker remarks that the crime which caused
David so much penitence and contrition was
one of which, probably, no other Oriental
monarch would have thought anything, and, if
there be any truth in history, it would have
occasioned few scruples to most defenders of
the Faith. The second crime ought not to be
judged apart from the first, of which it was the
natural and inevitable consequence ; David had
to choose between an honourable death for
Uriah and a horrible one for Bathsheba ; and
he chose the former. He who thinks Bathsheba
could have been safe while Uriah lived does not
see the whole hand. And when David is rebuked for the crime, he yields the point without

argument ; he is told that he has done wrong,
and he receives the prophet in a prophet's name.
When has this been done—before or since?
Mary Queen of Scots would declare that she
was above the law; Charles I. would have
thrown over Bathsheba ; James II. would have
hired witnesses to swear away her character ;
Mohammed would have produced a revelation
authorizing both crimes ; Charles II. would
have publicly abrogated the seventh command-
ment ; Queen Elizabeth would have suspended
Nathan. Who has ever acknowledged an error
of any magnitude, if it has been in his power to
maintain that he was right? A recent writer
has described the course of the ordinary man
who falls into the devil's meshes, and that writer
probably knows the human heart rather well.
Loyalty to the weaker sinner is not a spring
that works in the hero of that romance.[1] Cain's
plan—that of silencing the accuser, and Adam's
plan—that of shifting the responsibility, seem to
exhaust the range of human expedients when
an error is brought home. He who escaped
from both, though *semustulatus*, was a " man
after God's own heart."

[1] *The Silence of Dean Maitland.*

V

THE BIBLE OF THE JEWS

IF any one glances over a copy of the Rabbinic Bible, he will assuredly be struck by the care and trouble which the Jews have devoted to their Sacred Books. The vocalization and intonation of each word is elaborately marked by a system which also indicates the place of each word in the sentence. At the end of the column peculiarities are noted and registered with an accuracy which should prevent the possibility of alteration or error. Side by side with the Hebrew text is a translation into Aramaic, the language spoken by the Jews when they first left off Hebrew. References are further attached to most of the texts, guiding us to the vast volumes which contain the Tradition, or Talmud, which also claims Divine authority. The works which bear that name ordinarily occupy sixteen folios. Finally the text is surrounded by a series of commentaries which embody the results of grammatical, lexicographical, and archæo-

logical studies.   Compare this with what the
Indians have done for their Vedas, and it will
be doubtful whether the advantage rests with
the Indians.

But, alas ! there is a difference.   The Indian
can start an idea and the Jew cannot.   The
whole of the work at which we have glanced,
points, accents, Massorah, Talmud, grammar,
lexicography, is borrowed ; there is scarcely a
trace of originality anywhere.   The Jews have
in religious matters no ideas of their own.   This
is to our science what the Pythagorean proposition is to trigonometry, or the law of equal
pressure to hydrostatics.   Abandon that principle and traps of all sorts will ensnare you ;
keep firmly to it, and the source of every morsel
of non-Biblical literature which the Jews possess
will become clear.

The relation between Jews and Christians was
from the first exceedingly hostile.   We find in
the Acts of the Apostles that the work of the
Christian missionaries is definitely opposed by
the Jews in the different towns whither the
Apostles travel.   Until the fall of Jerusalem the
Jews had it in their power to persecute, and
they exercised that power with cruelty.[1]   The
fall of Jerusalem limited that power, but it did
not limit their ill-will.   For the fall of Jerusalem
had been foretold by Christ, and that prophecy
was preserved in a document composed in the

[1] Justin, *Dialogue,* § 17.

Hebrew of the time. The realization of the prophecy may have caused some conversions, but
in most cases it would excite only greater ani-
mosity.

When Constantine made Christianity the
state religion, the Christians had it in *their*
power to persecute,[1] and probably sporadic
cases of persecution of Jews by Christians had
occurred before. From the time of the con-
version of the Empire this persecution increased
in fierceness, and this insane policy laid the
seeds of greater disasters than its authors
deemed possible. Races of the stuff of the
Anglo-Saxons would, under this persecution,
have migrated to new lands and founded new
nations. The Jews have no such enterprise,
and so they wait.

Certain Jewish families had fled from persecution to free Arabia,[2] where their descendants
adopted the language and the manners of the
Arabs. The poems of Samuel of Tayma are
incorporated in the ballad book of the Arabs,[3]
and in martial spirit they are second to none in
the collection. Not one of his tribe, the author
boasts, ever dies in his bed. When taunted with
the paucity of its numbers, it replies that the
great are few. The death of a chief, however,

[1] Bedjan's *Acta Martyrum,* i. 335.
[2] Compare the Armenian historian, Kyrakus (Venice,
1865), p. 33. The *Aghani,* xvi. 94–96, has only fables.
[3] *Hamasah,* ed. Freytag, p. 49.

leaves another ready to speak the language and do the deeds of the brave.

Mohammed, when starting his calamitous career, was brought into contact with these Arabized Jews, and found them dangerous enemies. He took in many a Christian, and at an early part of his career obtained refuge for his followers in Abyssinia; but he never took in the Jews. Had the Jewish tribes been united, they might have crushed him ere he became powerful; but the Jews invariably divide when outside pressure is relaxed, and Mohammed cut them off in detail. His earliest efforts were thus helped by Christians and impeded by Jews, whence the Koran is favourable to the former and hostile to the latter. But when Islam became a mighty empire, things changed. The Jews were a force which could not hinder Islam, but which had power to help it; whereas the *jihad* was now directed against a powerful Christian empire, which was fast becoming aware of its danger. And now, for the persecutors of the Jews too, the day of reckoning had come. Plato well warns the states against being double, *i.e.* against harbouring a class who have an interest in the state being upset; and such an interest any class that is systematically oppressed must have. The Arabian hordes, after defeating the incompetent Christian generals in the field, proceeded to besiege the towns; there were Jews

in those towns, and they opened the gates.
Thus was the conquest of Asia Minor[1] and of
Spain[2] facilitated.   The Jews had taken advantage of the opportunity of making friends with
the new power, and the benefit which they had
conferred was not forgotten.   The terms which
Islam granted the Jews were far better than
those which they got from Christianity till long
after the Reformation.   Isolated rulers, like the
insane Al-Hakim, ill-used them terribly ;[3] but
under ordinary governors they enjoyed very
tolerable privileges, and on many of them posts
of importance and distinction were conferred.

To some unknown Jew Mohammed owed his
notion of a Divine revelation, and not a little of
the matter of his Koran.   The form of it he
owed to the old Arabian Prophets, and this
combination produced a new idea.   This was
that the inspiration of a book consisted in its
sound.   For the quasi-rhyme is characteristic
of the Koran, and this cannot be reproduced in
another language.   Whereas, then, it had long
been the custom of Christians to translate their
sacred books into the vernaculars of the countries where they proselytized, this could not be
done with the Bible of the new religion.   Instead
of its accommodating itself to other nations,
other nations had to accommodate themselves

---

[1] Dionysius of Tell Mahré, ed. Chabot, p. 27, 3.
[2] Makkari, i. 166, 7, etc.
[3] Ibn Iyās (Cairo, 1311 A.H.), i. 52.

to it.   Syria, Egypt, Africa, Spain, Persia,
Central Asia, were perforce Arabized.

If the inspiration of a book consist in its
sound, some obvious inferences follow.   It
should be communicated orally, and there
should be no variations.   In practice these two
inferences are hard to combine.   The first Caliph
wished to combine them,[1] but he had to give
way ; he allowed the Koran to be compiled.
The second inference was drawn by the third
Caliph, Othman ; he caused an official edition
to be issued, and had all unofficial copies destroyed.   This service cost him his life.

To those whose native language is not Arabic
acquaintance with the alphabet is of very mode-
rate help in reading texts.   The old Kufi
character is puzzling even to experts ; the
foreigners who had now to use the Koran for
devotional purposes could either make nothing
of it, or, by mispronouncing it, rendered the inspired word of none effect.   The fourth Caliph,
Ali, introduced some vowel signs to help the
Persians, and possibly thereby won their un-
dying attachment ; at least it is difficult to
conjecture any other grounds for it.   The whole
of the system as developed is of native growth :
save one suggestion which may have come from
Syrian Christians,[2] there is nothing in it which
is not derived from the Arabic alphabet.

[1] Ghazzali, *loc. cit and*.

[2] *i.e.* the place of the vowel *fathah*.

Although the art of writing is said to have
been encouraged by Mohammed, the use of it
appears to have been confined to the Koran,
and ephemeral communications such as letters,
for rather more than a century after the Flight.
Good authorities inform us that the first book
composed in Arabic after the Koran was of the
year 120 A.H., or later.[1]   Even till late times the
Arabic idea of a book was something like "a
memoria technica, to be supplemented by oral
tradition" rather than a subject for independent
study.   Everything seems to confirm the statement that has been quoted ; and where we meet
with conflicting assertions, *e.g.*, that a scholar
who died in 124 A.H. used to spend the whole
day with his *books*,[2] we must regard them as
anachronisms, or possibly explain them of ephemeral documents, such as the second Caliph is
reported to have composed.[3]   The Jews in the
Koran are called the people of the Book, and
the idea that a nation should possess only one
book probably came from them.   If there were
other books in Arabic besides the Koran, the
Koran would be less holy than the Jewish Bible,
for the Jews had no other book.   The anecdote
which connects the burning of the Alexandrian
library with the Caliph Omar may be insufficiently attested, but it does him no injustice.

[1] Ghazzali's *Ihyā* (Cairo, 1306 A.H.), i. 65.
[2] Ibn Khallikan, i. 572.
[3] *Muwatta*, ed. Zurkani (Cairo, 1279 A.H.), ii. 375.

Sprenger accepts a story that the dying Prophet wished to compose a code, but was forbidden by Omar on some such ground.   At the battle between Ali and Mu'awiyah, the followers of the latter were told to attach their Korans to their lances, and hold them up.   There being no other books in existence, Ali's followers immediately recognized them.   Thus for the 120 years mentioned there was only one Arabic book.   All else was transmitted orally.

The needs of a great empire presently proved too much for Omar's theory.   Government is possible only where there are rules, and these must be the outcome of experience.   The Prophet's practice was naturally taken as the norm of legislation and administration ; where that failed, the practice of his successors.   The first person who broke the ice is said to have been a certain Ibn Juraij,[1] who compiled a book of Tradition, consisting partly of interpretation of the Koran.   Presently authors began to multiply ; and while the field of Tradition and Law was naturally the most cultivated, other studies also began to find adherents.

For the language of the Koran was becoming antiquated, and that of the Moslems changing. Presently steps were taken to record the intonation authorized by famous readers, and to note down minute varieties of pronunciation. Those who had anecdotes to tell of the occasions

[1] Ghazzali, *loc. cit.*

on which certain texts had been "revealed," were not slow to make capital out of them. Hence that small volume, the Koran, by the year 200 of the Hijrah, has become the nucleus of a vast literature, which is constantly on the increase.

When once the idea that the Koran was the only book that might be written had been banished, attempts were made to collect and save every relic of Arabic antiquity. Grammars and dictionaries were compiled, the information being ordinarily derived from Bedouin chiefs, who were supposed to know. Tribal lays were collected and edited ; chairs of archæology were founded, at any rate temporarily ; and long journeys were undertaken by those who wished to acquire as full a knowledge as possible of the intricacies of the Arabic language, and of the history which explained the allusions in the old lays and proverbs.

And now let us return to the Jews, enjoying reasonable protection under the ægis of the Caliphate, and in many places privileged above other followers of sacred books owing to the service they had rendered in securing the conquest of Islam.

There were two callings especially which brought them into contact with Christians and Mohammedans. One of these was the wine trade. Although the drinking of wine was forbidden by Mohammed, for many centuries drunkenness was rather encouraged at the

Caliph's court. Not only were many famous poets notorious winebibbers, but the praise of wine became one of the recognized subjects of versification. The keepers of places of entertainment of this sort were either Jews or Christians. Abu Nuwas,[1] the chief of the Arabic encomiasts of wine, tells us how he and his companions went into one of these shops.[2] The *zunnar*, or girdle, told them that the keeper was not a Moslem; "so we thought better of him than he deserved. 'You are a follower of Jesus son of Mary, we presume?' He flushed up, and said, No! He was a Jew, one of those who profess to be your friends, while inwardly they detest you. We asked him his name. 'Samuel,' he replied; 'but I call myself Abu Amr; I have no son named Amr, but the name is an easy one to pronounce.'" Ibrahim of Mausil [3] related how, when summoned to Rakkah by Harun al-Rashid, he fell in with a Christian wine-dealer, the excellence of whose wine caused him to delay three days at the tavern. The excuse which he gave for his delay thoroughly satisfied the Caliph, who himself summoned the wine-dealer, and, after confirming Ibrahim's judgment of his wine, rewarded him richly. These taverns, then, were places where Jews, Christians, and Mohammedans met

[1] Ob. 810 A.D.
[2] *Divan* (Cairo, 1898 A.D.), p. 273.
   Aghani, v. 12.   He died in 828 A.D.

in a friendly manner ; and though the meetings
sometimes resulted in brutal outrages,[1] it is probable that they often went off harmlessly, and
did something to allay the bitterness of fana-
ticism.

A far more honourable calling which served
to conciliate the members of the three religions
was that of medicine. The fact of a physician
being a foreigner seems often to win him confidence ; and during the Caliphate the practising
physicians seem regularly to have been Jews or
Christians.[2] Nothing was known of the science
of medicine beyond what Hippocrates and the
Greek school had discovered ; their works were
translated by Christians[3] into Syriac and Arabic,
and perhaps, at an earlier period, into Pehlevi ;
men of science like Avicenna here and there
added an original observation, but this was rare.
The great physicians appear to have admitted
members of all recognized religions to their
courses ; and those who compiled medical
biographies narrate the lives of the physicians
irrespective of their religion. The social inter-
course established at these classes led to free
discussion of religious topics. A great Christian
doctor,[4] being ridiculed for taking part in the
ritual of a Christian Church, waited till some of

[1] *Aghani*, passim.
[2] Zamakhshari on Sura iii. 137. Ibn Abi Usaibi'ah,
passim.
[3] Rarely by Jews.   [4] Ibn Abi Usaibi'ah, i. 240.

his pupils had returned from the pilgrimage at Meccah, to ridicule them in turn on the subject of their antics there. Owing to the study of medicine being part of a cyclopædic curriculum, the teaching of it was often associated with the higher education, which included the sciences whence the material for religions metaphysics was drawn. Hence we find a science of comparative religion figuring among those pursued by the Mohammedans. The actual practice, however, as has already been said, appears to have been left mainly to Jews and Christians. In the anecdotes of the third Mohammedan century the Jewish doctors speak Persian.[1] By the fourth century they have taken to writing Arabic. As in several other departments of literature, the most celebrated medical treatises are by Moses Maimonides, contemporary and physician of Saladdin ; but it is unlikely that they are the best.

We have now to figure the Jews, possessed of their unpointed Bible and no other Hebrew literature,[2] brought into contact on friendly

[1] *Aghani,* passim.

[2] δευτέρωσις in Epiphanius, Jerome, etc., is a mistranslation of *Mishnah,* which means "Oral Tradition." That they were not written appears from Epiphanius. The correct translation is ἄγραφος παράδοσις. A line of Shammakh (contemporary of Omar I.) is quoted in *Lisan al-Arab,* ix. 46, about the way in which the Jewish doctors at Tayma write Hebrew, but it seems to refer to the writing of charms.

terms with Mohammedans, when the attention of the literary world is being attracted by the collections of Traditions, the grammatical treatises, the dictionaries, and collections of poetry and archæology which mark the second century of Islam. It is not difficult to reproduce in thought some of the scenes.

A Jewish physician finds a patient engaged in solacing himself with his Koran, and foregoes his fee on condition of being initiated in the mysteries of that volume. He observes that the pronunciation of the words is secured by vowel signs and other marks, and learns that great importance is attached to the style of reading authorized by certain scholars at the capitals. An idea enters his mind that at least as much might be done by the Jews for their Bible, and that it would be wise to record the proper pronunciation of the words before it has more seriously degenerated.[1] The wisdom of this suggestion meets with the approval of those to whom he dares to communicate it.[2]

At first the method that occurs to him is to use the vowel signs invented by the Arabs; but, as it would be highly improper to place these on a copy of the sacred text, his second thought is *to take down the pronunciation of the best readers*

---

[1] Jerome's teacher mispronounced badly.
[2] That the Jews consciously imitated Mohammedan practices is acknowledged by Maimonides, *Letters* (Amst., 472), p. 18*a*.

in Arabic letters. This is no conjecture; the British Museum contains a considerable number of Karaite MSS. in which the Hebrew text is transliterated into Arabic and pointed. It is soon seen that the Arabic vowel system is insufficient to represent the variety of the Hebrew vocalization ; so the physician asks one of his Christian colleagues to tell him how the Syrians deal with their Bible. He is shown a Nestorian text; and the Nestorian system will evidently serve the purpose far better than the Mohammedan. This is in effect adopted wholesale ; a few traces of the Mohammedan system are left ; but while in the " Assyrian " system these are still distinguishable, they are very faint in that which finally prevailed. On the other hand, there is very little that the Nestorian system does not explain at once. The differences are chiefly due to the reasonable desire to avoid the confusion caused in Syriac by the juxtaposition of several different systems of points.

The Karaites, who represent the conservative party among the Jews, adhered to the plan of employing the Arabic script for pointed texts till the end of the tenth century. The inconvenience, however, was so great that they were finally compelled to allow the points to appear on the sacred page.

The earliest Jewish writers [1] whose works we possess are well aware that the vocalization of

[1] So Seadyah.

the Old Testament is a recent achievement. That in the main it is correct need not be doubted ; but the nuances and minutiæ which it displays can have no scientific value. The exact colouring of a vowel is not transmitted with accuracy for a period of 1,000 years. The stout volumes in which German writers have collected all these minutiæ would have produced a curious sensation on those readers who deliberately invented many of them in order to be able to rival the "various readings" of the Koran.

The process of recording the pronunciation of itself introduced Othman's theory of literal and consonantal inspiration. In the Talmud this theory does not ordinarily appear. On the contrary, the Rabbis correct the text with great licence and with extreme infelicity. We are not entitled to regard their corrections as meant otherwise than seriously.

When the services of Mohammed to mankind are reckoned up, it will be remembered that it is due to him that the vocalization of the Hebrew Bible has been preserved.

When the vowels had been fixed, the grammarian could commence operations. Where the Arabic grammars provided guidance, the Hebrew grammarians got on tolerably well ; elsewhere they blundered badly. It would seem that even the names of their books were borrowed from those of the Mohammedan doctors.

In Jewish literature of the eleventh century [1]
Moses is spoken of as " the Apostle " or " the
Prophet," without further qualification. How
comes Moses to be an Apostle, a name which
belongs to the Christians ?   Clearly, because
Mohammed is the Apostle *par excellence* to the
Moslems.   How, then, can the Jews dispense
with one ?   The same writer proceeds to
enumerate the " sources of law " ; they are
three : the Book, Consensus of Authorities,
Analogy.   A member of the rival sect would
doubtless have enumerated four, giving Tradition
the second place.   Those who are acquainted
with Mohammedan law are very familiar with
the source of this discussion.   The same four
sources   are   enumerated   by   Mohammedan
lawyers, only with them the question is whether
Analogy counts or does not count.   The whole
of this doctrine of sources of law is therefore
borrowed by the Jews from the Moslems.   Next
we observe that those who recognize Tradition
as a source of law ascribe the Tradition to
Moses.   Writers of the tenth century are aghast
at the audacity of ascribing the Jewish tradition
to Moses.[2]   When the Jewish tradition does
little else than collect the opinions of doctors
who lived well within the Christian era, how can

[1] *Sefer   Ha-Miswoth*   (Bodleian MS.).   So too R.
Bachya, *Chobath ha-Lebaboth* (Warsaw, 1875), ii. 11, 150.
[2] Salmon Ben Jerucham, in Fürst's *Litteraturblatt des
Orients,* 1846.

it be by Moses ? To this question there is a
very practical answer. The Mohammedan
tradition goes back to Mohammed ; the Jewish
tradition cannot be less respectable in its line
than the other. Since Moses is to the Jews
what Mohammed is to the Moslems, the Talmud
must go back to Moses. This argument carried
the day.[1]

The Jews, in matters affecting their religion,
are forced to conceal their obligations, and hence
the reforms are sprung on the nation unawares.
Of the origin of the punctuation of the Bible, as
of the compilation of the Talmud, we have no
authentic record ; in the case of the latter the
origin is fraudulently misrepresented, in that of
the former it is hidden in the dark. Those who
introduced these reforms knew that to acknowledge obligations to Christians or Mohammedans
would be to wreck the chance of success that the
reform had ; whereas if flung on the nation
suddenly, they might win by their own merits.
The condition in which we have to think of the
Jews before the Abbasid period is somewhat
similar to that of the Copts[2] or the Parsees.
With the fall of Jerusalem Hebrew had ceased
to exist as a spoken or written language. There

[1] In the document printed by Gallandius, ii. 329, the
Mishnah is said *not* to be by Moses. Cf. Maimonides,
loc. cit. 19b.

[2] Jahiz (a careful writer) *loc. cit.* compares the Jews of
his time (early ninth century) to the Copts.

was, however, a tradition preserved of the way
to read the Hebrew Bible, and a certain number
of sayings in the same language, partly from
lost books, were preserved and taught in the
schools. Otherwise the Jews thought, spoke,
and wrote in the languages of the countries in
which they sojourned.

The Targum is no more an authentic document than the Mishnah. Of difficult words and
phrases in the Old Testament, there was here
and there a traditional interpretation in
Aramaic ; it is not impossible that some of
these glosses go back to the days of Nehemiah.
But the committal of this interpretation to writing
was forbidden ; [1] and the phrase by which the
Targum is quoted in the Talmud, "as we interpret," shows that it was not thought of as a
written book. Similarly, instead of "reading
the Targum," the formula used is "knowing
how to translate"; and the accurate Mas'udi in
the tenth century describes the Targum not as
a book, but as a *language* into which the Jews
translate their sacred books.[2] Where the Targum is mentioned as a book in the Talmud, the
Christian Syriac translation called Peshitta is
meant. Hence we can easily reconstruct the
history of the "Targum." When the movement
for preserving every monument of antiquity
which we see dominated Islam in the early

[1] Midrash *Tanchuma* (Warsaw, 1879), i. 25a.
[2] *Bibliotheca Geogr. Arab.*, viii. 79.

Abbasid period spread to the Jews, the pre-
servation of the old Aramaic interpretation was
considered desirable. But there was not enough
of it in stable form to put down. What was
done, therefore, was to *revise the Peshitta*, inserting the traditional interpretations where they
could be obtained. Hence it comes that Christian interpretations are found in the Targum,
and that the Peshitta is sometimes misrepresented
in it.

Novelists who are well acquainted with human
nature sometimes show how a quarrel between
masters is taken up by servants. Two officers
are on bad terms ; so their servants come to
blows. Between Kais and Kalb there is an
immemorial feud ; if the theory be true that
David was chief of Kalb, then we can understand how it came about that there was no
peace between him and the son of Kais (Kish).
Similar to, if not identical with, this feud was
that between the people of Syria and the people
of Irak ; the Umayyad dynasty represented the
hegemony of Syria, whereas the Abbasid
dynasty represented that of Irak. The Christian chronicler known as Dionysius of Tell-
Mahré speaks of the Abbasid conquest as the
conquest of the Arabs by the Persians. It
would be surprising if the Jews, though subjects
and not directly involved in the quarrel, had not
taken it up. They did take it up ; the Syrian
Jews by no means approved of the domination

of their Eastern brethren. Hence we find a duplication of the new literature. The Babylonian Talmud finds a rival in the Jerusalem Talmud. The Targum of "Onkelos" has a rival in the Jerusalem Targum. But just as Irak prevailed in the contest for political power, so the school of Babylon won an easy victory over the school of Palestine.

For the rest, the literature which the Jews now produce in large quantities is the merest imitation of what the Mohammedans have got. A writer, confused with Nissim of Kairawan, about the year 1,000, writes a book of "Anecdotes," and gives the following reason for doing so : [1] " Since the sectarians (*i.e.*, the Moslems) have books which they call *Deliverance after Stress*, I thought our people ought to have a work of the same kind." The idea of collecting stories of providential escapes in order to console the afflicted appears to require but little originative power for its conception ; but the author is incapable of conceiving it without external aid. A couple of generations before, R. Seadyah, the greatest of Jewish writers, writes on Creeds ; he would not have done this, had not the comparison of beliefs been a recognised part of the Kalam. The period after the compiling of the Tradition is with the Mohammedans the period of the composition of the legal codes ; so the Jews begin to compose codes. Some of the

---

[1] This translation is not literal.

Moslem codes are called "Pandects," *i.e.*, "All containing"; ere long these are matched by a Jewish work bearing the elegant title "All-in-it." The pride of the Arabic language is its poetry, which, while observing the measure of syllables as carefully as Greek, adds thereto a rhyming system of extraordinary elaboration. The Jews find that Hebrew will scan and rhyme no less than Arabic, and so they become poets. Letters are written by the heads of Mohammedan communities to distinguished jurisconsults, requesting opinions on difficult points of law; presently the Jews find themselves in possession of a whole literature of Responsa, at first in the Yiddish of the time, *i.e.*, Nabatæan Aramaic, presently in Arabic, and then in Hebrew. In the fourth century of Islam continuous commentaries on the Koran come to be substituted for the older and less formal style of desultory homilies. The Jews, who had matched the latter with their Midrashim, can soon boast of a Rashi and an Ibn Ezra.

The canon that the Jews have in religious matters no ideas of their own has therefore proved itself the solvent for all questions which attach themselves to what is called Rabbinical literature; if you see a Jewish book, you have only to look through an Arabic bibliography, and you will speedily detect the source of the former. Few Jewish writers acknowledge their obligations so candidly as Pseudo-Nissim, but the reason of this has been seen. What, then, were the Jews doing between the fall of Jerusalem and the Mohammedan conquest? This question cannot be answered easily; but the point whence we start is the definite assertion of the Talmud that the Jews were allowed to write nothing except the Old Testament. This assertion is rightly regarded as indisputable by Seadyah in the tenth century and Rashi in the eleventh; Krochmal and Frankel in the nineteenth century think they know better, but they are mistaken. The Talmud can be no more mistaken about that matter than can Ghazzali be about the age of the literature of the Mohammedans. Hence the latest event mentioned in the Talmud gives us the *terminus a quo* for the renaissance of Jewish writing. This is probably the slaughter of the Umayyads[1] in 750 A.D., which is used as an illustration in the Mishnah of the tractate " New Year's Day."

But the idea of a canon, containing books which might be written to the exclusion of all others, must have some origin; and how far can

---

[1] The spelling מרון for *Merwan* is the same as that employed by Dionysius of Tell-Mahré. *Banu Merwan* is used for the Umayyads by early Arabic writers, Ibn Kutaibah, Istakhri, etc. If the anecdote in Ibn Khallikan i. 258 be authentic, it was used before 100 A.H. The Gemara first glosses the phrase rightly as " sons of our Prince," but proceeds to give some impossible explanations. The massacre was at Anbar (*Ikd Farid*, ii. 280), a Jewish centre.

we trace either the prohibition against writing or
the constitution of the canon? The canon of
Leontius of Byzantium of the seventh century
shows that the rule existed then; but its commencement is not so easy to trace. Jerome professes to have seen the original of Ecclesiasticus,
but he was easily taken in, and deserves little
credence. The words of Epiphanius, who is a
little earlier, imply that the Apocrypha once
existed in Hebrew, but do not imply that they
still existed. From Origen we might expect
fuller information on this point, but we fail to
obtain it. He is, however, familiar with the
word *Apocrypha*, and the meaning of that word
is worth considering. It is a translation of the
Hebrew word which, in this context, means to
destroy. The Talmudists bless a man for not
having allowed Ezekiel to be rendered apocryphal; thereby implying that Ezekiel would
otherwise have been lost to the community.
Hence apocryphal books mean "destroyed
books," and Origen's suggestion that certain
narratives might be preserved among the
destroyed books involves a humorous contradiction. Hence the rule that only the canonical
books might be written is as early as Origen;
and when Melito enumerates the canonical books
as those possessed by the Jews, we are justified
in inferring that they had no others. The last
copy of the original of Ecclesiasticus was that
used by the Syriac translator somewhen in the

second century A.D.; it was faint and obliterated with age, and was probably thrown away by him when he had done with it.

To him who reflects on the origins of Christianity it will be apparent that the earliest Christian literature must have been largely in Hebrew. In the Gospel of the Nativity the Hebrew often glimmers through, and here and there in the Acts of Thomas, where indeed we are expressly told that Thomas sings in Hebrew, and therefore is understood by a Jewess. The fall of Jerusalem doubtless led to the disappearance of Hebrew as a spoken language. The books of the Christians, invigorated by the fulfilment of their Master's prophecy, were a positive danger. A rule, therefore, is made, prohibiting the writing of any Hebrew books besides those included in the Canon. Ben-Sira has the name *Jesus ;* though his book is harmless, it is better to destroy it, for, if books by a Jesus were allowed, Christian productions might be smuggled in. The Wisdom of Solomon is likely to be used for polemical purposes, owing to the predictions which it contains ; therefore it may be allowed to perish. From the rigid censure which the Salomonic writings underwent, and whence Proverbs and Ecclesiastes narrowly escaped, we may infer without hardihood that some of them are likely to have perished.

Whether the anti-Christian interpolations which the Hebrew Bible contains were all made at once seems uncertain. Probably they were introduced according as controversy rendered it necessary. The most striking of all is the alteration of the name of the follower of Moses from Jesus to Joshua (Jeshua to Jehoshua). This personage is called Jesus by Nehemiah, the LXX., the Peshitta, Philo, and Josephus; and Ben-Sira, in a remarkable grammatical note, observes that his name is an intensive form of the word "saviour,"[1] which can only apply to the name Jeshua, since Jehoshua must mean "Jehovah is a rock," and has no connection with this root. Ben-Sira's nine-syllable metre also testifies in a manner which perhaps the revisers of the Canon could not foresee. The Latin fathers before Jerome speak regularly of *Jesus* in this context. The reason for this alteration was not only dislike of the name Jeshua, or Jesus, but the fact that the Christian controversialists based an argument on Moses having altered his follower's name from Hoshea to Jesus. This appears in Augustine, Jerome's contemporary,[2] but also in the Dialogue of Justin, which is of

[1] Ecclus. xlvi. 1 :   גִּבּוֹר חַיִל יְשׁוּעַ בִּן־נוּן

וְיוֹרֵשׁ מֹשֶׁה בַּנְּבִיּוּת

אֲשֶׁר הָיָה כִשְׁמוֹ [מוֹשִׁיעַ]

גָּדוֹל עַל יְשׁוּעַת חֲבֵרָיו

The Samaritan Pentateuch agrees with the Jewish Bible.

[2] *Contra Faustum*, xvi. (viii. 249B).

the second century ; [1] and, since the spelling of
the name Jehoshua in the Hebrew Bible is such
as to render the pronunciation Jeshua impossible,
this alteration would be quite sufficient to silence
the Christians.   If we knew whether Justin was
the first person [2] who based an argument for
Christianity on the passage of Numbers in
which the name of Hoshea is changed, we
should have a *terminus a quo* for this alteration ;
for the introduction of the form Joshua into
Christian books Jerome is apparently responsible.

The purpose, therefore, of the revision of the
Canon which took place before Melito's time was
restrictive.   Only those books which were to
form part of the Law were to be preserved ; the
rest were to be destroyed.   From this time dates
the great distinction between " reading " and
" reciting " which pervades the Talmud.   To
read means to study the Old Testament ; to
recite means to study something else.   The Old
Testament is Mikra ; everything else Mishnah.[3]
This means that nothing but the Old Testament
might be written ; the rest of the matter possessed
by the Jews was to be preserved orally.[4]   Where

[1] *Dialogue*, §§ 106, 131, 132.

[2] *The Epistle of Barnabas*, § 12, cannot be quoted.

[3] Ordinarily Rashi understands this, *e.g. Ketuboth*, 17a
ult. ; but on *Nedarim*, 62a, he forgets it. Cf. *Tosefta*,
ed. Zuckermandel, p. 374, 25.

[4] This is regularly *assumed* in the Talmud ; *e.g.*,
Nedarim, 41a : " Rab Joseph was ill ; so all his knowledge was uprooted. Ubayy repeated it to him ; he

oral tradition has to take charge of a mass of matter that is neither in verse nor in counted sentences, accretion and loss cannot be avoided. Hence the Talmud contains matter belonging to some nine different centuries. It is not likely, however, that the tradition really claimed to be a second law till the Mohammedan tradition had acquired that value. The Karaites are in reality no more averse to tradition than the Rabbanites. What they disapprove is that the oral tradition should be written and assigned an importance equal to that of the Bible.

Before the revision of the Canon, there was the state of things which Josephus describes : there were a number of sacred books of primary authority ; but there was no objection to multiplying literature in Hebrew. How then came the Jews to think of a Canon? For we see that the Bible contains post-exilian matter. Whence came the Jews to think of separating books of authority from the rest? As before, we have only to glance round to find the source of this idea.

To the Jews of Ben-Sira's time the Greeks were what the Arabs were to Seadyah and his contemporaries. We have seen that Seadyah

---

said, I have never *heard* this *oral tradition.*" *Kiddushin,* 30*a* : " When Rab Assi died, the Rabbis met to pick out his dicta." This means, says Rashi, " they met and said, Let every one who has *heard* a fresh dictum from his mouth *say* it in the ears of his companion."

convinces the Jews of the authority of the
Talmud, although it was not reduced to writing
more than a century before Seadyah's time.
Hence the completion of the Canon need not
have preceded Ben-Sira's birth by many generations, notwithstanding his glorification of it.
The destruction of Greek liberty by Philip of
Macedon, followed by the world conquest of
Alexander, had made Attic Greek the literary
language of the world.   Entering upon the
heritage of free Hellas, the world of the Epigoni
took stock of its possessions.   Just as Aristotle
collects constitutions by scores, so he has on his
shelves a row of classics furnishing the matter
whence he can generalize for his philosophy of
taste.   That any nation besides the Hellenes
had a literature is an idea from which the father
of science seems to be very far.

The classical age of Greek literature stops at
the battle of Chæronea ; and within sixty years
of that event the Alexandrian library is founded.
Contemporary with its foundation is the first
editor of Greek classics, Zenodotus.   He is the
father of all who collect various readings.   The
generation that separates him from the battle of
Chæronea represents the period of transition
from the productive period to the reproductive.
The Greek authors have become *classics*, *i.e.*,
authors divided into classes, and arranged in
rows.

That the Hebrew Canon closes at this time

can be no more accidental than the fact that
Hebrew grammar and lexicography flourish a
little later than Arabic grammar and lexicography. The attitude of Alexandria towards
Judæa was friendly, whence the latter was willing
to learn from the former. The heirs of free
Greece were proud of its legacy of classics, hence
the Jews find themselves in possession of classics ;
only, as usual, they can surpass what the Greeks
have. The Greeks have their canon of orators,
their epic cycle, their old, middle, and new
comedy, their twenty-four books of the Iliad and
twenty-four books of the Odyssey. The Jews
have their five books of Moses and their twelve
minor prophets, etc., etc. Just as in the case
of the oral law and the vocalization of the Old
Testament, the Jews have to learn from foreigners
the value of what they have. They learn it ; but
they are forced to disown the obligation.

Just as for the writing down and editing of the
Talmud we have the narrow limits drawn by
the dates of Ibn Juraij and Seadyah, so for the
completion of the Canon we have the boundaries
marked by the dates of Aristotle and Ben-Sira.
The name given to the Hebrew classics was at
first *either* the Law, *or* the Prophets, *or* the Book
of the Covenant ; the practice of the Talmud, in
which the Law means the Old Testament, is as
old as the New Testament, and is also found in
Ben-Sira.[1] That the name "the Prophets"

[1] Ecclus. xxiv.

covered the whole appears from the passage cited above, in which Joshua is said to come after Moses in the prophetic office, whence the books of Moses would clearly come under the category prophecy. The term "Written Books" is also applied in the New Testament to the whole collection; but this must be an abridgment for "Divine" or "Prophetical Books," and is to be compared with the use of the word "Poet" for Homer by Greek writers.

That all existing copies of the Hebrew Old Testament are ultimately derived from one is proved by the *puncta extraordinaria*, or points placed above certain letters to indicate that those letters should be *expunged*. This inference (first drawn, it would appear, by Lagarde) commends itself at once to any one who is familiar with MSS. If, then, we could discover when the process of expunging was invented, we should have a *terminus a quo* for this copy. For this it is worth while observing that the word *expunge* is Latin, and refers properly to an operation performed with the Roman pen, the *stylus*. The earliest context in which it is apparently found is a place in Plautus, where it is applied to the erasion of the name of a soldier from a roll,[1] an operation for which both the Hebrew and Greek languages use a word meaning "to wipe out"; *pricking* out would be done with a stylus on a tablet of wax. The

[1] Compare Jahn on Persius, ii. 13.

single point, then, by which erasion is indicated
is symbolic of this process, and must have come
from Italy to Greece and Palestine. The word
used by the Rabbis for "pointing" means
originally "cleansing"; it is derived from a
Syriac adjective which means "pure," "clean."
This, again, seems to come from an Arabic verb,
which means "to discriminate," "select." The
process, then, which we call "pointing," originally meant "purifying," and was done by putting
points above unnecessary letters, and inserting in
a minute hand others that had been omitted.
The former process gives its name to *expunging* in
Latin, but not in Greek or Hebrew, and is connected with purely Italian processes. Therefore,
it cannot have come to Palestine before Latin
influence waxed strong, *i.e.*, before about 60 B.C.
Hence all our copies of the Old Testament are
derived from one that is not earlier than 60 B.C.

A fast in the Jewish calendar which commemorates the burning of the Law by Apostomus
confirms the hypothesis that at some time the
copies of the Law were reduced to one. Who
was this Apostomus? The name appears to be
Latin, Postumus or Postumius. The Persian
calendar [1] calls him "king of the Greeks," which
may be an error for "Romans."

That it could be possible to destroy all the
existing copies of the Hebrew Bible, when the
Jews were scattered over so many countries,

[1] See next chapter.

seems surprising.   But then we probably have
no means of telling in what number such copies
existed.   If, however, the burning of the Law by
Postumus was an event worth celebrating by a
yearly fast, it must clearly have been a very
serious misfortune ;   and this would not have
been the case had it been possible to replace the
Law easily.   The inference suggests itself that
the restoration of the Law, which followed this
catastrophe, was the occasion on which the
negative fixing of the Canon, of which the
Talmud retains a tradition, took place.

The meaning of the " extraordinary points "
and hanging letters was unknown to the Talmudists, who assign ridiculous explanations to
them, to which references are faithfully given by
many of those German commentators from
whom we fancy we can learn criticism.   So
hard is it for mankind to be really *critical, i.e.*, to
gather the wheat into their garners, and allow
the chaff to burn away.

The purpose of this sketch of literary history
is to secure our lines of communication in
dealing with the Old Testament as the prepara-
tion for the New.   That we possess the Old
Testament in a partially anti-Christian recension
is shown by the name *Jehoshua ;*   that interpolation must be after the time of Justin, who
bases an argument against a Jew on the occurrence of the name *Jesus* in the Pentateuch, but
earlier than Jerome.   And yet even in Justin's

time the Jews were charged with anti-Christian
alterations. This fact excites suspicion where
arguments based on passages of the Old Testament are, according to our present text, futile.
The process of deliberately falsifying evidence
in order to avoid a painful conclusion does not
commend itself as either honest or intelligent ;
but he knows little of human nature who
supposes that less than 99 per cent. of mankind would resort to it if tempted.

Secondly, some reason must be given for the
fact that the interpretation of the Bible current
among the Jews before Seadyah's time is (as is
generally agreed) worthless. It is to be found
in the rule that the writing of traditions was
forbidden. If we consider what confusion and
obscurity have been brought into the history of
Islam by one hundred and twenty years of oral
tradition, what the effect of eight hundred years
of it among the Jews would be may be con-
jectured. The grammatical sense fails the
Talmudists altogether. Where they come
across unusual words, they interpret them
according to the language of the country in
which they happen to be residing.[1] Words
in the Old Testament are thus interpreted as
Coptic and Greek ; some one in Persia hears

[1] Theodoret, *Quæstt.* in Gen. lxi. : " You can nowhere
find Hebrew children speaking Hebrew, but only the
language of the country in which they happen to be
born " (fifth century).

the word *shighāl* (" jackal ") and, coming across
the Hebrew *sheghāl* (" queen ") [1] thinks it may
be this Persian word.   The endeavours made by
many writers to get history out of the Jewish
books   are   absolute   failures ;   the   sense   of
chronology is as much lost as that of philology.

The scientific study of the Old Testament
among the Jews begins with Seadyah, or a little
earlier.   That the Arabic language was the best
possible source for Hebrew grammar and lexicography is certain ; but the chain of circumstances
which led the Mohammedans to provide the
Jews with both is so remarkable that it may
well be termed providential.   The Jews would,
in any case, have explained words they did not
know from the language of the country in which
they had taken up their abode ; since Arabic
happened to be the real source of those words,
the explanation of the Bible at last had fallen
on ground where it could thrive.   Seadyah
began by translating the Old Testament into
Arabic.   The probability is that he utilized
previous translations made by Christians from
Syriac or Coptic ; so that here was another gate
by which Christian glosses came into Jewish
books.

What, however, is a more interesting subject
for speculation is this : Until Jewish history
merges in Biblical history, so far back as it can
be traced, *originality* seems absolutely to fail

[1] Nehem. ii. 6.

the race. All their non-Biblical literature is
borrowed (at any rate in form) from Mohammedans or Christians ; their idea of a canon
from Greeks ; their pointing MSS. for different
purposes from Romans and Syrians. In some
of these matters they appear able to outdo those
from whom they borrow. The counting of
letters and the arranging of dots, the Kabbalah
and the Tradition, are thought by mankind to
be peculiarly Jewish, but all these things have
come to the Jews from others. And if we consider what the Bible tells us about them, we
should expect that this would be so. The desire
of Israel appears to be to resemble others.
Other nations have a king, so they want a king.
The fact that the institution is not altogether
desirable does not count. Other nations are
idolatrous, whence they display an unreasoning
attachment to idolatry ; no amount of preaching
is of avail. How are we to reconcile with this
most patent want of originality the extraordinary
phenomenon of such a race having produced a
literature which, after having once taken its place
at the head of the literature of the world, has no
intention of quitting that post ? The lost
literatures that come to light rarely have any
value of their own. Egypt and Assyria produced monuments which were long lost, but
now are found and deciphered. Who reads
them except out of mere curiosity, or to aid him
in some other study ? Indian literature is now

as easy of access as Greek ; but who cares for
it ? One or two isolated morsels, perhaps, are
known beyond professional circles, but nothing
else. The Bible itself explains this problem by
the theory that the best of Israelitish literature
was communicated to its authors from *without*—
that it was the result of special favours conferred
on privileged members of the race. "Men spake
as they were moved." The nation which of
itself could do nothing for science or philosophy,
which could not observe and could not experiment, which could not compile a grammar nor
invent a metre, produced the books which, owing
to the profundity of their contents, " the first
man did not fully know, and the last man has
not sounded to the bottom." Truly this is the
Lord's doing, and it is marvellous in our eyes.

It is not altogether fair to expect of the Jews
in dependence the qualities which they exhibited
when independent, if that be the epithet to apply
to an oriental monarchy. But, as Pindar well
says, even if you cut down an oak, it is still an
oak ; though it be sawn for a pillar or burnt on
the hearth, it is still the king of trees. For
whatever purpose it be employed, the great
qualities of the wood show themselves. The
Athenians of St. Paul's time have still the intellectual keenness of the Athenians of the fifth
and fourth centuries B.C. From being the
university of Hellas, Athens has become the
university of the world. The singular purity

with which the Jewish race maintains itself does much to eliminate the factor which in the case of all the modern representatives of ancient races has cut away the ground for such an argument. If we fail to find in the Greeks of to-day the qualities of the Greeks of old, the explanation is to be sought in the paucity of Hellenic blood in the former. But if race count for anything, there is no reason for supposing that since the first exile the Jews have mingled with other races in such a manner as would seriously alter their national qualities.

That the great gifts which members of the race once possessed did not disappear with the first Captivity is certain ; some post-exilian matter got into the Canon ; and though Ben-Sira could not be called a prophet, there are passages in his book which are worthy of a writer of the first class. It seems, however, clear that these gifts were not *racial*, but isolated. The Israelites were not like the Greeks, whose intellectual ability was such as to cause the word " clever " to be naturally associated with their name. But to particular individuals extra-ordinary powers were granted, which they could neither communicate nor hand down, and the very form of which they could not lucidly explain. Hence what they produced differed from the productions of other races more in kind than in quality, and its efficiency for the purpose of evolution has been proportionately great.

The descent from the Old Testament to the Mishnah is, in consequence, steeper than that from the greatest of the Greek poets to the feeblest, or from the most brilliant of the productions of India to the least tolerable. And the underlying fact is that the value of the former is due to the presence in it of a factor which the intellectual capital of the race did not provide. The literature produced by the race unaided wanted that antiseptic, and also showed but a small measure of the gifts whence mankind has derived its stores of philosophy and science.

VI

THE CALENDAR OF THE SYNA-GOGUE.

IN the first half of the eleventh century Abd Al-Hayy of Kardiz compiled a history,[1] mainly intended to glorify the Sultans of Ghaznah, his masters, but also incorporating a variety of interesting matter. Several chapters are taken up with accounts of the feasts of the Eastern nations, among whom he included Moham-medans, Jews, Christians, Parsees, and Hindus. The devastating hordes of Janghiz Khan had not then swept Asia, and much precious litera-ture was still in existence to which we no longer have access. Kardizi, as we shall call this writer, went to authoritative sources for his Calendars, and his chapters, which are in Persian, have some curious marks indicating the authentic character of the documents whence they

[1] It is called *Zain al-akhbār* ; the Bodleian Library has the unique copy.

were drawn.[1]   The Jews learned from the Greeks
to count by the letters of the alphabet, but for 15
they write 9, 6, to avoid employing the Divine
name Jah for so mundane a purpose.   To the
Persians the letters JH have no such association,
so that when they count by letters they make no
exception is this case, but let 15 follow the same
system as the others.   In the Persian account
of the feasts of the Jews, 9, 6 appears to have
been used in place of 15, which, taken together
with some peculiarities of the numeration in the
twenties, gives us a certain trace of the character
in which the underlying document was written.
Kardiz, which is sometimes included in Ghaznah,
is far removed from those communities of Sora
and Anbar to which we owe our ordinary
information concerning Jewish affairs, so that
we are justified in expecting something out of
the way.

This expectation would appear to be fulfilled.
Kardizi   commences   by   enumerating   the
categories of acts which might not be done on
the Sabbath.   He counts 38 ; and his list cannot
possibly be dissociated from the Talmudic list
of 39.   But when we compare the lists, we find
that they differ widely.   Of the categories
enumerated only half tally ; and even by
correcting the text and assuming occasional

[1] He also used Al-Biruni's *Chronology of Ancient
Nations.* Most of the matter to which attention is called
below is not in Al-Biruni.

mistranslation of Hebrew words we cannot, without exceeding the limits of probability, bring many more into harmony. Which list is then the earlier? The Talmudic list begins with Sowing, Ploughing. That this is an intentional inversion is obvious; for every one knows that ploughing precedes sowing. But the first letter of the verb to sow comes in the Hebrew alphabet immediately before the first letter of the verb to plough.[1] The purpose of the inversion is therefore to aid the memory, and is characteristic of a Mishnah or unwritten book. But the Persian list has the natural order, Ploughing, Sowing.

What, however, is more important and striking is the fact that the Persian Mishnah contains categories which we know from the New Testament to have been among the acts forbidden in our Lord's time, whereas the Talmudic list does not contain them. One of these is *plucking an ear of corn*. Every one remembers how the disciples were rebuked for doing this on the Sabbath. It would, however, be difficult to bring this act under any of the 39 categories of the Mishnah. The nearest would be "reaping"; and, indeed, "pulling up" is repeatedly said to be a subdivision of "reaping." [2] Against this it might be urged that reaping is done with an instrument, whereas the act of the disciples was scarcely distinguishable from ordinary eating;

[1] ‏חרש‎, ‏זרע‎.   [2] Rashi on *Betsah*, 3*a*.

and, in the second place, that the list makes a
distinction between acts of which the law forbids
a minimum, and acts of which a minimum is
not forbidden ; and clearly "reaping" is of the
latter class.   Hence the disciples might easily
have defended their action.   But the Persian
Mishnah has "plucking an ear of corn" as a
special category, No. 27.   If, therefore, the
Persian Mishnah were in vogue in our Lord's
time, the act of the disciples could not be
defended.   The occurrence of this category
would excite grave suspicion if the list of forbidden acts were given by a Christian or in a
document which betrayed Christian influence.
But in Kardizi's case such a suspicion would
be illgrounded.   His misrenderings of Hebrew
words show that his source was Jewish, and the
agreement between his No. 38 and the Talmudic
No. 39 cannot possibly be accidental.   Neither
a Jew nor a Mohammedan would have had any
interest in interpolating the list so as to confirm
the Gospel ; but the Mishnah which accords
with the usage of New Testament times has a
right to be considered earlier than the Mishnah
which disagrees with it.   If it be added that the
Mishnah of the treatise *Sabbath* teems with late
words, which are likely to have been learned by
the Jews after the Mohammedan conquest, it is
evident that it can lay no claim to antiquity.

A case similar to this, in which there can be
no suspicion of interpolation, is No. 3 of the

Persian list, which appears to mean " watering
the fields," combined with No. 28, "digging a
thing up from its place." Neither of these
categories is to be found in the Talmudic
Mishnah ; both, however, were forbidden, and
elsewhere in the Talmud there is an interesting
discussion about the categories under which
they come. " On what grounds,"[1] asks a Rabbi,
" do we warn any one who waters or weeds on
the Sabbath?" Rabbah said, because these
operations come under the head of ploughing.
Rab Joseph said, because they come under the
head of sowing. The first explained that watering was, like ploughing, a mode of softening the
earth ; whereas the latter held that, like sowing,
it contributed to the growth of the plant. The
Persian Mishnah, by assigning these operations
special categories, rendered such a discussion
unnecessary.

To only one more of these categories need
attention be called. The Gospels make much
of the prohibition against moving objects on the
Sabbath. A man who took up his bed and
walked thereby violated the Sabbath. This,
too, cannot easily be got into the Talmudic
categories. No. 39, " removing from region to
region," is the most likely; but this implies the
elaborate doctrine of regions, which has about it
no semblance of antiquity. The Persian Mishnah has three categories which are connected

[1] *Moed Kalon, 2b.*

with this subject, and No. 35, "removing furniture from place to place," exactly corresponds with the theory recorded in the Gospel. The question, then, does not depend on the doctrine of regions, which has not yet been worked out.

The remainder of the categories offer scope for observations that are not devoid of interest, but would be irrelevant here. The examples given make it likely that we are tapping a source of Jewish tradition that is older than the collections of which the genesis was described in the last chapter. It is certain that only specialists in Judaic matters would have even heard of the categories of acts ; there can be no doubt therefore that Kardizi gets his facts from a Jewish book. The book known to him must have been in Judæo-Arabic or Judæo-Persian. For the Feast of Tabernacles was called *Matal* in it, and Kardizi mistakes this for a Hebrew word ; whereas it is really an Arabic word which might have been used in either of the languages mentioned. But this work must have been a rather unlearned translation of a work in New Hebrew, as shall be seen presently, when we consider what it says of the numbering of the people. This work (called by Kardizi the Book of Fasts) cannot have been the existing Book of Fasts (*Megillath Ta'anith*), for that does not contain all the matter known to Kardizi. There are, moreover, grounds for thinking that the

Book of Fasts in the existing form is of no great antiquity ; for the Talmud, while quoting it, declares it abrogated. Rashi, whose opinions are always deserving of consideration, supposed that an exception was made in favour of the Book of Fasts when the prohibition against writing anything save the Bible was introduced.[1] But it seems more probable that the Talmud refers to a lost book, of which the Fast-Scroll known to us was a later reconstruction.

For the present the document which, as has been seen, was known to Kardizi at third hand, may be identified with an apocryphal scroll quoted in the Talmud,[2] which contained the 39 categories of acts, though we cannot be sure with which list they agreed. That apocryphal scroll was probably the source not only of Kardizi's lists, but of the matter afterwards written down in the Fast-Scroll,[3] and of the supplement to it, containing a list of days on which fasting was incumbent, which the latter Jewish codes copy without being able to make anything of it. The antiquity of the matter contained in that Appendix can be proved very curiously. A day is there set apart for the commemoration of the struggle between the parties of Hillel and Shammai, wherein blood was shed. Of this event there is a casual notice in the ˉPalestinian Talmud, but none in the

---

[1] *Sabbath*, 13*b*. [2] Ibid., 6*b*.
[3] Neubauer, *Medieval Jewish Chronicles*, ii. *init.*

more popular Talmud of Babylon, whence it
came that in the second quarter of the tenth
century the most learned Jew of the time knew
nothing of it.[1]   That he knew nothing of an
event commemorated in the Calendar is explicable only on the supposition that either it was
inserted in the Calendar after his time, or that
the Calendar, though old, was known to only
a few persons in the tenth century.   Since the
memory of the struggle was so painful that the
Rabbanite Jews preferred to forget about it, the
former supposition is exceedingly unlikely.   The
latter therefore remains, and it is confirmed by the
occurrence of this fast in the Persian Calendar.
Kardizi mistakes the parties for tribes, but that is
a natural blunder for a Mohammedan to make.

The Persian Calendar differs from the Fast-
Scroll in that it commences the year with Tisri,
which is the practice of the ordinary communities, whereas the latter commences with Nisan.
New Year's Day was called the Fast of the Ten
Days by the Jews known to Kardizi, and even
the babe in the cradle, he tells us, was not
allowed any milk.   It was kept for two days,
a practice about which we read much in the
Talmud, and in the controversial literature of
the tenth century.   In what follows we shall
collect other notices in this Calendar that seem
to be ancient.

[1] Frankel, *Introduction to the Jerusalem Talmud*,
p. 132*b*.

Feast 9 "is called 'Barek' which means
'blessing' in the Hebrew tongue." The name
Barek was sometimes given to Mount Gerizim,
where the blessing was to be recited.[1] The
Persian catalogue connects it with the pro-
traction of the life of Moses, a legend to which
Mohammedan writers occasionally refer.[2] That
the Persian writer should have invented a
Jewish festival, or interpreted its import out of
his own head, is highly improbable ; therefore
he must have obtained both the name and the
interpretation from his Jewish authority. It
might indeed have been expected that the
blessing on Mount Gerizim would have been
commemorated by a day in the Calendar.
There may perhaps be a reference to both the
points noticed in the Persian Calendar in the
words of Ecclesiasticus about Moses, " And he
brought out of him a merciful man, finding
favour in the eyes of all flesh, beloved of God
and man, Moses, whose memory is in blessings."[3]
These verses can be restored to their metrical
shape by the most literal retranslation ; and

[1] Commentators on Josephus, i. 252.
[2] *Letters* of Abu 'l-Ala, p. 107.
[3] xlv. 1 :

וַיּוֹצֵא מִמֶּנּוּ אִישׁ חָסִיד

מוֹצֵא חֵן בְּעֵינֵי כָּל־בָּשָׂר

אָהוּב מֵאֱלֹהִים וְאָדָם

מֹשֶׁה אֲשֶׁר זִכְרוֹ בִּבְרָכוֹת

since where syllables are numbered not every clause need be forcible, it is possible that this means no more than the familiar "whose memory is blessed" which the Jews, perhaps in imitation of Mohammedan practice, put after the names of dead saints. On the other hand, if an event in the life of Moses was really commemorated at a feast called Blessings, the last clause would be much more pointed.

It is noteworthy that the legend about Moses is preserved by Mohammedan writers rather than by Jews. Something of the same sort occurs in the notice of the trumpet-blowing on New Year's Day. This, Kardizi tells us, is to imitate the sound which Satan caused Sarah to hear at the time of the sacrifice of Isaac. That New Year's Day with the Jews commemorates the sacrifice of Isaac we learn rather from the practice of their ritual than from any express statement to that effect. Of an interview between Satan and Sarah that took place at that time we read little in Jewish books except in one very late Catena ;[1] whereas the historian Tabari gives a very detailed account of one. What we should infer hence is that we are not entitled to neglect the Biblical legends of the Mohammedans when they are found in early and careful reports like that of Tabari. Instead of looking for the source of these in the Talmuds,

[1] See *Yalkut Sofer* (Pax, 1894), 126a.

we should regard them as an independent current of tradition.

Fast 4 is "the Day of Visitation," and commemorates the numbering of the people by David. This is not noticed in the Appendix to the Fast-Scroll, and the Talmud seems to know nothing of such a commemoration. Yet the account is here authentic. In the first place the name of the Fast is represented by the Arabic word for punishment. In Hebrew the word for census-taking is identical with the word for visitation in the sense of punishment : [1] so that we have no difficulty in restoring the Hebrew name of this Fast. There is also another indication of the source of this notice. The choice offered David is between " famine, defeat, and death." The word used in New-Hebrew for "pestilence" [2] differs by one letter added from the word for " death " ; and in the paraphrase of the chapter in 2 Samuel, where this story is told, the ordinary edition several times gives " death " for " pestilence " in consequence. Similarly in Ecclesiasticus xxxix. 29 we read " fire and hail, famine and death, all these were created for vengeance," where " death " must be a mistranslation for " pestilence." [3]

As has been seen, the Persian Calendar is not supported by the Appendix in mentioning this Fast. Yet it is clear that it was mentioned in

[1] פְּקוּדָה.   [2] מוֹתָן.   [3] אֵשׁ וּבָרָד כָּפָן וּמוֹרָתָן.

the New-Hebrew document on which the Persian Calendar is based. The facts collected above, which prove this document to contain matter that goes back to New Testament times, allow us to infer that the notice of this Fast goes back to the time before the destruction of the second temple. But where are we to stop? That a fast-day should have been instituted between the first and second captivities to commemorate David's numbering of the people seems unlikely : the consequences of that event were not sufficiently disastrous to make this likely. On the other hand, the purpose of the Appendix to the second Book of Samuel might very possibly be to explain the purpose of a fast. Hence the calendars might seem to contain relics of oral tradition of great value.

Of the other notices which the Persian Calendar only contains, the most interesting is certainly post-Christian. This is that at the Feast of Purim it was the custom of the Jews to have a sort of miracle-play, at which the figure of Haman was *burned ;* but the Feast was called "Haman *Crucified.*" In the formula of abjuration for converted Jews, printed as an appendix to Clement of Rome, the practice of crucifying a figure ostensibly meant for Haman is mentioned and condemned ; apparently in the community known to Kardizi burning was substituted, but the name " crucified," [1] which Kardizi gives

[1] *Nizkop.*

with the Mesopotamian pronunciation, was retained.

It would be expected that a nation which had passed through so many vicissitudes as the Israelites would have a very full calendar of days commemorating national joys and sorrows. Certain days would count as specially unlucky, being marked by the recurrence of calamities ; and the fact of a day being already signalized by a calamity would render the occurrence of a fresh one more striking, and serve to keep it in the recollection of the people. Days which marked minor victories or defeats, or such as were too ephemeral in their effect to count as of great importance, would presently drop out of the reckoning. Hence the fact of a fast being retained, the cause of which was unknown to the Rabbis, seems a sign of good faith. Such a fast is mentioned in both the Appendix and the Persian Calendar as coming after the Days of Darkness. If the compiler had intended to falsify his table, he would surely have found no difficulty in assigning a reason for it from among the many national disasters recorded in the Bible. And, indeed, in one of the late codes [1] a suggestion is made for it : whereas Kardizi's authority made out that the nature of the disaster has been intentionally concealed.

It is clear that both the Fast-Scroll and the Persian Calendar show traces of a considerable

[1] *Sefer Kol-bo.*

amount of information that is otherwise lost to
the Jews. So much of the Fast-Scroll deals
with the glorious period of the Maccabees that
it is sometimes called the Maccabean Scroll. [1]
Some of the feasts which it mentions tally with
notices in Josephus, whereas in the case of others
it stands alone. The fact that many Jewish
scholars in the first nine centuries of Christen-
dom had access to Josephus and the other books
concerning the Jews, which are preserved in
Greek, [2] renders it particularly difficult to sever
purely Jewish tradition from that which has
been contaminated from Greek sources ; but the
general appearance of the Fast-Scroll suggests
that the text represents an authentic oral
tradition, whereas the commentary is of a very
mixed nature.

The latest event mentioned is probably the
death of Rabbi Akiba, who is supposed to have
been executed in the time of Trajan, and whom
we know from the notices in Epiphanius to
have been a historical personage. The Persian
Calendar notes the day as a Fast-day, but the
name of Akiba has dropped out, though the
words which it contains about him leave no
room for doubt as to his identity. But from
this period the Calendar goes back with
apparent continuity to the remotest antiquity

[1] So in the *Halachoth Gedoloth*.
[2] See Justinian *Nov.* 146, where they are recommended to use the LXX and Aquila.

of the Hebrews. And it is remarkable for both what it omits and what it includes.

As was seen above, the numbering of the people is told in an Appendix to David's biography, which might seem to have been suggested by the need for the explanation of a Fast-day. The Bible once or twice points out that future generations will want to know the reason for certain practices, and therefore a record of them is left in writing. Fast 18, "the Death of the Tribes," seems to admit of a similar analysis. The Appendix to the Fast-Scroll and the Persian Calendar agree in commemorating the almost total extinction of the tribe of Benjamin. The story is told in the Appendix to the Book of Judges. The Book of Judges also names a day on which the death of Jephthah's daughter was commemorated, of which neither of the calendars take notice. The obvious reason is that that Fast-day was celebrated by a tribe which went into captivity and never returned thence, whereas the tribe of Benjamin did return from captivity. If we were to regard the Calendar as a conscious fabrication, it would be hard to account for the insertion of a fast not mentioned in the Book of Judges, and the omission of a fast that is mentioned there.

Fast 29, "the Fast of the Ark," commemorating the capture of the ark by the Philistines, is also common to the Hebrew and Persian

Calendars. That the event is historical is probably granted by even the most sceptical; what is doubted is whether the ark ever returned. There can be no doubt that its capture would be regarded as the gravest of national disasters, which, therefore, we should expect the Calendar to commemorate. With regard to the story as told in the first Book of Samuel, there is a passage in the valuable chronicle published with the title "Fragments of the Arabic Historians,"[1] which bears so curious a resemblance to it that it seems right to quote it here. One of the early battles of Islam is being described. "Said the Persians: Ye have slain Kutaibah; had he been one of us, and died among us, we should have regarded him as a martyr, and kept his *ark* (coffin) till the Day of Judgment, to ask aid thereof when we went on a campaign." Were it not for the shape of the ark being so carefully recorded in Exodus, we might have supposed the Israelitish ark to have had the same origin and the same purpose; but the measurements are given too accurately to admit of such a possibility.

The Jewish prayer books would seem to have been compiled in the 10th and 11th centuries. These contain services for very few of the days the observance of which is not prescribed in the Pentateuch. One of these, however, the Fast of Gedaliah, is commemorated in the Service

[1] *Fragmenta Historicorum Arabum,* i. 19.

Books. This must assuredly represent a continuous tradition ; for the murder of Gedaliah was too insignificant a disaster to attract the attention of a fabricator ; whereas at the time when it occurred it would be of sufficient importance to cause the anniversary of the day whereon it occurred to have melancholy associations.

Both the Persian Calendar and the Appendix state that the Day of Atonement commemorates the worship of the Calf. And, indeed, the Appendix, instead of speaking of the Day of Atonement, has the succinct notice : " On this day the worship of the Calf was expiated." The learned Jewish editor [1] of the Fast-Scroll tells us that he consulted the best authorities to find confirmation of this statement, but did not succeed. Modern critics regard the Day of Atonement as a very late institution, and very few of them would assign the episode of the Calf any historical value. It is clear that if monotheism came in with Elijah, the worship of the Calf in the wilderness would not have been criminal. It seems a bold suggestion that the calendars are here preserving a fragment of genuine tradition, yet there are grounds for making it. The worship of the Calf is as much the great national sin of the Israelites as the Exodus was the great national miracle. That a fabricator would find a day to commemorate this event and its

[1] J. Lev.

disastrous consequences is likely; but would he have fixed on the great national Fast without some authority from tradition? This appears to be unlikely; and the fact that in the narrative of the Exodus Aaron takes part in the worship of the Calf agrees curiously with the doctrine that on the Day of Atonement the high priest first makes atonement for himself. The ceremonies of the Day of Atonement would appear to belong to a very extreme antiquity; and the choice remains whether we are to regard the statement of the calendars as the conjecture of a heortologist, or a fragment of genuine tradition.

If the Day of Atonement were a late innovation, it should be possible to account for its origin. This could scarcely be done with ease, and it would seem that the attempt to derive Purim from a Persian festival has been of dubious success.

Of the fasts which commemorate events connected with the history of the Bible we have already had occasion to allude to two. One is the Fast called Darkness, supposed to commemorate the darkening of the world for three days, owing to Ptolemy Philadelphus having ordered the LXX. translation to be made. The Persian Calendar exhibits on this occasion more knowledge than was possessed by the compiler of either Talmud, for he knows the name Philadelphus, which the Talmudists have lost.

The conflicting notices of this holy day show us the difficulty of dealing with oral tradition. According to Philo, who ought to know, the Egyptian Jews celebrated a feast at Pharos, in memory of the LXX. translation, which they regarded justly as a national benefit. According to Josephus it was Ptolemy who celebrated a feast. And here we have the Jewish tradition maintaining that the Jews kept the day as a fast! The traditions concerning the LXX. which the Talmud contains by no means favour the view that the LXX. translation would be regarded as a national misfortune ; they, moreover, contain (curiously enough) a stratum of true tradition which we gratefully accept, while numerous errors of detail prove that they have passed through a number of inaccurate memories before being committed to paper. Perhaps the name Philadelphus was purposely omitted by the earliest recorders owing to the associations connected with that word, which would have been so painful to the Jews. The words of the Persian writer, which seem to mean " Ptolemy at the same time that he liberated Egypt, conferred favours on the Jews, and sent them back to their own country," seem to go back to Josephus, whom it is surprising to find even so well-informed an author as Kardizi quoting in this context ; but it has already been observed that the Archæology was accessible to many Jews while the Byzantine

empire flourished.   Whether the Darkness from
which this Fast took its name was real or
fictitious cannot easily be determined.   It seems
indeed, analogous to the earthquake which, the
Talmud tells us, signalized the translation of the
prophets by Jonathan Ben Uzziel, probably a
mythical personage ; and it is in favour of the
antiquity and trustworthiness of the calendars
that they know nothing about this ; for the
origin of the Targums has already been seen to
be unworthy of such celebration.

Of the burning of the Law by Apostomus,
which is also known to the Talmud and the
Jewish liturgy, notice has already been taken.
On another day the burning of the Scroll of
Jeremiah was commemorated ; the Fast was,
according to the Persian writer, called *Kinoth*—
the Hebrew for "Lamentations"; and his
account of it differs somewhat from the account
of the Appendix. Finally, the Fast-Scroll
appears to contain a notice of the enactment
forbidding the writing of other books in addition
to the Law. The day whereon this event was
celebrated was Tammuz 14. The reason
assigned for it is that the existence of a Sad-
ducean Scroll made it necessary to interpret
literally certain passages of Scripture which it
was desirable to gloss. The particular cases
cited include the precept "An eye for an eye,"
which, it will be remembered, is abrogated in
the Gospel. The whole story, as it appears in

the Fast-Scroll, seems to represent the memory of a real event, very much disfigured by alterations, intentional and unintentional.

The remaining days commemorate the deaths of leading members of the community—Moses, Aaron and his sons, Miriam, Joshua, and Samuel. In the case of some of these the date is argued out in the existing Talmud, so that there is no reason for assigning these days any high antiquity. The Appendix and the Persian Calendar agree in noticing a Fast of the Death of the Righteous, who, they say, were the leaders of the people in the time of Joshua, son of Nun.

A calendar is, it may be observed, the kind of work to which the theory of accretion is not only applicable, but best suited. As the events occur, the day of their occurrence is noted ; and some days, like the ninth of Ab, are likely to acquire notoriety for ill luck. The names of the months used by the Jews were probably adopted by them in the first exile. The dates of pre-exilian disasters could then be remembered, and some of them may have been translated into the new Calendar. This collection of lucky and unlucky days was probably preserved orally, and added to as new events of importance occurred ; the Maccabean period provided a number of memorable days. Whether there is any truth in the story of the composition of the Fast-Scroll narrated in the Talmud is doubtful; but the reference which has been quoted to an Apocryphal Scroll seems genuine, and this may have been the basis of the three documents which have furnished the matter for this chapter. The memory of it was best retained in an obscure and distant community, whence we owe our best knowledge of it to Abd Al-Hayy of Kardiz, who wrote in the eleventh century, and of whose work a transcript of the eighteenth century appears to be the sole copy that remains! If a document of so late a date seem a strange source to draw from, how old, it may be asked, are the oldest known copies of the Hebrew Bible?

The place which this discussion occupies in the defence of Revelation is due to the continuity of history that such a Calendar exhibits. At each point where we can test it, it appears to display collateral knowledge to that recorded in the ordinary sources of information. At the commencement we have seen that it agrees curiously with the Gospels on the question of the acts forbidden on a Sabbath. Then it knows about Maccabean victories which the historians, having only the books of the Bible to read, have forgotten. So strange even to learned mediæval Jews was the history of the Maccabean period that the author of the famous work *Khazari* (called by the Jews *Cusari*) puts Alexander Jannæus after Christ. The destruction of written literature, the occasion of which is forgotten by the nation at large, is remembered here. The building of the Egyptian Temple by Onias, which is remembered also by the Talmudists, is commemorated, owing to its having been associated with the unlucky ninth of Ab. Where it deals with events recorded in the Bible, the Biblical passages, from the fact of their being supplements, seem rather to be commentaries on its statements than the texts which gave rise to the notices in the Calendar. For surely, had the Calendar been a compilation, in which arbitrary dates were assigned to important events of importance, such memorable days as those of the finding of the Law and the recitation of the law by Ezra ought not to have been neglected, seeing especially that the later tradition makes the former the commencement of an epoch.[1] Going back to the beginnings of Israelitish history, we find that it has an account of the Day of Atonement which is unknown to both the Bible and the tradition, and that it professes to retain the memory of an event of the time of Joshua which the ordinary tradition at any rate has forgotten.

If we compare this Calendar with the Calendar of Mohammedan Feasts that precedes it, the first fact which strikes the reader is that all the Mohammedan days commemorate events of actual, and indeed modern, history, except those of which the origin is explained by deliberate

[1] Targum on Ezekiel.

fabrication. In such cases both the time and the source of the fabrication are fairly clear. Elsewhere, though there may be some doubt concerning the correctness of the date, there is no reason to doubt the historical character of the fact recorded. If this list of Mohammedan feasts of the eleventh century be compared with that of the Mohammedan feasts of the year 1900, it will appear that many of the old holydays have fallen into desuetude, but that there are no events of early history commemorated now, which were not commemorated in Kardizi's time.

Of a Calendar borrowed from another nation this would not be true. The Abyssinians strangely fast three days in commemoration of the fasting of the people of Nineveh ; but nothing can be concluded therefrom except that at some time or other the example of the people of Nineveh, as recorded in the Book of Jonah, was held out to them for imitation. And, indeed, the whole Abyssinian Calendar is that of another community introduced when the Abyssinians were converted. But in the case of national calendars like those of the Jews and the Mohammedans, the point at which deliberate fiction comes in is hard to fix. The Feast of the Dedication commemorates, as we know, a historical event ; the Jews had for centuries no book in which it was recorded ; but the fact of the festival recurring served to retain a vague

notion of the important epoch in the national
history to which it belonged. In the old
Calendar (which the Persian text represents)
that event is already embellished with details
taken from other histories ; but there is as yet
nothing miraculous. By the time the Talmud
is committed to writing a miracle is introduced.
From the Dedication the next step takes us to
the translation of the Bible and the building of
the temple of Onias, both of them events that
are well known to be historical, but of which
the Jews preserved only vague notions. A few
more steps take us to Purim, the account of the
origin of which appears to be the latest book
included in the Canon, and which, indeed, may
be still said to be hovering about the Canon,
since the Talmud has doubts about the question
whether it may be written, and in a work of the
eleventh century it is excluded from the
XXIV. Canonical Books. Thence we are
carried back by easy stages to the time before
the Exile, to the splitting of the nation, to the
time of David, to that of Samuel, that of Eli,
that of the Judges, that of Joshua, that of Moses,
till we come to the sacrifice of Isaac, with
which the sacred year commences, though there
is a tradition that its date has been altered.
The Calendar is so purely national that the
commencement of Israel's influence on the
nations of the world is signalized by a fast.
Nothing before the time of Abraham is worthy

of commemoration, but from that period on-
wards it continues to collect until the last relics
of a Jewish state are extinguished in the time
of Trajan.   Of the great national Fast it can
give a good account, viz., that it is for the great
national sin.

Although, then, the evidence of a document so
late as the Calendar, which lies at the basis of the
works we have discussed, must be accepted with
great caution, we seem justified in regarding it
as a barrier against the wholesale discrediting
of the Old Testament narratives.   The distinction between good and bad days was of no
slight   consequence   to   the   ancient   nations ;
among some of them it constituted a science ;
and Ben-Sira parallels the inequality of different
men by the inequality of different days.   The fact
that men, though all of the same clay, are yet
unequal is, he thinks, analogous to the unequal
value of different days, all of which are produced
by the same sunlight.   This observation, made
before the time of the Maccabees, shows that
the extreme importance of the holy days which
constitute the Calendar would strike any thinking man.   The more celebrated of these were of
course enjoined by the Law, and their observance even in Justin's time was regarded as one
of the chief differences between Jews and
Christians.   But even those enjoined by the
Law were commemorations of definite events.
And this fact enabled the Calendar to grow

continuously. Where the celebration was not prescribed by the Law, it was prescribed by the Rabbis.

That in certain cases, where a day counted as of good omen or as of evil omen, a cause was assigned to it by conjecture, is conceivable ; but yet the acknowledgment of ignorance made by the Calendar with respect to the day which followed the Days of Darkness seems a decided mark of good faith. And another is found in the comparative unimportance of the events commemorated : thus the death of the sons of Aaron would appear to have been of very trivial consequence in the evolution of Israelitish history, but it has a day, whereas the deaths of Saul and David have none. The ordinary sign of natural growth as opposed to fabrication is the absence of system ; for in performances of the latter kind the effects of accident, though not negligible, are considerably restricted. Whereas in the case of what grows by nature the range of accident (by which the working of forces that cannot be mathematically measured is meant) is very wide.

The more, then, we regard the Biblical grouping of Israelitish history as correct, the more easily shall we be able to interpret the Calendar by it, and it by the Calendar. If the legend of the compiling of the Fast-Scroll some time during the century before the destruction of the second temple be correct, and the number

of days assigned in it to events connected with
the Maccabees lends it some colour, the work
then done will rather have been the regulation
and codification of existing practice than the
assignation of dates to events deserving of commemoration. Possibly at the time when it was
compiled the list of acts that might not be
done on the Sabbath was also provisionally
fixed ; polemical interests may have caused its
later alteration. And here it may be regretted
that so little of the talent that has been spent
on the analysis and grouping of partly imaginary
codes, supposed to be contained in the Bible,
has been devoted to the comparison of the
codes actually existing among the Jews ; for
any scientific description of the Old Testament
must deal primarily with the form of it current
among the Jews, and communication therewith
can only be secured by advancing to it through
the outworks of comments wherewith the
Rabbis have surrounded it.

VII

THE PRINCIPLES OF CRITICISM

THE principles of science scarcely differ from those of virtue; indeed, the latter may be regarded as a case of the former. A virtuous act is a specimen of a rule to be observed in all cases, irrespectively of the pleasure or pain which the performance of it gives to the doer. Similarly a sound argument is one in which the major premise claims assent on all occasions, whether the particular consequence deduced give pain or pleasure to him who deduces it. The first and greatest writer on logic, therefore, made the universality of the major premise the criterion whereby a scientific argument could be distinguished from one that had merely rhetorical value. The purpose of the latter being merely to convince a particular audience, the work of the major premise is done when the audience is convinced. For the next cause which he may have to plead the orator may employ propositions which directly contradict those whereby he

won the first.   The scientific reasoner, on the
other hand, has not to care whether his audience
are convinced or not.   His sole care must be
that his reasoning is conclusive, and this quality
it can have only if the major premises are
universal.   He cannot vary them with the nature
of his audience, or with the pleasure or pain
produced by the consequences in each case.
For him they either hold good in all cases or in
none.

Owing to the important consequences flowing
from modern Biblical Criticism, which threatened
either the divorce of religion from science or
the eventual abandonment of the former, it was
desirable that the world should have some
opportunity of knowing what value was really
set on the arguments which it employed by
those who had made it popular ; and this could
best be done if some case arose wherein the
same premises which had been employed to
discredit prophets and apostles involved consequences discrediting to the critics themselves.
A few years ago there seemed little chance of
such a case arising ; but various causes combined
to bring one about.   The document to which
reference has occasionally been made in these
papers, called the Cairene Ecclesiasticus, was
discovered between the years 1896 and 1900,
and was accepted by all the leading Hebraists
of the time as a work of the second century B.C.,
whence the existing Greek and Syriac transla-

tions were derived. In reality it is shown to be a work of the eleventh century A.D., compiled from those two existing translations. This is proved by arguments similar to those employed for the discrediting of Holy Scripture, only with certainties substituted for the conjectures whence the minor premises in the latter region are frequently derived. The choice which lay before the Hebraists, to whom reference is made, was either to acknowledge that they had committed the most serious error that had ever been made in the dating and analysing of documents, while relying on the arguments whereby they had dissected the Bible to maintain themselves, owing to their intrinsic force, which would not be affected by the temporary discredit into which the authors of those arguments would, by such a confession, fall ; or to throw up all the major premises which they had employed in the hope that a public which is so slow to move would fail to see that these major premises, being discredited, dragged the *whole* of the Higher Criticism into discredit with them. Their choice was soon made. All the arguments that had ever been employed in literary criticism, and all the laws of nature might go to the wall rather than so colossal an error should be acknowledged. Four lines of argument in particular may be noticed.

1. The argument from Tendentious Alterations occupies a large space in Biblical Criticism. It

is found, *e.g.*, that the author of the Chronicles makes the pious kings observe certain institutions which the author of the Kings makes them neglect ; it is inferred that the purpose of the chronicler is to make these pious kings act in accordance with the portion of the Pentateuch called the Priestly Code ; whence it follows (or is thought to follow) that the introduction of this code comes between the composition of the Kings and that of the Chronicles. The thought that the author of the Kings may have accidentally misstated is dismissed.

Now let us study in the Cairene Ecclesiasticus a real case of a tendentious alteration ; real, because the whole controversy which it illustrates is not based on hypotheses, but recorded in faithful monuments. As is well known, Abraham is repeatedly promised in Genesis that all nations shall be blessed or shall bless themselves in his seed. Two parts of the Hebrew verb are used in different places in Genesis, but there can be no doubt that they mean the same. One of these forms [1] would more naturally mean "shall bless themselves," *i.e.*, shall take Abraham's seed as a type of blessedness ; whereas the other [2] might more naturally be thought to mean "shall be blessed." St. Paul, in his Epistle to the Galatians, adopted the view that the promise meant that all nations should be blessed in

[1] הִתְבָּרְכוּ.   [2] נִבְרְכוּ.

Abraham's seed, viz., Christ; thus using it as
an argument for Christianity, which, avalanche-
like, gained in force as the ages went on. The
Jews,[1] to evade this, declare that it can only
mean "shall take Abraham's seed as a type of
felicity." We have two early witnesses, neither
of whom is likely to have been influenced by St.
Paul's use of the passage, who deserve to be
heard, viz., Philo and Josephus. The latter,[2]
who had access to the Hebrew, paraphrases the
words elegantly, "shall be envied of all mankind," adopting the Jewish interpretation. The
former,[3] who only had the LXX. rendering,
paraphrases it, "shall derive a blessing." His
idea is that the existence of one excellent man
sheds glory on the others. Although, therefore,
his interpretation differs from that adopted by
the Jews, he does not venture to alter the
form of words in which the promise is given
in the LXX.

The Greek text of Ecclesiasticus, of about
125 B.C., reproduces the LXX. of Genesis, merely
substituting the infinitive for the indicative and
"nations" for "all the nations of the earth."[4]
The first of these alterations is due to the form
of the sentence, the second (evidently) due to
the desire to obtain a certain number of syllables.

---

[1] Rashi on Gen. xii. 3.
[2] i. 235, ζηλωτοὺς ἔσεσθαι πᾶσιν ἀνθρώποις.
[3] i. 454, ed. Mangey.
[4] xliv. 21, ἐνευλογηθῆναι ἔθνη ἐν σπέρματι αὐτοῦ.

The Syriac version (of about 200 A.D.) reproduces
the phrase employed in the Peshitta of Genesis
without alteration. This may easily be accounted
for by the desire to harmonise.

After the first century controversy became
rife, and by the time these primary versions
came to be translated into other languages,
Christians and Jews had each an interest in
rendering Ben-Sira's words in the way which
favoured their respective theories. The Jewish
translators who, in the eighteenth [1] and nineteenth [2] centuries rendered the LXX. and Syriac
versions into Hebrew, both employed the word
which meant "shall take as a type of blessedness" least ambiguously. The Christian translators of both the Syriac [3] and the Greek [4] versions
wilfully substituted " that he would bless nations
in his seed " for the passive of the originals. In
the case of the Arabic translation of the Syriac
there was no excuse for this. In the case of the
LXX. it appears that one MS.[5] has a reading
which, though evidently erroneous, might lend
colour to this proceeding. The purpose is ex-

---

[1] Ben-Zev (Wolfsohn).   [2] Frankel.
[3] Polyglot Arabic version.
[4] Vatablus and Tremellius ; Latin of Polyglots ; English
A.V.
[5] MS. 248, ἐνευλογεῖν. This is clearly a corruption
caused by the following ἔθνη : for (1) all the other
infinitives are aorists (πληθῦναι, ἀννψῶσαι, κατακληρονομῆσαι);
(2) the transitive verb would be εὐλογεῖν, not ἐνευλογεῖν.

ceedingly plain. If Ben-Sira distinctly interpreted the promise in St. Paul's way some
centuries before any controversy attached to the
verse, the Jewish objection was finally disposed
of. And probably some of these translators
made the alteration without *mala fides*, not
having any doubt of the correctness of St. Paul's
interpretation.

The Hebrew Ecclesiasticus has distinctly and
unambiguously, "to bless in his seed nations." [1]
If this is a translation of a secondary version
made by some Christian from the LXX., or of
the Arabic version of the Syriac, the source of
the rendering is certain ; the Jewish translator
copied it carelessly, not, perhaps, having heard
of the controversy. But if we dream that it is
the original, what must we infer ? That the
author *accidentally* and *to serve no purpose* altered
the words of Genesis exactly as the Christian
translators afterwards altered them to serve a
definite purpose ; and that the author's grandson altered the words back accidentally and to
serve no purpose (for if he were bent on har-
monising, clearly he would have substituted "all
the nations of the earth " for " nations "), just as
a Jew of the Christian era would alter them to
serve a definite purpose.

This, therefore, may be regarded as a case
of a tendentious alteration of the clearest sort

[1] לברך בזרעו גוים׃

because we are acquainted with the history of the controversy to which it appertains, and we know that the phrase was altered *in the same passage* by others to serve the same purpose.

This alteration does not stand by itself. Ben-Sira, versifying, as usual, the prose of the Old Testament, goes on, "to multiply him as the dust of the earth, and like the stars exalt his seed. And to cause them to inherit from sea to sea." The Hebrew omits the first two of these clauses, and represents the passage thus : "to bless in his seed nations and to cause them to inherit from sea to sea." The omission is either intentional or unintentional ; and in either case it must have a reason. If it be intentional, its purpose must be to make the nations (*i.e.*, the Gentiles) the inheritors of "from sea to sea"; and this purpose can only have been entertained by a Christian. If it be unintentional, it must be due to two successive verses ending with the word for "his seed." But it is only in the Greek that the verse which both preserve ends with "his seed"; in the Hebrew the order is "to bless in his seed nations." Therefore this omission must be due either to interpolation by a Christian, or to translating from the Greek. But Christian interpolations would only be possible in a book that had come through Christians to Jews.

When this argument was produced in the *Guardian* by the present writer, a leader of

Biblical Criticism in this country replied that it did not "appeal to his mind." Of course the rejoinder must be that in that case *no* arguments from tendentious alterations appeal to his mind, since a clearer case is not to be found. The differences between Kings and Chronicles which the criticism of the Pentateuch attributes to design are therefore due to accident. And therefore the criticism of the Pentateuch collapses.

2. Of the Argument from Silence a little was said in Chapter IV. It is now conceded that the most learned Jew of the early tenth century knew nothing of the existence of a Hebrew Ecclesiasticus before 934 A.D.; and it is also certain that the most learned Jew of the later tenth century, who occupied the same rank as the former, knew nothing of the existence of such a book about the year 1000. The most learned Jew [1] of the eleventh century likewise denies its existence; and the most distinguished Jew [2] of the twelfth century also knows so little of the nature of Ben-Sira's work that he guesses at its contents from the author's name. The sole work in which it is cited is ostensibly by the first person mentioned in this list—R. Seadyah. R. Seadyah, it is therefore supposed, discovered the book in the year 934. Since, however, he couples the ascription of this work to Ben-Sira with errors of the grossest sort in

[1] Rashi.   [2] Maimonides.

literary history, his testimony as to its genuineness is worth nothing at all ; and since, in spite
of his testimony, the scholars who did their best
to save every remnant of Hebrew, old or new,
paid no attention to the work, albeit they were
all Seadyah's pupils, it must immediately after
discovery have been recognised as a fabrication.
The work wherein it is cited is, however,
certainly a forgery, which can have no other
object than to ridicule the Cairene Ecclesiasticus
itself. Here, then, we have the strongest possible
case of the Argument from Silence, and it is
rather interesting to compare the inferences
drawn in the case of the Book of Deuteronomy
with those that are drawn in the case of the
Cairene Ecclesiasticus. Deuteronomy was, we
know, discovered in the Temple in the reign of
Josiah. Who does not infer hence that it must
have been fabricated and put there ? The Jews,
however, uncritically supposed it to be genuine,
and it has ever since remained part of their
national literature. The Cairene Ecclesiasticus
was discovered in 934 by the Rabbi who counts
as the founder of modern Judaism, and who
succeeded in winning the case for the Talmud
against fierce opposition. This Rabbi was so
uncritical and ignorant that he thought Judas
Maccabæus had written a book in which the
taking of Jerusalem by the Romans in A.D. 70
is described as an event in the remote past, and
that points and accents had been invented 900

years before any one ever thought of them. His own pupils, though they had been persuaded into accepting the Talmud, refused to believe in the genuineness of the Cairene Ecclesiasticus ; but the modern Hebraists, who reject Deuteronomy, are prepared to accept the genuineness of the other document on the supposed Seadyah's word !

As before, if the Argument from Silence is rejected when it is most powerful, then it is to be rejected when it is weak. If a book equal in size to the longest of the Bible, and so important that Talmudic authorities often confused it with the Canon, could exist in the heart of Jewish communities of the tenth and eleventh centuries without the most learned of their body ever having heard of it, and escape the vigilance of those who were searching for every monument of the Hebrew language ; then it is clear that the Argument from Silence must be used for no purpose whatever. For of Jewish literature of the tenth and eleventh centuries we possess a knowledge with which no part of our knowledge of Biblical antiquity can compare.

3. Of the keenness wherewith research was pursued at the Mohammedan capitals in the tenth and eleventh centuries we have many monuments ; among the most remarkable is the work of Al-Biruni on the chronology of ancient nations, wherein the differences between the Hebrew Bible, the Samaritan Pentateuch, and

the LXX., in regard to the age of the patriarchs are tabulated. To this period also belongs the *Fihrist*, or Scientific Bibliography of Al-Nadim, wherein there is a comparative Canon of Jewish and Christian Scriptures. Mas'udi's work on Comparative Religion, if we possessed it, would doubtless contain fresh observations on the differences between the Christian and the Jewish Bibles. The Arabic version of Ben-Sira, which is known to the author of the *Fihrist*, is made from the Syriac; but it professes to be made from the Greek, and gives the author's name in the Greek form. Since no falsehood is told without some reason, the purpose of this must be to gain the book credit. This would be gained because it was generally known that the Greek version was the work of the author's grandson, and therefore likely to be correct. What we may therefore infer is that the Greek translation was generally known to be better than the Syriac, though the Arabic translator had access only to the latter.

It was shown that the Cairene Ecclesiasticus was made up of our two existing versions, except that the Greek had been used in a daughter version, apparently in Persian. This result was made certain by the fact (which came to light after it had been stated) that the Hebrew repeatedly gave alternate renderings of the same verse, following the Greek for one and the Syriac for the other, and ordinarily in such cases mistranslating one or both very grossly. The process was exactly analogous to that followed in the last century by the retranslator Ben-Zev, who compiled his retranslation from the Syriac and probably a German version of the Greek.

The account given then was that the document before us was made up from one document which we possess, and a lost translation of another document which we possess : in an age in which the differences between the different recensions of the Scriptures had attracted the attention of the educated ; and on a plan exactly analogous to that followed by a retranslator of no critical reputation in the eighteenth century. The boldness and complication of this hypothesis were too great for those to whom the conflation of Biblical documents from a variety of utterly unknown sources, and on plans to which there is no known analogy, offered no difficulty whatever. "How complicated! Only think of the wildness of the suggestion that a document had been compiled out of two, one of which no longer existed in precisely the form in which it had been used ! How fantastic ! You cannot expect so intricate a theory as that to be accepted ! " Once again, then, we apply the *a fortiori* argument. If complication renders a theory improbable in a case to which we have the precisest analogy, and in which the docu-

20

ments which we suppose to have been conflated are preserved : what must be the improbability of the hypotheses which assume the conflation of documents for the existence of which there is no warrant, on a system for the employment of which there is no evidence ! Our age, then, can offer a very tolerable illustration of men who strain out a gnat and swallow a camel. If complication renders a hypothesis improbable, then let us hear no more of J and E and P !

4. We have already seen that it was owing to the conquest of Islam, which led to the compilation of Arabic grammars and dictionaries, that Hebrew grammars and dictionaries began to be compiled. During the period in which Hebrew was a dead language we cannot say how far a Rabbi would have been competent to write it, supposing that he had been allowed to ; but he would probably have mixed it with whatever language happened to be his vernacular. When the Jews in the ninth century took to writing Hebrew after Arabic models, they adopted a quantity of Arabic words, partly because the Bible had no expressions for the ideas which they wished to handle, and partly with the view of enriching a vocabulary which the general loss of non-Biblical literature had rendered meagre. Some of these words, *e.g.*, those for *centre*,[1] *nature*,[2] *pole*,[3] have remained part of the New-

---

[1] מרכז.   [2] טבע.   [3] קוטב.

Hebrew vocabulary, and are used by Rabbis utterly unfamiliar with Arabic. Now the date of Arabic words cannot always be ascertained, but it is often possible to locate them. For firstly stress was laid on purity of language at the Caliphs' court from the beginning of the Abbasid period, whence words that are not registered in the collections which go back to the early Arabic philologers are most likely to be late ; and secondly the growth of a religious and political vocabulary can be traced in the Koran and the early literature.

A word of the second sort is that which signifies in the developed theology " to create." [1] The idea of *creation* in the sense of production without matter implies reflexion ; it would be surprising if the Arabs of the " time of Ignorance " had possessed an expression for it. Now in the Koran we can trace the process by which a certain word acquired that meaning. The word with which it is at first coupled [2] means " to equalise," and the adverb with which it is ordinarily accompanied is " accurately." This agrees with what the Arabic grammarians tell us of its meaning " to measure out " properly, they say, a piece of leather before stitching it into a wallet, &c. The Ethiopic language uses the same verb for " to number," whereas the Hebrew uses it for " to apportion." Probably the word " prepare " would represent the early

[1] *Khalaka.*　　　　　[2] *Sawwā.*

use of the word in the Koran and the early
poets with sufficient accuracy.

But the Prophet in the course of controversy
with Jews and Christians learns about creation
from nothing, and to express this borrows
Hebrew [1] and Ethiopic [2] words. Since *making*,
as predicated of God, implies creating, the word
which at first signified "to prepare," having
been used by the Prophet of the Deity, comes
to mean "create." Since the earlier usage of
the Koran, in which the matter whence the
object was "created" is regularly expressed,
is opposed to the later usage, according to
which it signifies making from nothing, the
grammarians have to distinguish the two senses,
which they do very carefully.

This Arabic word is found in the Cairene
Ecclesiasticus, where the two primary versions
have "create." [3] As an Arabism employed by
a Jew of the Abbasid period, it presents no
difficulty ; in the original of Ben-Sira it would
represent an anachronism of 850 years. To
this argument the reply is, How do you know
that the word had not the sense which
Mohammed is known to have given it eight
and a half centuries before Mohammed's time?

This reply can only be accepted on the
condition that wherever the argument from
dated words is employed it may be evaded by
a similar subterfuge. The Talmud speaks of

[1] ברא.   [2] פטר.   [3] *E.g.*, xxxviii. 1.

King Josiah consulting the *Sanhedrin.* We infer that this story is after the time of Alexander the Great, because *Sanhedrin* or *Synhedrion* is a word which the Jews learnt from the post - Alexandrian Greeks. But it may be urged, How do we know that the Jews of Josiah's time did not hit on the same word?

Given these four points, that the Argument from Silence is worthless, that the Argument from Tendentious Alterations is worthless, that a complicated hypothesis cannot be accepted, and that arguments from dated words are valueless, and we can indeed walk through the camp of the Biblical critics (as an American writer once said) without striking a blow. For *that* science is worthless in which the validity of a method depends on either the reputation of the person who employs it or the agreeableness of individual results.

The plan of discrediting the witness is not indeed one to which it is often desirable in scientific matters to resort. It would be better if we could accustom ourselves to consider arguments entirely on their own merits, without troubling about the name or character of the person who happened first to call attention to them. But in the present case it was highly desirable that the world should have some opportunity of gauging the skill of those on whose faith the old - fashioned belief in the authenticity of Scripture had been abandoned. Any one, indeed, who desired to have his skill tested could easily get this done. By discovering the number of leader-writers employed on a London daily in a month and assigning to them their respective contributions to the paper a critic might give proof of the cogency of his reasoning in the analysis of documents which offer far greater difficulty. It does not, however, appear that this experiment has been tried. The Ecclesiasticus experiment was forced on the Hebraists of our time, and, though an easy problem, belonged to precisely the same region as that in which the criticism of our time was accustomed to run riot. And it resulted in hopeless failure.

If ever the criticism of the Old Testament be started aright, it will be desirable to see that its premises are everywhere taken from the region of the certain or the probable, and that these regions be carefully distinguished. Too great scepticism cannot be recommended in respect of the statements which at present are made the basis of far-reaching propositions. We saw in Chapter III. that of two criteria whereby the true Isaiah was to be distinguished from the false, one begged the question of the possibility of prophecy, whereas the other was an untenable proposition about the date of the introduction of Aramaic loan-words into Canaanitish. In the same work it was assumed that the com-

piler of the Oracles of Isaiah must have taken
chapters xxxvi.–xxxix. from the Kings; but the
fact that the hymn of Hezekiah is preserved in
Isaiah whereas it is omitted from the Kings
ruins this assumption ; either the Kings must
take the chapters from Isaiah, or both " com-
pilers " must be drawing from a third source.
At different periods in the Ecclesiasticus controversy the same scholars have assumed that
the Talmudic quotations from that work are
absolutely accurate and wholly inaccurate ; that
Ben-Sira cannot have used Arabic words and
that Arabic words found in him should occasion
no surprise ; that the Greek translation is so
accurate that it would neither add nor omit an
" and," nor substitute a singular for a plural ;
and that it is so inaccurate that it need not
even approximate to either the sense or the
words of its original.   Clearly contrary propositions cannot both be true, though they may
both be false.   Now the introduction of any
false premise into a chain of reasoning ruins
it when there are no collateral links, and has a
tendency to discredit it when there are some.

The few who have ever understood the
critical art—Bentley, Porson, Cobet—constantly
warn us against neglecting trifles. The reason
for this is that nature does not recognise the
distinction between what is important and what
is trifling ; and that in the case of human action,
where it is conscious, it is the result of motives,

and where it is unconscious, of reasons.   Hence
any ascertained fact, however insignificant in
appearance, may resemble a narrow channel
connecting great reservoirs.   Grotefend's reading of a few names in Persian cuneiform was
a narrow enough conduit ; but through it the
whole of the history of Assyria and Babylonia
has permeated to our age.   In detective
romances the real detective is he whom
nothing escapes ; human motives and human
devices are not so many, but that the ground
for a slight deviation from the normal may
often be circumscribed within a limited number
of possibilities.   The next deviation from the
normal which meets us in the same inquiry will
also be explicable by only a limited number of
possibilities ; and a single possibility which is
common to the two sets may be regarded as
a certainty.

The clue which leads to the discovery of the
metre of Ecclesiasticus (of which use has been
made in the foregoing papers) may be taken
as an illustration of this principle.   Ben-Sira
expresses such loud appreciation of the Law
that we may be sure he would not alter the
phrases of Holy Writ without some reason.   Yet
in his account of Abraham, he improves on the
etymology given by the Divine Being Himself.
" Abraham a *great* father of a multitude of
nations," [1] he writes, whereas in Genesis he is

_____
[1] Ecclus. xliv. 19.

called "a father of a multitude of nations."[1]
The word "great" must be added for some
purpose. Then in Genesis Abraham is promised
that "all the nations of the earth shall bless
themselves in his seed."[2] Ben-Sira *reduces* this
to "that nations should bless themselves in his
seed."[3] There must be a ground for *reduction*
in this case just as for *addition* in the other case.
Procrustean operations are conducted with one
particular end, viz., to adjust an object to a
particular measure. The words added and
taken away in each of these clauses are such
as affect the sense least; therefore the writer's
purpose is to *versify* Genesis, *i.e.*, reduce it to a
fixed number of syllables, with as little alteration
as possible of the text. If we had before us a
French translation of any English metrical
version of the Psalms, we could deduce the
fact of the English version being in metre by
analogous reasoning. "As pants the hart for
cooling streams": Why, we should ask, is the
word "cooling" added, when the Psalm has
only "the waterbrooks"? Since it adds
nothing to the sense, its purpose is probably
to add to the number of the syllables. "O,
when shall I behold Thy face": the Psalm
has "when shall I *come and* behold the face
of God," in which "come and" are the words
that can be omitted with least detriment to the
sense. Since the paraphrast *omits* in this clause,

[1] Gen. xvii. 5.   [2] Gen. xxii. 18, &c.   [3] Ecclus. xliv. 21.

whereas he *adds* in the foregoing clause, we
should argue, he must be composing in a fixed
number of syllables. For that is the one possibility which gives an adequate explanation of
both operations.

The two clauses of Ecclesiasticus quoted can
be restored as certainly as if we had a copy of
the original ; [1] measure them, and you will find
that they are each of nine syllables, and that
the principle of scansion is similar to that which
the Jews at the renaissance of Hebrew literature
adopted from the Arabs.[2] But an author does
not employ Procrustean operations for the purpose of obtaining nine syllables of a certain sort
in two verses of his book. Unless there is
evidence to the contrary we assume that the
whole of his book was in nine-syllable metre
of the same style ; that becomes our working
hypothesis, which every verse that goes naturally
into this shape strengthens. Where the verses
do not fall into it naturally, we look about to
see whether there is anything about them that
suggests that the translation is untrustworthy.
' The discourse of the righteous is wisdom
always, but the fool changeth as the moon." [3]
The first line (if restored) gives eight syllables
and is unmetrical. But without knowledge of

[1] *Abrāhām āb rab hamon goyim* and *Lĕhithbārech goyim
bĕzar'ō.*

[2] This fact ruins Bickell's metrical theories.

[3] Ecclus. xxvii. 11.

Hebrew any one who can think should be able to correct the sense. If the variability of the fool is compared to the phases of the *moon*, then the constancy of the wise man will be compared to the constancy of the *sun ;* and the transposition of two letters gives us the words " like the sun," and this alteration makes the line metrical and restores the nine syllables.[1] Then we observe that the old Latin version has actually the words " like the sun," and this teaches us to take the old Latin occasionally into our counsels.

But what is the advantage of the metre of Ecclesiasticus, now that we have acquired it ? Nothing less than this—that whereas we have hitherto trusted for the vocalisation of the Hebrew Bible a tradition not written down till the eighth century A.D., we can now test it, and here and there correct it, by a document of the third or second century B.C.

The canons, then, which we follow in these operations are—(1) That nature never deceives ; (2) that human action when intentional is the result of motives, and when unintentional of reasons ; (3) that these are to be inferred from deflexions from the normal. We thus believe that it is normal to speak the truth : where there is a falsehood there must be a cause for it. And from a very few cases of deflexion it is possible to infer a certain cause.

[1] שיחת צדיק תמיד כחמה.

From the fact that the Greek text of Judith has in one place "the saw of Judæa," where "the plain of Judæa" is meant, we may infer with certainty that the book is a translation from the Hebrew. For that error is easily explained by the Hebrew *script;* if it could be explained by the Hebrew *pronunciation* it would be conceivable that the writer's native language was Hebrew, though he wrote in Greek. The supposition, then, that any one by an accidental miswriting could have put instead of "plain" a word differing from it so much both in meaning and in form, and that the identity of the names for these objects in Hebrew should be a coincidence only, violates the canon that nature never deceives.

Where deflexion is intentional it is well to know the motives which have produced deflexion of the same sort, if possible in the same case, but if not, in some case that is closely parallel. Thus the whole of the modern theory of the Pentateuch is liable to be wrecked on a verse of 1 Samuel,[1] where it is stated that the sons of Eli "misused the women who assembled (A.V.) at the door of the Tabernacle of the congregation." That clause is omitted by the LXX. translator. Here, then, is a case of deflexion. Either the editor of the Hebrew interpolated the clause, or the LXX. translation omitted it. Omission can happen accidentally, whereas addi-

[1] ii. 22.

tion in such a case must be intentional ; whence
the supposition that it can have got accidentally
into the Hebrew may be dismissed, whereas the
possibility that it may have been accidentally
omitted by the translator must be allowed.
Was there, then, any motive for omitting it,
supposing the omission to be intentional ? One
has but to glance at the Rabbinical commentaries to see ; the Rabbis do their utmost
to clear Eli's sons from this terrible charge.
The oldest exegesis made the words allegorical ;
the crime Eli's sons committed was so bad that
the text is supposed to *compare* it to the crime
with which it really charges them. The later
exegesis gives the words senses which they
certainly do not possess. Hence it is clear that
there was a motive for the omission of the
words.

Was there an equally strong motive for
adding them *after* 300 B.C. ? for the witness of
the LXX. takes us back no further than that
date. Against this it is to be observed that
there is a second difficulty in the clause, which
the Jewish exegesis has to overcome. Who
were the *women* that served at the door of the
Tabernacle ? The word translated " assembled,"
but really meaning "served," is of great antiquity,
and corresponds with the word " serve " in being
specialised in certain contexts. " One who has
served " means, if used of a man, one who has
been a soldier ; and the word used in Hebrew

for "the army" means literally "the service."
But just as the word "service" in other contexts
means religious service, so this Hebrew word
used of something done at the door of the Tabernacle of the Covenant means some religious
performance done by these women as *func-
tionaries*. The crime committed by Eli's sons,
as the author meant it, was, though not light,
considerably less grievous than that with which
the text, as it is ordinarily construed, charges
them ; their fellow-offenders were the women in
attendance, not those who had come from a
distance to worship.   But the idea of *women in
attendance* at the Tabernacle is so odious that
it has to be got rid of.   The Peshitta renders
"the women who *prayed*" there ; and this the
Targum adopts.   The Rabbis, followed by our
Authorised Version, render it "the women who
thronged."   In Exodus xxxviii. 8, where there
is another reference to these women, the same
objection is felt.   The Aramaic translators
make them women who *prayed*, the LXX.
women who *fasted*.   Thus it is evident that by
the time when the LXX. translation of the
Pentateuch was made, the idea of women
ministering at the door of the Tabernacle had
become so odious that it was wilfully mis-
translated.   What chance is there, then, that
any one would have wilfully added an allusion
to them after that date?

This, then, is a case in which an argument, at

first sight powerful, if steadily glanced at,
vanishes. The LXX. rendering of Exodus is
most likely earlier (certainly not later) than
that of 1 Samuel. From that rendering,
coupled with those of other authorities, we
learn that a certain phrase had become odious
by the time when the translation was made.
What we infer thence is surely that no one
would have wilfully inserted the same phrase
where it did not occur. Hence the possibility
of the addition of the clause we are discussing
to the text after the date acquired may be dismissed. Whereas, therefore, at first sight we
fancy that the LXX. is against the genuineness
of that clause, a little examination shows that
the LXX. furnishes a date after which it cannot
have been added.

The deflexion exhibited by the LXX. in
1 Samuel ii. 22 is thus fully accounted for.
The text either charged Eli's sons with an
offence of the greatest heinousness, discredit-
able to the whole nation, or it revealed the
existence of female attendants on the Tabernacle, which the Jews desired to conceal
When confronted with such difficulties, many
persons think the wisest course is to flee.
And this is what the LXX. translator has
done.

But if we imagine the deflexion in the
Hebrew, we find that the deflexion can only
have been wilful, and that it would have been

introducing matter which was repugnant to the nation. This alternative may therefore be dismissed.

And what time the idea of ministering women became odious cannot perhaps be determined ; but the clause must go back to a time before it had become so.

In treating this difficulty, therefore, we are on firm ground, because the motives by which editors and translators were guided are to be learned from documents of which some are as early as the text with which we are dealing. Sometimes motives are of such universal validity that general principles may be deduced from them. Sometimes they are of so personal a character that they might easily remain unsuspected. When Velleius Paterculus mentions Vergil and Rabirius as the great poets of the Augustan age, those who do not understand criticism suppose Rabirius a mistake for *Horace ;* those who understand it suppose that Rabirius was substituted for Horace owing to the working of some motive ; but to locate that motive is not so easy a matter.

In dealing above with the fact that Ben-Sira omits Daniel from his list of heroes, we saw that this was not owing to his being unacquainted with Daniel's personality ; and also that he omitted Ezra, though he dwelt on the merits of Nehemiah. The name of Nehemiah must have suggested that of Ezra, and the name of Job that of Daniel; hence these omissions are intentional. Is there, then, anything common to Daniel and Ezra which might induce Ben-Sira to omit their names? for clearly the fewer the motives we suppose working, the less complicated will be our explanations. Daniel and Ezra have this in common—that their books are partly in Aramaic. Nehemiah, as we saw before, insisted on the Jews speaking Hebrew. Hence Ben-Sira may have omitted their names with the idea of punishing them for unfaithfulness to the sacred tongue.

Where the critical art faces factors wherewith it is acquainted, it can thus proceed to results that are certain or probable, provided that it follows clues rather than effaces them. In a document of any considerable size something can be learned of the character of the author, and though conduct is not absolutely uniform, it can be brought within the dominion of rules, provided that the critic be capable of placing himself in the situation of the writer whose work he is handling. The restoration of Ben-Sira's verses is an easy task, because a modern scholar could write a book of the kind. If, *e.g.*, he wished to versify Hosea xiv. 10, "Straight are the ways of the Lord, and the righteous shall walk in them, and sinners shall stumble in them," he would do it as Ben-Sira does it (xxxix. 24), "His ways to the holy are

21

plain, so to the ungodly stumbling-blocks." [1]
Hence, having to move between the Old
Testament and the Greek version, with independent authorities here and there to hold him
up, and with the knowledge that there is a
definite number of syllables of a certain sort
and neither more nor less in each line, he can
make progress, there being no forces present
the neglect of which could overthrow his calculations. But if Ben-Sira had been in possession
of a Bible many times larger than ours, or of
abilities greater than those with which a paraphrast can ordinarily be credited, the difficulty
would be very greatly increased. Now if there
be any truth at all in the pretensions of the
prophets, we cannot place ourselves in their
situation, because it is beyond our experience.
Hence we cannot analyse the principles which
underlie their compositions. In this they differ
from pagan oracles, of which the explanation is
to be found in a sort of cunning which most
minds are able to grasp. A cautious oracle-
monger in any age would have given Croesus
the oracle which he is supposed to have received
from Delphi ; we have only to fancy ourselves
oracle-mongers, and we are capable of delivering
it. But the answer whereby the king's confi-

[1]
דְּרָכָיו לַצַּדִּיקִים מֵישָׁ־
רִים כֵּן לָרְשָׁעִים מִכְשׁוֹלִים

dence was won is of a different sort. In any case it was a revelation of what was going on, not of what was to come. If, therefore, the story be true, and there was no treachery employed, it comes under the category of second sight, the existence of which is probably not to be denied without hardihood, whatever be the account which science may ultimately give of the occasions whereon it has been displayed. As, however, the reward to be received by the oracle for a successful answer was a vast sum of gold, it is probable that more normal means were employed for discovering the king's intention, and it must be remembered that Greek ingenuity was hard to beat. The ordinary commentator can, however, put himself in the position neither of one possessed of second sight nor of a specially ingenious impostor. Whereas, then, he is in sympathy with the oracle where it was helpless, he is no match for it where it succeeded.

In the case of the analysis of historical books, the difficulty of arriving at any results which deserve to be called scientific is of a different sort. Where we are in possession of the earlier histories it is not ordinarily difficult to deduce the later histories from them. We know that the earlier histories have to be abridged, because the later generation has not an unlimited amount of time; but the principle of abridg-

ment will often vary with personal proclivities.
Carelessness and wilful falsification with the
view of serving a variety of interests will
often intervene.   But that it is possible to
work   backwards   and   from   a   compilation
evolve its sources, where their number, character,
and date are not recorded, has not yet been
proved.

To the compiler whose plan is to read and
excerpt written books, and then amalgamate
his results, it is difficult to recall the days when
a book was communicated orally, sometimes also
existing somewhere on a stone, whence the recital
might perhaps be checked.   There is a considerable chance of each person, through whom it is
transmitted, leaving some mark on the narrative ; the human memory is not to be trusted,
even where scientific notions of accuracy are
already current.   But at what period in literary
history do they become current ?   That is a
question that cannot be answered, because the
bulk of mankind never can assimilate the notion
at all.

Supposing, therefore, that a recital is first put
into shape at a period Q, by the time it has
reached X the number of factors introduced will
have become so numerous, so small, and indivi-
dually for the most part so insignificant, that
science has at present no instruments capable of
severing them.   The reasons for slight variations
will no longer be apparent, whereas the motives

which dictated greater changes are likely to be entirely forgotten.

Our chief hope, therefore, for the satisfactory analysis of the documents of the Old Testament lies in the fact that ancient history in Palestine was written on stone, and that this material has a tendency to survive. Excavation in the Holy Land may lead to results which, lying outside the range of conjecture, will not be liable to be overthrown. But the same, as we have seen, is the characteristic of any result which is based on sound reasoning from certain premises.

To publish theories which are, to a great extent, at variance with received opinions, is only justifiable in an age which has proved itself uncritical in the region to which those opinions belong. In differing about the date and analysis of Hebrew documents from a school which could be deceived for a day by the document to which reference has been made at the beginning of this chapter, and could spend a year in defending it, I do not seem, to myself, to be incurring any serious risk. And that risk is slightest where external evidence, so far as it exists, is in favour of the opinions advocated.

INDEX OF NAMES AND MATTERS

INDEX OF TEXTS

UNWIN BROTHERS, THE GRESHAM PRESS, WOKING AND LONDON.

Date Due